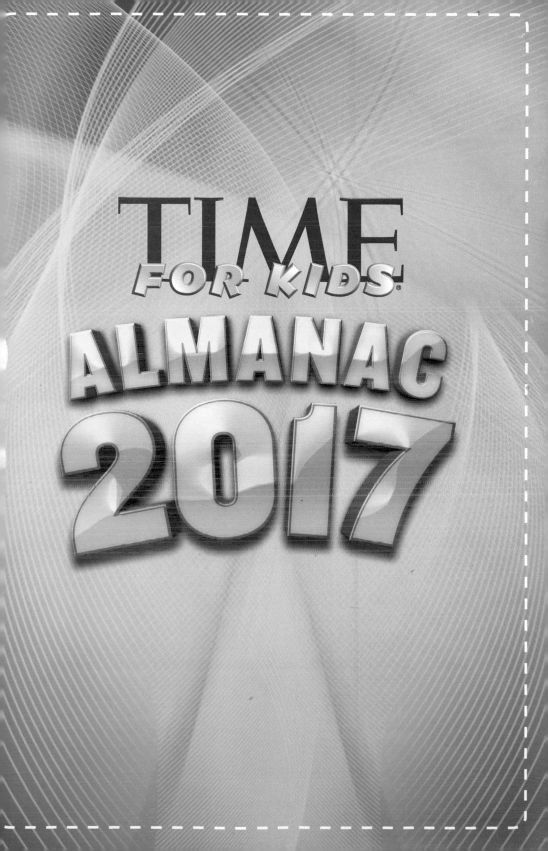

TIME FOR KIDS®
ALMANAC 2017

Published by Liberty Street, an imprint of Time Inc. Books
225 Liberty Street
New York, New York 10281

© 2016 Time Inc. Books

LIBERTY
STREET

LIBERTY STREET and TIME FOR KIDS are trademarks of Time Inc.

Special thanks to the TIME for Kids team: Nellie Gonzalez Cutler, Andrea Delbanco, Don Heiny, Jennifer Kraemer-Smith and Drew Willis; and the Time Inc. Books team: Margot Schupf, Anja Schmidt, Beth Sutinis, Deirdre Langeland, Georgia Morrissey, and Hillary Leary

Produced by:
10Ten Media
Project Editor: Andrea Woo
Writers: Vickie An, Ethan Back, Kaci Borowski, Catherine Worley
Editors: Tim Gramling, Ed McGrogan
Art Director: Ian Knowles
Designers: Chris Delisle, Crhistian Rodriguez
Special Thanks: Bob Der, Scott Gramling, Zachary Cohen, Brad Kallet, Nina Pantic, Joe Scarpulla

ISBN 10: 1-61893-415-5
ISBN 13: 978-1-61893-415-4

First Edition, 2016

1 QGT 16
10 9 8 7 6 5 4 3 2 1

Time Inc. Books products may be purchased for business or promotional use. For information on bulk purchases, please contact Christi Crowley in the Special Sales Department at (845) 895-9858.

We welcome your comments and suggestions about Time Inc. Books. Please write to us at:
Time Inc. Books
Attention: Book Editors
P.O. Box 62310
Tampa, Florida 33662-2310

timeincbooks.com

Contents

CONTENTS

CONTENTS

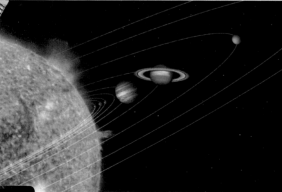

196–229 Sports

230–275 The United States

The information in this book is current as of March 1, 2016.

Bei Bei

A Look Back

Raúl Castro and Barack Obama

Iran's foreign minister Mohammad Javad Zarif (left) and U.S. Secretary of State John Kerry (right) shake hands.

Greece Gets Bailed Out, Again

Greece's financial problems stem from economic troubles that many countries faced in 2008. In August 2015, the country accepted a deal from 18 Eurozone nations that would rescue the country from its money woes for a third time in five years. The agreement came after months of tense negotiations. Terms of the new bailout include loans of up to 86 billion euros (about 96 billion U.S. dollars) over three years. But the aid came at a high price: Greece had to agree to harsh measures that would affect ordinary citizens, such as higher taxes and more spending cuts.

World Powers Reach Nuclear Deal With Iran

More than 20 months of talks between world leaders, including U.S. Secretary of State John Kerry and Iranian officials, produced a landmark agreement on Iran's nuclear program in July 2015. The deal limits Iran's access to nuclear materials in order to prevent the country from developing a nuclear weapon for at least the next 10 years. In return, the U.S. and other nations will remove financial and trade restrictions on Iran.

The Refugee Crisis Deepens

The summer of 2015 saw hundreds of thousands of refugees and migrants risking their lives to reach Europe as they fled violence, persecution, and economic hardships in the Middle East and Africa. Under international law, refugees are people who flee their country because of war or persecution. Migrants are people who move to another country for jobs, in an effort to improve their lives. Most of the refugees who made the dangerous trek were from Syria, where a civil war has raged since 2011. Thousands died attempting to cross the sea in unsafe vessels.

Migrants leave their village for a refugee camp in Slovenia.

Tragedy in Paris

On November 13, 2015, terrorist attacks in Paris, France, left the world in shock. Attackers armed with guns and explosive vests carried out assaults in six different sites across the French capital that evening. The coordinated attacks killed 129 people and injured more than 350.

The Islamic State militant group, sometimes called ISIS or ISIL, took responsibility. World leaders vowed to stand with France. U.S. President Barack Obama called the tragedy an "attack on all humanity." French president François Hollande called the events "an act of war." France began bombing ISIS targets in Syria in retaliation two days later.

A memorial in Place de la République Square in Paris honors the victims of the terror attacks.

The biggest power is not the weapon but the Prayer

Pray for

A Powerful Earthquake Rocks Nepal

A massive earthquake struck the South Asian nation of Nepal on April 25, 2015, leaving a trail of devastation in its wake. The magnitude 7.8 quake was the largest to hit Nepal since 1934.

The earthquake's epicenter was located 50 miles northwest of Nepal's capital, Kathmandu. The tremor reduced hundreds of thousands of homes to rubble and triggered a deadly avalanche on Mount Everest, the world's tallest mountain peak.

Cuban President Raúl Castro (left) and U.S. President Barack Obama (right) meet in April 2015.

Old Foes, New Friends

President Barack Obama and Cuban president Raúl Castro met in Panama City, Panama, in April 2015, marking the first face-to-face talk between the leaders of the nations since the U.S. cut diplomatic ties with Cuba in 1961. The sit-down signaled a new relationship between the Cold War foes. "We can develop a friendship between our two peoples," said Castro.

11

A First for Women in the Army

Captain Kristen Griest (left) and First Lieutenant Shaye Haver (right) wave at their graduation ceremony.

In August 2015, Captain Kristen Griest and First Lieutenant Shaye Haver became the first women to graduate from Army Ranger School. Allowing women to take part in the Ranger course is part of the U.S. military's push to open more combat jobs to women. "Each Ranger School graduate has shown the physical and mental toughness to successfully lead organizations at any level," Army Secretary John McHugh said in a statement. "This course has proven that every soldier, regardless of gender, can achieve his or her full potential."

Future Face of Money

Move over, Alexander Hamilton! It's time to share the limelight. The U.S. Treasury Department announced in June 2015 that the next $10 bill will feature a woman who played a major role in American history. The new bill is planned for release in 2020. That year marks the 100-year anniversary of the passage of the 19th Amendment to the United States Constitution, which gave women the right to vote.

The Founding Father won't be completely replaced, however. It's possible that the new design will feature a picture of Hamilton as well as a woman (or women).

The current $10 bill features Alexander Hamilton.

Mount McKinley No More

President Barack Obama became the first sitting U.S. president to spend time in Arctic Alaska, north of the Arctic Circle, when he toured the region during a three-day trip in September 2015. On August 30, a day before his historic visit, the president declared that Alaska's Mount McKinley, North America's tallest peak, would be renamed Denali, which means "the high one" in the Athabascan languages spoken by many Alaska Natives. Alaskans have called the mountain Denali for centuries.

South Carolina Removes Confederate Flag

In July 2015, South Carolina Governor Nikki Haley signed into law the removal of the Confederate flag from statehouse grounds. The flag has long been a topic of controversy. During the Civil War (1861–65), the states that broke away from the Union called themselves the Confederate States of America. The flag's defenders see it as a symbol of Southern heritage. Opponents consider it a reminder of a history of racism and slave ownership that has no place on government property.

A New House Speaker

Republican Paul Ryan of Wisconsin became the 54th speaker of the U.S. House of Representatives in October 2015. In this powerful position, Ryan is next in line for the presidency after the vice president.

Ryan was the top choice for many House Republicans after Speaker John Boehner of Ohio announced his resignation in September 2015. "We are wiping the slate clean," he said. "Only a fully functioning House can truly represent the people."

A LOOK BACK

The Pope Visits the U.S.

In September 2015, Pope Francis made his first visit to the U.S. During the visit, Francis met with leaders and schoolchildren, held religious services, and gave speeches in Washington, D.C., New York City, and Philadelphia. Thousands of people lined the streets to greet the pope over the course of his six-day stay.

Pope Francis acknowledges the crowd in Philadelphia.

In 2015, a super blood moon eclipse occurred for the first time in 33 years.

A Super Special Eclipse

Sky gazers in the U.S., Europe, Africa, and western Asia were treated to a rare celestial double feature in September 2015 when a total lunar eclipse coincided with a so-called supermoon. That combination hasn't happened since 1982, and won't occur again until 2033.

A supermoon happens when a full moon reaches the closest point to Earth in its orbit. A full lunar eclipse occurs when the sun, Earth, and moon line up, with Earth directly between the moon and the sun. The moon, completely in Earth's shadow, takes on a reddish tint. This is why a total lunar eclipse is sometimes called a blood moon.

Bei Bei relaxes in an enclosure at the Smithsonian's National Zoo.

World, Meet Bei Bei!

Two giant pandas at the Smithsonian's National Zoo, in Washington, D.C., are the proud parents of a baby boy! Mama bear Mei Xiang (may shang) gave birth to twins on August 22, 2015. But, sadly, the smaller cub lived only four days. The first week of life can be hard for panda cubs. That's one reason giant pandas are endangered. However, the surviving cub is healthy and growing.

A month after the surviving cub was born, he officially received a name: Bei Bei. The name, chosen by First Lady Michelle Obama and Chinese first lady Peng Liyuan, means "precious treasure." Bei Bei's older sister, Bao Bao, was born in 2013.

Water on Mars

In September 2015, NASA scientists discovered evidence of liquid water flowing on Mars. These findings boost the odds that there is life on the Red Planet. A study published in the journal *Nature Geoscience* reveals that Mars has multiple dribbles of salt-laden water. In 2008, scientists confirmed the existence of frozen water, but instruments aboard NASA's Mars Reconnaissance Orbiter have found the strongest evidence yet that salt water in liquid form trickles down certain Martian slopes each summer. Mars is now the only planet in our solar system, other than our own, to show signs of water on its surface.

Dark streaks on the slopes of Mars could be proof of flowing water.

A Mammoth Find

Michigan farmer James Bristle stumbled on a mammoth discovery. On September 28, 2015, while digging in his field, Bristle found what he thought was a fence post. Upon closer inspection, he realized that it was a three-foot-long woolly mammoth bone.

Dan Fisher, a University of Michigan professor who studies mammoth and mastodon extinctions, confirmed the find. In addition to the skull and tusks, Fisher and a team of scientists excavated vertebrae, ribs, and shoulder blades. It is believed the animal lived between 11,000 and 15,000 years ago.

A Record Start

The Golden State Warriors started the 2015–16 season with a streak for the ages. The reigning NBA champions kicked off the year with a record 23 consecutive victories. Warriors point guard Stephen Curry fueled the run, averaging 33.9 points per game during that span. "Like Michael Jordan was a whole other thing, this guy is his own thing," 15-time NBA All-Star Kevin Garnett said of Curry's play. "It's beautiful for basketball." Previously, the 1948–49 Washington Capitols and 1993–94 Houston Rockets shared the record with a 15–0 start. Golden State's win streak was finally snapped on December 12, 2015, in a 108–95 loss to the Milwaukee Bucks.

Triple Threat

On June 6, 2015, American Pharoah rode into history after winning the Belmont Stakes horse race in Long Island, New York. With the win, the horse won the prestigious Triple Crown. The Triple Crown is a victory by a horse in three different races—the Kentucky Derby, the Preakness, and the Belmont Stakes—in the same year. The 3-year-old bay colt is the first horse in 37 years to win the Triple Crown and only the 12th in horse racing history to accomplish the feat.

Broncos linebacker Von Miller celebrates at the Super Bowl.

Super Bowl Triumph

On February 7, 2016, defense shined at Super Bowl 50. The Denver Broncos, led by linebacker Von Miller, shut down the Carolina Panthers, 24–10. Miller, who was named the game's MVP, put heavy pressure on Panthers quarterback Cam Newton, stripping him twice of the ball. One of those turnovers resulted in a defensive touchdown. The win gave Broncos QB Peyton Manning his second Super Bowl title.

Warriors point guard Stephen Curry goes up for a lay-up.

Shear Madness

What a load off! Chris the Sheep is the new world record holder for having the heaviest fleece. In September 2015, Guinness World Record officials declared the 89 pounds of wool shaved from the animal to be the most shorn from a sheep in a single shearing. (It's enough to knit 30 sweaters!)

Chris was found wandering near Canberra, Australia, and rescued earlier in the year. The weight of the wool made walking difficult for the lost sheep, and he was suffering from skin sores caused by his dirty fleece. Normally, merino sheep are shaved regularly, but Chris had never been trimmed. Ian Elkins, a champion sheep shearer, spent 42 minutes giving the sheep his first shave.

Chris the Sheep was rescued near Canberra, Australia.

Buzz Word

The Oxford Dictionaries 2015 "Word of the Year" is one that many texting teens know well: an emoji. The selection shows how popular these pictures have become in our daily lives. Oxford University Press partnered with the company SwiftKey to see which emoji was getting the most play in 2015. According to their data, the Face With Tears of Joy emoji, also known as Laughing Emoji, made up nearly 20% of emoji use in the U.S. and the U.K. The runner-up in the U.S., with 9% of usage, was the Face Throwing a Kiss.

Striking Gold

In June 2015, a family of professional treasure hunters discovered gold coins and jewelry worth more than $1 million in a 300-year-old shipwreck off the coast of Florida. A company hired the Schmitt family to search the *Capitana*, the flagship vessel of a Spanish fleet that sank during a 1715 hurricane. The loot included an extremely rare Spanish coin, valued at more than $500,000, that was meant to be delivered to the king of Spain.

Butterflies

Animals

Types of Animals

Scientists use many different indicators to group, or classify, animals. One way that animals can be classified involves their body structure. Animals that have backbones are called **vertebrates** . Animals without backbones are known as **invertebrates** .

Vertebrates

Amphibians are cold-blooded and begin life in the water, breathing through gills. When they are fully grown, they breathe through lungs and can walk on land. They lay eggs. Some examples of amphibians are frogs, toads, newts, and salamanders.

Red Eyed Tree Frog

American Bald Eagle

Birds are warm-blooded and have wings and feathers. All birds lay eggs and most can fly (though several, including emus, cassowaries, and penguins, cannot). Some other examples of birds are ducks, vultures, macaws, woodpeckers, wrens, puffins, orioles, eagles, and peacocks.

Pueblan Milk Snake

Great White Shark

Fish are cold-blooded and live in water. They have scaly skin and breathe using gills. Most fish lay eggs. Betta, catfish, koi, sharks, pufferfish, stingrays, and trout are examples of fish.

Reptiles are cold-blooded and have lungs. Their skin is scaly. Most reptiles lay eggs. Reptiles include alligators, crocodiles, tuataras, iguanas, snakes, and tortoises.

ANIMALS

Mammals are warm-blooded and, with the exception of the platypus and the echidna, give birth to live young. Mammal mothers breast-feed their young. Most mammals have hair or fur and live on land (except for porpoises, dolphins, and whales, which live in the water). Wolves, pandas, orangutans, bears, meerkats, dogs, elephants, tigers, seals, horses, and humans are all mammals.

Elephants

Invertebrates

Coelenterates have stinging tentacles around their mouths. They use their mouths not only to eat with but also to eliminate waste. Examples of coelenterates are jellyfish, corals, hydras, sea wasps, and sea anemones.

Glowing Blue Jellyfish

Echinoderms live in the sea and have exoskeletons, which means that their skeletons or supporting structures are located on the outsides of their bodies. Echinoderms include sand dollars, sea stars, sea cucumbers, and sea urchins.

Mollusks have soft bodies. To protect themselves, some have hard shells. Oysters, snails, octopuses, slugs, clams, scallops, squid, and mussels are all mollusks.

Sea Urchins

Garden Snail

Butterflies

Sponges live in water and are immobile. They get their food by filtering tiny organisms that swim by.

Arthropods have bodies that are divided into different parts, or segments. They also have exoskeletons. Arthropods include crustaceans (such as prawns, shrimp, and barnacles), arachnids (tarantulas, mites, and scorpions), centipedes, millipedes, and insects (such as butterflies, maggots, wasps, and ants).

Earthworm

Worms live in a variety of places, including underwater, in the ground, and even inside other living creatures. Examples of worms include hookworms, earthworms, leeches, peanut worms, and tapeworms.

Vanishing Act

Scientists say there have been five major extinction events on Earth—and a sixth has begun. They also say we can stop it.

The last time there was a major extinction event on Earth, the dinosaurs were wiped out. That happened 65 million years ago, after a giant asteroid struck the planet. Scientists say the Earth has had five major extinction events over the past 450 million years. Their causes are uncertain, though some were likely caused by massive volcanic eruptions. Each time, up to 90% of the species on the planet were killed off.

And each time, Earth bounced back.

Researchers say a sixth extinction has begun. This time, humans are the cause. Experts also say there is time for us to change our ways.

Species in Trouble

According to studies published in the journal *Science*, humans are responsible for a 25% drop in the populations of all species over the past 500 years. "Species are going extinct 1,000 times faster than they should be," scientist Stuart Pimm told TFK. He is a professor at Duke University and an expert on present-day extinctions.

Up to a third of all types of vertebrates are considered threatened. These include large animals such as rhinoceroses, elephants, and polar bears. Amphibians are also getting clobbered, with 41% of species in

Every year, hundreds of rhinos are hunted illegally.

The oceanic whitetip shark is a victim of overfishing. Its fins are used to make soup.

Orangutans are disappearing because the forests where they live are being cut down.

trouble. The number of invertebrates, including species of butterflies, worms, and spiders, has dropped by 45%.

What are we doing to cause creatures to disappear? Killing animals for food, clothing, and sport plays a big role. Elephants are hunted for their tusks and rhinos for their horns. Tigers are shot for their fur. Sharks end up in soup.

Humans are destroying habitats, particularly rain forests. People invade, building farms and homes and cutting animals off from sources of food and water. Trees are cut to build roads. Every year, about 25,000 miles of trees in the rain forests are lost.

Climate change is also responsible for putting many species at risk. Habitats become too hot, too dry, or too stormy for species that have adapted to different conditions.

Finally, there are invasive species. Foreign species, often introduced by people,

take over ecosystems, putting native species at risk.

It's Not Too Late

Experts say we can stop this sixth extinction—but it will take work. "We have choices," says Pimm. For example, "We can be careful to eat fish that are not being overharvested. We don't have to harvest fish to extinction."

Pimm runs Saving Species, a group that raises money to buy

up land in rain forests. Local people plant trees and reforest the areas. "There are things we can all—including kids—do as individuals," he says. "The future is not yet written. I'm very optimistic."

—*By Jeffrey Kluger for TIME, with reporting by Glenn Greenberg*

Golden lion tamarins from Brazil's rain forests were taken to zoos, where they produced babies. Their numbers grew and scientists were able to release the species back into its habitat. Today, there are about 1,500 living in the wild.

Animal Habitats

There's No Place Like Home

A habitat is an animal's natural home. And animals have habitats in every corner of the globe. Monkeys, snakes, toucans, and more live in rain forests. Camels, fennec foxes, and scorpions live in hot deserts. Deer, squirrels, and raccoons call temperate forests home. The tundra is the habitat for wolves, polar bears, and snowy owls. In the grasslands, you will find elephants, lions, and ostriches.

An animal is able to survive in the physical environment of its habitat. It can find food, water, mates, and shelter, and deal with the weather conditions. Let's take a quick look at some of the more unusual habitats that animals call home.

Raccoons

MYSTERY PERSON

I was born in London, England, in 1934. I am known for my study of chimpanzees in Africa. I have a Ph.D. from Cambridge University and established an institute to protect chimpanzees and their habitats. From 1998 to 2008, I served as president of Advocate for Animals.

◄ **Who am I?** Answer on page 276

Shrublands

Shrublands, true to their name, have a lot of shrubs. Shrubs are strong, woody plants that are smaller than trees. A shrubland has four seasons, including hot, dry summers and mild, rainy winters. These habitats are home to many animals, such as insects, like bees and butterflies; reptiles, including pythons, boas, tortoises, and rattlesnakes; birds, like mockingbirds, eagles, and quail; and mammals, including antelope, wild boar, sheep, and goats.

Antelope

Tide Pools

Tide pools form in rocks along the shoreline in coastal areas around the world. When the ocean is at high tide, which generally happens twice a day, water fills up around the rocks. When the tide goes out (also twice a day), the water level in the tide pools gets lower. Animals that live in tide pools have to be able to adjust to these daily changes in water level and temperature, as well as changes in sunlight. To survive in this habitat, sea stars attach themselves to rocks so they don't get swept out to sea during low tide. Clams use their shells to dig holes in the sand and into rock for the same reason.

Sea Stars

The Bathypelagic Zone: The Deep, Dark Sea

There is life at various levels in the sea, including the completely dark zone that starts at about 3,300 feet (1,006 m) below the surface. The water exerts a crushing force of 5,800 pounds per square inch (408 kg per square cm)! And the temperature hovers around a chilly 39°F (3.9°C). Giant squid, some kinds of sharks, and some eels call this place home, as do bioluminescent creatures—animals that make their own light using special light-producing organs. The anglerfish makes light in order to attract mates and to lure in prey.

Deep Sea Anglerfish

Pets

Meet the Most Popular

Most Popular Dog Breeds

1. Labrador retriever
2. German shepherd
3. Golden retriever
4. Bulldog
5. Beagle
6. Yorkshire terrier
7. Poodle
8. Boxer
9. French bulldog
10. Rottweiler

Source: American Kennel Club

Labrador Retriever

Most Popular Dog Names

1. Bella
2. Bailey
3. Max
4. Lucy
5. Molly
6. Charlie
7. Daisy
8. Buddy
9. Maggie
10. Sophie

Source: Veterinary Pet Insurance

German Shepherd

Most Popular Cat Breeds

1. Exotic
2. Persian
3. Maine coon
4. Ragdoll
5. British shorthair
6. American shorthair
7. Abyssinian
8. Sphynx
9. Siamese
10. Scottish fold

Source: Cat Fanciers' Association

Most Popular Cat Names

1. Bella
2. Max
3. Chloe
4. Oliver
5. Lucy
6. Charlie
7. Lily
8. Sophie
9. Tiger
10. Shadow

Source: Veterinary Pet Insurance

Persian Cat

ANIMALS

Most Popular Pets in the United States

Animal	Households	Population
Dogs	54.4 million	77.8 million
Cats	42.9 million	85.8 million
Fish	12.3 million	95.5 million
Birds	6.1 million	14.3 million
Small Pets (guinea pigs, hamsters, rabbits)	5.4 million	12.4 million

Source: American Pet Products Association

Hardworking Dogs

A new school for dogs is training the animals to use their amazing sense of smell to save lives.

Balancing Act
Ronnie practices walking on a slanted surface. Soon he'll use his skills on the job.

"Go find him," says trainer Jonathan Ball, and Jake takes off. The yellow Lab races toward a giant pile of rubble, with an expression that means business. The pile is a heap of wood, rocks, and metal. It's the kind of mess you might expect to find after an earthquake. But Jake climbs right up.

He hops around, sniffing and searching. And then he stops. He barks as he paws at a wooden board, trying to tear it off the container it is covering. Seconds later, the board comes loose, and out pops college student Patrick Robbins.

"Good boy, Jake!" Robbins yells. Jake's tail is wagging wildly. He's done exactly what he set out to do—find the hidden person.

Practice Run

For now, Jake's hard work is just for practice. Robbins was not really trapped. But someday, Jake may be called on to search for people buried in collapsed buildings after an earthquake, tornado, or other disaster has struck.

Jake is one of 16 detection dogs in training at the Penn Vet Working Dog Center, in Philadelphia, Pennsylvania. He and his canine classmates are learning how to use their keen sense of smell to search not only for missing people, but also for other things.

Some of the dogs may save lives by locating bombs. Others could protect kids who have serious nut allergies by sniffing out peanuts. And a few may be put to work identifying cancer so that patients can receive the treatments they need. Dogs are ideal candidates for these jobs because of "the bond that they have with humans," veterinarian Cindy Otto, director of the center, told TFK.

A Typical Day

In many ways, the center is like any other school. The dogs live with families nearby, and they arrive at

the center each morning by 9 a.m. They spend the day learning from their teachers. They practice following directions. And they even have their own version of gym class, in which they exercise and work to improve their balance and agility.

"If a building collapses, nothing is going to be steady," says training director Annemarie DeAngelo. "It's important for the dogs to be confident when they're climbing."

For their good work, the dogs do not earn an A on a report card. Instead, they are rewarded with playtime. Often, a trainer will engage a dog in a quick game of tug-of-war over a toy. "That is like winning the lottery, for the dogs," says Otto.

Since the Working Dog Center opened, the dogs have learned a great deal, and so have the people. "The goal," she says, "is to help future generations of dogs and handlers to be the best that they can possibly be."

—By Suzanne Zimbler

Lifesaving Skills McBaine figures out which bucket holds cancer cells. Trainer Jonathan Ball praises his good work.

Found! Patrick Robbins climbs out of his hiding place in a pile of rubble once Jake finds him. At nine months old, Jake is a quick learner.

Amazing Animal Facts

Fastest, Biggest, Smartest—and More

Fastest
Cheetahs
This speedy animal has been recorded running at speeds as high as 75 miles per hour!

Most talkative
Prairie Dogs
These animals have one of the most sophisticated languages in the animal kingdom. Their bark contains surprising amounts of information that can describe colors, sizes, directions of travel, and even speed. They use specific calls for different types of predators.

Most poisonous
Box Jellyfish
If stung by these deadly animals, a victim will most likely suffer a heart attack from the venom in the jellyfish's tentacles.

Longest lifespan
Bowhead Whales
Bowhead whales can live more than 200 years!

Sleepiest
Brown Bats
These creatures conserve energy by sleeping an average of 19.9 hours per day.

Biggest
Blue Whales
Their tongues alone can weigh as much as an elephant and their hearts as much as a car!

Tallest land animal
Giraffes
With long necks that stretch more than six feet in length, giraffes can tower as high as 20 feet tall.

Smallest mammal
Etruscan Pygmy Shrews
These tiny creatures weigh only about 1.8 grams on average, with a body length of four centimeters (excluding the tail).

Smartest
Dolphins
The sea mammals are second only to humans in intelligence.

Slowest
Three-toed Sloths
The top speed for sloths is 0.15 miles per hour. They move so slowly that algae can grow on their fur!

Flamingo Party

These photos of the pink tropical birds may look slmllar, but examine them closely and you'll see that not everything is quite the same. Can you spot all 10 differences?

ANIMALS

Answers on page 276

Art

The Origins of Art

A study shows that the art uncovered in caves in Indonesia is about 39,000 years old—the oldest ever discovered.

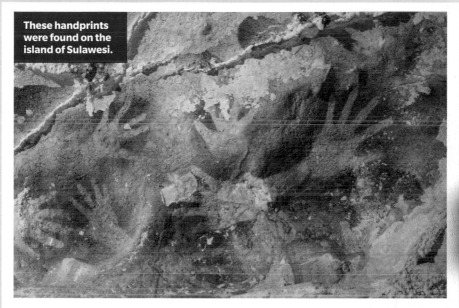

These handprints were found on the island of Sulawesi.

ART

According to a study published in the science journal *Nature*, cave paintings in Indonesia are as old as similar cave art in Europe. The paintings of animals and hands are located in seven caves on Sulawesi, an Indonesian island (see map). One of the handprints is at least 39,000 years old, making it the oldest handprint ever discovered. A painting of an animal known as a pig deer is also among the oldest of its kind.

Historians had thought that the oldest art was created in Europe. But a study of mineral deposits in the Sulawesi caves concludes that the art there is as old as, if not older than, prehistoric cave paintings from France and Spain. The findings cast new light on the origins of human creativity. "Whoa, it was not expected," said Maxime Aubert, who led the study.

Painting Through the Ages

Art has always been a form of communication and expression for people. The world's oldest paintings date back as much as 40,000 years. Found on the walls of caves, these paintings often feature large animals. Finger flutings are another type of cave art. They are impressions in the walls of caves made by people's fingers. Over the years and centuries, there have been many different styles of painting. Here are a few examples.

Italian Renaissance Painting

Renaissance means rebirth, and the Renaissance in Europe, which lasted from the 14th century to the 17th century, was a time of great growth for all kinds of learning, culture, and art. The city of Florence, Italy, was considered the birthplace and center of the Renaissance art movement. Many Renaissance paintings were commissioned by the Catholic Church and feature religious themes. One of the most famous is Leonardo da Vinci's *The Last Supper*.

The Last Supper

Dutch Golden Age

In the 17th century, the Dutch Republic (which is now the Netherlands) was the richest country in Europe. During this time, Dutch painters were known for several styles of painting. Many paintings depicted scenes of middle-class and peasant life, such as *The Milkmaid*, by Johannes Vermeer. Other themes included landscapes, still lifes, and seascapes. Wealthy families posed for many portraits. Rembrandt van Rijn painted both individual and group portraits. Painters from this period often emphasized light and shadow.

The Milkmaid

Impressionism

Paris, France, was the center of the art world in the late 1800s, when a painting style called Impressionism became popular. These paintings featured ordinary people, landscapes, and still lifes. Impressionist artists painted with a brighter range of colors than many previous artists. They also used shorter brushstrokes that are visible to the viewer, such as in Claude Monet's *Impression, Sunrise* and in portraits by Auguste Renoir, including *Madame Georges Charpentier and Her Children*.

Madame Georges Charpentier and Her Children

Modernism

Modern art is all about an artist's individual experimentation with paint and materials and his or her interpretation of objects and emotions. That explains why these works of art are incredibly varied and inventive. Modern artists include the early-20th-century painters Henri Matisse and Pablo Picasso, as well as Piet Mondrian, who worked mostly in the 1930s, and Jackson Pollock, who painted mainly in the 1940s. Some modern artists who became well known in the 1950s and 1960s are Andy Warhol, Roy Lichtenstein, Mark Rothko, Frank Stella, Jasper Johns, and Helen Frankenthaler.

Artist Roy Lichtenstein stands in front of one of his works.

ART

Grand Masters

Throughout history, many talented artists have impacted the art world with their memorable paintings, drawings, sculptures, and photographs. Here are five influential artists through the ages whose works we continue to celebrate today.

MICHELANGELO
1475–1564
Birthplace: Caprese, Italy
Movement: Renaissance
Michelangelo was a sculptor, painter, architect, and poet. From a young age, he served as an artist's apprentice, before moving to Florence as a teenager. He soon became a star thanks to the precise detail, realism, and intensity displayed in his art. His famous painting of the ceiling of the Sistine Chapel (above) took four years to complete and depicts scenes from the Book of Genesis.

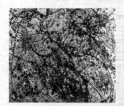

CLAUDE MONET
1840–1926
Birthplace: Paris, France
Movement: Impressionism
Monet was initially criticized for his loose forms and lack of realism. In fact, his style was the origin of Impressionism, paintings that depict the artist's "impressions" rather than the actual subject. Impressionism, known for its focus on light, transformed the art world. Monet's works were often a series of paintings, like haystacks and water lilies (above) shown over the course of a day in different light.

PABLO PICASSO
1881–1973
Birthplace: Malaga, Spain
Movement: Cubism
Picasso was destined to be a great artist. His father was an artist and Picasso held his first art exhibition at age 13. Picasso went through several periods in his art before he and artist Georges Braque founded Cubism, a movement that used geometrical shapes to express their vision of objects. This movement, showcased in *The Three Musicians* (above), established Picasso as one of the most important figures in the art world.

FRIDA KAHLO
1907–1954
Birthplace: Mexico City, Mexico
Movement: Surrealism
Kahlo is one of Mexico's greatest artists, known for her somber self-portraits (above) and honesty in her work. She suffered from crippling medical issues her entire life. In 1925, Kahlo's spine and pelvis were severely injured in a bus crash. During her recovery, she discovered her passion for painting. Using the canvas to reflect her pain, she included herself in 55 of her 143 known paintings.

JACKSON POLLOCK
1912–1956
Birthplace: Cody, Wyoming
Movement: Abstract expressionism
Pollock pushed the boundaries of art with his abstract works. The American painter's pieces were created with a drip technique: He'd place the canvases on the floor and splatter paint, letting it drip off the brush. Pollock's art is filled with action, expressing his emotions and mood, as seen in pieces such as *Reflection of the Big Dipper* (above). He remains a revolutionary figure in modern art.

Name That Movement

Popular styles of art have varied throughout history. Here are some more art movements with a description of the characteristics that defined them. Read about each period, then match it with the well-known masterpiece that was created during that time. Then, note the letter next to the work and fill in the box below that shows the corresponding number. Once that's done, you will learn the answer to this question:

What is the Italian name for the Mona Lisa, the famous portrait artist Leonardo Da Vinci painted around 1503?

MOVEMENTS

1. Ancient Greece (Hellenistic period)
Ancient Greeks were famous for their sculptures, which began to look more realistic during this period.

2. Italian Renaissance
This was a golden age in art led by famous Italian masters who created grand, realistic-looking works.

3. Baroque
Paintings that show dramatic moments and feature extreme realism and clever use of light and perspective are typical of this period.

4. Romanticism
This movement was defined by art that expresses raw emotion, showing the fury of nature and war.

5. Post Impressionism
This modern art style used vivid colors and heavy brushstrokes to express the emotion behind the work.

6. Expressionism
The pieces during this period focused on feelings. Often the figures are distorted and painted in bright colors for shock value.

7. Cubism
Artists during this period often portrayed objects and people with geometric shapes.

8. Pop Art
This style refers to art that reflects popular culture, often featuring well-known people and everyday objects.

ART

MASTERPIECES

Les Demoiselles d'Avignon by Pablo Picasso (D)

Liberty Leading the People by Eugene Delacroix (N)

The Scream by Edvard Munch (O)

Campbell Soup Can by Andy Warhol (C)

The Birth of Venus by Botticelli (I)

The Calling of St. Matthew by Caravaggio (L)

Venus de Milo by Alexandros of Antioch (A)

Starry Night by Vincent Van Gogh (G)

THE ANSWER

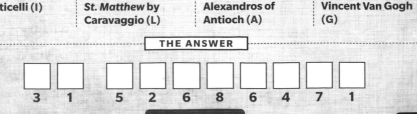

3	1	5	2	6	8	6	4	7	1

Answer on page 276

Body and Health

Inside Out

The human body is an amazing machine. The organs work together in perfect harmony and keep your body running. Here's a look at some of the important roles the major organs play.

Brain
- Controls bodily functions
- Home to the nerve center
- Made of soft tissue

Heart
- Pumps oxygenated blood through the body
- Helps keep other organs working

Lungs
- Takes in oxygen to pump into the circulatory system
- Expels carbon dioxide from the body

Pancreas
- Produces enzymes necessary for digestion

Liver
- Creates bile to help aid stomach with digestion
- Filters toxins
- Regulates blood sugar
- Largest internal organ in the body

Kidneys
- Help filter water and salt out of blood
- Produce urine to eliminate waste
- Help regulate blood pressure

Small Intestine
- Digests food
- Absorbs nutrients and delivers them to blood

Stomach
- Breaks down food to be further processed in the small intestine

Skin
- Protects inner organs
- Regulates body's temperature through sweat and oil glands

Large Intestine
- Helps break down any food not digested by the small intestine
- Expels waste

Go to Sleep!

Tired? Falling asleep in class? Maybe you are skimping on sleep. Unplugging before bed can help you get rest and stay alert.

Kids who keep electronic devices in their room get less sleep at night.

Trixie Johnson, 10, likes to stay up late playing Minecraft and watching videos on her iPad. The fifth grader from New York City says she can tell when she has not had enough sleep. "It can be hard to get up for school," she says.

Trixie is not alone in feeling tired. According to the National Sleep Foundation (NSF), kids between the ages of 6 and 13 need nine to 11 hours of sleep each night. Most are getting far less than that.

New research shows that a good night's rest affects how your brain works and how well you learn. "The things you learn in school stick better in your brain when you sleep enough," Lisa Meltzer told TFK. She is a sleep expert.

Meltzer and other experts say that getting the proper amount of sleep is particularly important for learning complex subjects, such as math and foreign languages. Not getting enough Zs can affect your concentration and your mood and can impact your behavior. "You don't do well even in activities that you enjoy," Meltzer says.

Screen-Free Zones

What is stealing kids' valuable sleep time? According to the NSF, electronic devices play a big role. The NSF reports that nearly three out of four kids ages 6 to 17 keep at least one electronic device in the bedroom. Kids with smartphones and tablets in their room get nearly half an hour less sleep than those without. "Smartphones and devices should stay in the living room at night," says pediatrician Matt M. Davis.

Other behaviors can also contribute to bad sleep habits. A poor diet, an irregular bedtime, and too many after-school activities can affect how well and how long you sleep. Davis urges families to work together to help kids find the right

balance of after-school activities so kids are not overscheduled.

Making sure you get the right amount of sleep takes work. But it is worth the effort. The American Academy of Pediatrics (AAP) advises kids to stop looking at screens at least half an hour before bedtime. Doing so will help your brain slow down and get your body ready for sleep. The AAP says bedrooms should be "screen-free zones."

Trixie's mom, Ally Johnson,

> **When you are well rested, your brain is ready to do math and other complex work.**

says her family has changed its routines. "We are limiting Trixie's screen time and have set an earlier bedtime," she says. "Doing relaxing things like reading a book before bed really helps her get a good night's rest."

Keep track of your sleep hours. Is it time to change up your bedtime routine?

—By Melanie Kletter

A Good Night

Researchers say there are four stages of sleep. All are important. The cycle repeats every 90 minutes.

STAGE ONE
As you first begin to drift off, you close your eyes, but you can be awakened easily.

STAGE TWO
You enter into a phase of light sleep. Your body temperature drops and your heart rate slows down. You start to feel removed from your surroundings.

STAGE THREE
This is the deepest sleep. During this stage, your muscles relax, blood pressure drops, and blood supply to the muscles increases. Substances that the body needs for growth and development are released. Tissues repair themselves. Energy is restored.

STAGE FOUR
During rapid eye movement—or REM—sleep, your brain is active and your eyes move back and forth. Your body is still and relaxed. You dream.

All in Your Mind

Experts say you have the ability to boost your brainpower.

Last year, when she was in the fifth grade, Kayla Thompson dreaded math class, especially when it came to adding and subtracting fractions. "I knew there was only one correct answer," Kayla told TFK. "And when I didn't get it, I felt discouraged."

This year, Kayla has a different point of view. Since September, she and her classmates at Lenox Academy, in Brooklyn, New York, have been taking a course called Brainology. The program teaches that the brain works like a muscle: The more you use it, the stronger it gets.

Now, when Kayla faces a challenge in math, she doesn't shut down. And she doesn't feel bad about making mistakes, either. After all, she says, "mistakes help us learn."

Work Your Brain!

Psychologist Carol Dweck, at Stanford University, in California, developed Brainology after years of studying students' attitudes toward learning. She found that when kids realize it's possible to increase their intelligence, they do better in school. "We teach kids that every time they work on something hard and stick to it, their brain forms stronger connections. And these connections can make them smarter," she says.

So how can you give your brain a good workout? When you have a choice between an easy task and a challenging one, says Dweck, you should always take the challenge. "Struggle is good," she says. "Working hard at something really grows your brain."

Dweck also recommends embracing mistakes. "Don't run away from it," she says. "Instead, think about it. Ask your teacher about it."

Brain Game
Place your pencil on the red dot. Without lifting your pencil from the paper, can you connect the nine dots with only four straight lines?
Answer on page 276

Smart Science

According to Dan Hurley, author of *Smarter: The New Science of Building Brain Power*, certain activities could sharpen the mind. Studies show that being physically active is a good way to improve your mental abilities. "Physical activity seems to stimulate the growth of neurons," says Hurley.

What else can you do to give your brain a boost? "Learning to play a musical instrument seems to have benefits that go beyond just learning the instrument," Hurley says. "And playing chess is really mind-expanding."

But no matter what you are doing, Hurley stresses the importance of stepping outside your comfort zone. "The more you challenge your mind," he says, "the more it responds."

—By Suzanne Zimbler

Head Scratchers

**How well do you know the human body?
Put your knowledge to the test with this trivia challenge.**

1. How many bones are in each of your hands?
A. 2 ○
B. 5 ○
C. 15 ○
D. 27 ○

2. Which part of the body does not perform a clear function?
A. Appendix ○
B. Tonsils ○
C. Gallbladder ○
D. Pinky finger ○

3. How are fingerprints formed?
A. The prints are created when babies suck on their fingers. ○
B. They are inherited from the parents and are a combination of the mother's and father's prints. ○
C. The prints are formed based on the environment in the womb. ○
D. The prints are a reflection of how we use our fingers and hands and can change through the years. ○

4. What are the strongest muscles in the body?
A. Biceps ○
B. Jaw muscles ○
C. Heart ○
D. Glutes ○

5. What are your five senses?
A. Understanding, Talking, Seeing, Listening, Eating ○
B. Seeing, Hearing, Touching, Tasting, Smelling ○
C. Laughing, Crying, Shouting, Shaking, Smiling ○
D. Running, Walking, Jumping, Sleeping, Standing ○

6. How much does the average brain weigh?
A. 1 pound ○
B. 2 pounds ○
C. 3 pounds ○
D. 4 pounds ○

7. What is the largest organ in the human body?
A. Brain ○
B. Skin ○
C. Liver ○
D. Heart ○

8. What part of your body is responsible for balance?
A. Ears ○
B. Eyes ○
C. Legs ○
D. Arms ○

BODY AND HEALTH

Answers on page 276

45

Books

All-Time Classics

These great books are the favorites of kids of all ages.

Harry Potter and the Sorcerer's Stone
By J.K. Rowling
Published: 1997
This global favorite about the adventures of a young boy wizard and his friends at a magical boarding school took author J.K. Rowling five years to write. The successful book series has since been turned into multiple feature films and amusement parks.

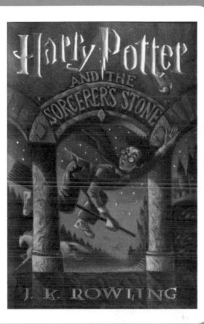

Charlotte's Web
By E.B. White
Published: 1952
The classic tale of friendship between animals on a farm is the best-selling children's paperback of all time. White found inspiration for the story after moving his family from New York City to a farm in eastern Maine in 1939.

The Hunger Games
By Suzanne Collins
Published: 2008
Centered on heroine Katniss Everdeen and a world in which children compete in the annual Hunger Games, this book, part of a trilogy, became a worldwide sensation. It has been translated into 26 languages and a film franchise.

The Giver
By Lois Lowry
Published: 1993
The 1994 Newbery Medal winner tells a tale of a seemingly perfect society that has no pain or knowledge of the past. Jonas is assigned to be the "Receiver of Memory" and must learn to cope with the emotions that come with his role.

The Lion, The Witch and The Wardrobe
By C.S. Lewis
Published: 1950
The first book in the Chronicles of Narnia series, this fantasy tale introduces readers to a land of endless winters that can only be accessed through a wardrobe. It was named one of TIME's All-TIME 100 Novels.

To Kill a Mockingbird
By Harper Lee
Published: 1960
This Pulitzer Prize-winner about the Finch family is a beloved classic that addresses issues of race relations in the South. The novel was made into an Oscar-nominated movie in 1962 and ranked as the fourth-most influential book in a survey taken by the Library of Congress in 1991.

Holes
By Louis Sachar
Published: 1998
A favorite of young-adult readers everywhere, this silly, treasure-hunting tale tells the story of a group of misfits sent to a detention camp. Forced to dig holes in the desert as a way to build character, they uncover buried secrets.

The Phantom Tollbooth
By Norton Juster
Published: 1961
Juster was inspired to write this book after a young boy asked him what the biggest number in existence was. According to the author, that conversation created the spark for the novel, which tells the story of "a boy who asked too many questions."

Bridge to Terabithia
By Katherine Paterson
Published: 1977
This is the tale of Jesse and Leslie, two unlikely friends who create an imaginary place in the forest near their home and make themselves king and queen of the land. The book, inspired by real-life events, won the Newbery Medal in 1978.

Where the Red Fern Grows
By Wilson Rawls
Published: 1961
This novel about a young boy named Billy and his two dogs, Old Dan and Little Ann, is a heartbreaking classic that has been read in schools for decades. But it almost wasn't to be: Rawls received two rejections before the story was finally accepted for publication.

MYSTERY PERSON

I was born on July 31,1965, in England, and liked writing fantasy stories as a child. Using a pen name of my first and middle initials, I wrote the best-selling book series of all time. I came up with the idea for the book in 1990 while on a train. Because I didn't have a pen, I spent four hours going over the details of the magical world in my mind.

Answer on page 276

New and Noteworthy

From a modern spin on fairytales to talking animals, here are some recent books to check out.

Brown Girl Dreaming
By Jacqueline Woodson
In this book, a 2015 National Book Award winner, Woodson shares what it was like to grow up as an African-American in the 1960s and 1970s and pays tribute to her family by telling their story in poems.

Crenshaw
By Katherine Applegate
This magical tale from Newbery Medal-winner Applegate follows a young boy named Jackson and an old imaginary pal, a large cat named Crenshaw. The book shows that the power of imagination is greater than you think!

The Crossover
By Kwame Alexander
This rhythmic, 2015 Newbery Medal-winning novel combines the art of poetry with narrative storytelling. Told entirely in verse, the book follows 12-year-old narrator Josh as he navigates life with his family and on the basketball court.

El Deafo
By Cece Bell, Color by David Lasky
In this loosely autobiographical graphic novel, Newbery-winning author/illustrator Bell chronicles her hearing loss at a young age—and what it's like to grow up with a giant hearing aid strapped to your chest!

Island Treasures: Growing Up in Cuba
By Alma Flor Ada
As a child living in Cuba, Ada, an award-winning author, loved to spend time exploring the fields near her home. In this book, she shares vivid details of the adventures and Cuban traditions she grew up with.

The Isle of the Lost: A Descendants Novel
By Melissa de la Cruz
In this fresh spin on old fairytales, the children of Disney villains embark on a quest to retrieve the Dragon's Eye, the key to true darkness. But along the way they realize that an evil family tree doesn't always produce bad apples.

The Marvels
By Brian Selznick
Caldecott-winning author and illustrator Selznick tells two tales here: the first in pictures and the second in words. Together, the stories create a captivating narrative about a young shipwreck survivor and a runaway.

The Story of Diva and Flea
By Mo Willems, Illustrated by Tony DiTerlizzi
Cats and dogs don't always get along. But not so in this tale! Set in Paris, France, this book follows happy-go-lucky cat Flea and pampered pooch Diva as they develop an unexpected friendship.

BOOKS

49

10 Questions for Gail Carson Levine

TFK Kid Reporter Dahlia Suiter spoke with the author of *Ella Enchanted*.

Kid Reporter Dahlia Suiter got writing tips from Levine. A big piece of advice: Keep writing!

1. You've said that you didn't think you'd become a writer. Why?
I didn't know what I would be. There were times when I wanted to be a scientist. I loved reading about dinosaurs and biology.

2. Why do you write children's books?
I never thought about writing stories for adults. It was always for children because when I was a child, books were so important to me.

3. What do you enjoy most about writing?
Revision is my favorite part. I also love developing characters. If I can be surprising, I'm happy about that, too. I want to make the reader care about what's going on.

4. How do you keep a story going?
Generally, I'm not going to let a story go. I'm willing to throw out hundreds of pages, and I've done that many times.

5. What fascinates you about the fantasy genre?
It's a combination of being able to do anything, but having to make it real. I like to imagine creatures, and I like to make them mine.

6. In your book, *Writer to Writer: From Think to Ink*, you end each chapter with "Have fun, and save what you write!" Why?
Writing is hard, and if you're not having fun with it, why do it? "Save what you write" is crucial because you may need it. You may need that scene you cut.

7. What are some other tips?
Writing is something you get better and better at. You never get perfect at it. I continue to learn. Major advice: Keep writing because writers write.

8. What do you hope kids will learn from *Writer to Writer*?
I hope the book will suggest new directions and open up new places to go with writing. For kids who don't like to write, I hope the prompts will make that less onerous, less of a hardship. I hope writing becomes a friendlier thing to do.

9. Can you give me a good prompt?
Write this scene: In "The Frog Prince," the frog turns into a prince not when the princess kisses him but when she throws him against a wall as hard as she can.

10. Why is it important for kids to practice writing?
Writing is self-discovery. You learn about yourself when you write. The process of writing slows your thinking down, and you can make discoveries and go places that you don't expect.

Levine shares the tricks of her trade in her book *Writer to Writer: From Think to Ink.*

GAIL CARSON LEVINE
WRITER to WRITER

The Wisdom of Words

Use the chart below to match a letter to each symbol. Fill in the blanks to reveal a famous quotation by author Mark Twain.

—MARK TWAIN

January, February, March, April, May, June, July, August, September, October, November, December

2017

Calendar and Holidays

JAN
1

2017

January

S	M	T	W	T	F	S
1	2	3	4	5	6	7
8	9	10	11	12	13	14
15	16	17	18	19	20	21
22	23	24	25	26	27	28
29	30	31				

February

S	M	T	W	T	F	S
			1	2	3	4
5	6	7	8	9	10	11
12	13	14	15	16	17	18
19	20	21	22	23	24	25
26	27	28				

March

S	M	T	W	T	F	S
			1	2	3	4
5	6	7	8	9	10	11
12	13	14	15	16	17	18
19	20	21	22	23	24	25
26	27	28	29	30	31	

April

S	M	T	W	T	F	S
						1
2	3	4	5	6	7	8
9	10	11	12	13	14	15
16	17	18	19	20	21	22
23	24	25	26	27	28	29
30						

May

S	M	T	W	T	F	S
	1	2	3	4	5	6
7	8	9	10	11	12	13
14	15	16	17	18	19	20
21	22	23	24	25	26	27
28	29	30	31			

June

S	M	T	W	T	F	S
				1	2	3
4	5	6	7	8	9	10
11	12	13	14	15	16	17
18	19	20	21	22	23	24
25	26	27	28	29	30	

July

S	M	T	W	T	F	S
						1
2	3	4	5	6	7	8
9	10	11	12	13	14	15
16	17	18	19	20	21	22
23	24	25	26	27	28	29
30	31					

August

S	M	T	W	T	F	S
		1	2	3	4	5
6	7	8	9	10	11	12
13	14	15	16	17	18	19
20	21	22	23	24	25	26
27	28	29	30	31		

September

S	M	T	W	T	F	S
					1	2
3	4	5	6	7	8	9
10	11	12	13	14	15	16
17	18	19	20	21	22	23
24	25	26	27	28	29	30

October

S	M	T	W	T	F	S
1	2	3	4	5	6	7
8	9	10	11	12	13	14
15	16	17	18	19	20	21
22	23	24	25	26	27	28
29	30	31				

November

S	M	T	W	T	F	S
			1	2	3	4
5	6	7	8	9	10	11
12	13	14	15	16	17	18
19	20	21	22	23	24	25
26	27	28	29	30		

December

S	M	T	W	T	F	S
					1	2
3	4	5	6	7	8	9
10	11	12	13	14	15	16
17	18	19	20	21	22	23
24	25	26	27	28	29	30
31						

CALENDAR AND HOLIDAYS

Every Month Is Special

Each month we celebrate important topics—both serious and fun.

January
- Braille Literacy
- National Mentoring

February
- Black History
- American Heart

March
- Women's History
- Reading Awareness

April
- Autism Awareness
- Volunteer

May
- Asian American and Pacific Islanders Heritage
- Mental Awareness

June
- Oceans
- LGBT Pride

July
- Ice Cream
- Parks and Recreation Month

August
- Water Quality

September
- Wilderness
- Guide Dog

October
- Bullying Prevention
- Breast Cancer Awareness Month

November
- Military Family
- Native American Heritage

December
- Human Rights
- Read a New Book

Time to Celebrate 2017

January 1: New Year's Day

January 16: Martin Luther King Jr. Day

January 20: Inauguration Day

January 28: Lunar New Year

February 2: Groundhog Day

February 12: Lincoln's Birthday

February 14: Valentine's Day

February 20: Presidents' Day

March 1: Ash Wednesday

March 12: Purim*

March 12: Māgha Pujā Day

March 12: Daylight Savings Time Begins

March 13: Holi

April 1: April Fool's Day

April 9: Palm Sunday

April 11-18: Passover*

April 13: Holy Thursday

April 14: Good Friday

April 16: Easter

April 17: Dyngus Day

April 22: Earth Day

May 5: Cinco de Mayo

May 10: Buddha Day

May 14: Mother's Day

May 20: Armed Forces Day

May 25: Ascension Day

May 27-June 25: Ramadan

May 29: Memorial Day

May 31-June 1: Shavuot*

June 6: D-Day

June 14: Flag Day

June 18: Father's Day

June 26: Eid al-Fitr

July 4: Independence Day

July 8: Dhamma Day

August 15: Assumption of Mary

August 21: Total Solar Eclipse in the U.S.

September 2: Eid al-Adha

September 4: Labor Day

September 10: National Grandparents Day

September 21-22: Rosh Hashanah*

September 30: Yom Kippur*

October 5-11: Sukkot*

October 9: Columbus Day

October 19: Diwali

October 31: Halloween

November 1: All Saints' Day

November 5: Daylight Savings Time Ends

November 7: Election Day

November 11: Veterans Day

November 23: Thanksgiving

December 7: Pearl Harbor Remembrance Day

December 8: Feast of the Immaculate Conception

December 13-20: Hanukkah*

December 26-January 1: Kwanzaa

*Jewish holidays begin at sundown the evening before

CALENDAR AND HOLIDAYS

Basler Fasnacht

Monday through Thursday after Ash Wednesday

• The largest popular festival in Switzerland is Basler Fasnacht, or the Carnival of Basel. Starting at 4 a.m. on Monday, people in huge, cartoonish masks and colorful costumes begin to march through the streets. They carry lanterns, play instruments, sing songs, and act out scenes from the year before.

Dyngus Day

Monday after Easter

• Some Christians take part in Lent, which is a period of 40 days before Easter, during which they fast—give up something they enjoy—and reflect on their sins. Celebrated in Poland, Dyngus Day is a day of fun and silliness that follows Lent. Boys chase girls and try to drench them with buckets of water or squirt guns. Girls have a chance to do the same on the following day.

Gai Jatra

A day in August or September

- A popular celebration in Nepal is Gai Jatra, which means "festival of the cows." Any person who has lost a family member in the year leading up to the festival leads a cow in a parade. If a person does not have a cow handy, he or she will lead a young child dressed as a cow. The kids may be fed milk or given money or gifts. Cows are sacred to members of the Hindu religion. According to the tradition, the cows in the parade help usher people's ancestors into heaven. Even though the festival commemorates the dead, it is not a somber event. After the parade, people dress up, wear masks, make jokes, and have a great time.

Eid al-Fitr

End of Ramadan (date changes every year, but it will be celebrated on June 25 in 2017)

- Ramadan is the holiest month of the year for Muslims. During Ramadan, Muslims pray, perform acts of charity, and refrain from eating or drinking during the day. Eid al-Fitr (eed al-fit-tuhr) is the festival at the end of the month. It's celebrated with prayers, gifts, charity, new clothing, and big family meals that include lots of sweet dishes.

Ring in the New Year

People around the world have many different ways of celebrating January 1.

No Sour Grapes In Spain, people eat 12 grapes at the stroke of midnight for good luck.

• **Greeks** bake a cake called a vasilopita and hide a coin inside. The diner who finds the coin in his or her piece of cake will be extra lucky all year long.

• Many **Japanese** people clean their houses and forgive any grudges they may be holding in order to start off the year in a good place. Decorations called *shimekazari*, which are made of twisted rice-straw rope, are hung in doorways. They are often adorned with shide, which are paper strips cut in zigzag patterns. These decorations keep bad spirits away. Other good luck items, such as ferns and oranges, may be included in a shimekazari.

• **In the Netherlands**, people eat a deep-fried, donut-like treat called an *oliebol*. They also set off fireworks and light bonfires, often burning their Christmas trees.

• At the stroke of midnight, many **Kenyans** howl at the top of their lungs. They cheer, sing, dance, and honk car horns.

• **The Spanish** pop 12 grapes into their mouths at midnight. It is considered good luck.

• **In Peru**, some people play a game with potatoes. A peeled potato (symbolizing having no money), a partially peeled potato (symbolizing an average amount of money), and a potato with its skin on (representing having a lot of money) are placed under a chair. Without looking, party guests choose a potato. The potato they pick predicts what kind of financial success they'll have that year.

Trick or Treat!

It's Halloween—that means time to trick or treat.
Help the kids find their way to the house, but be sure to avoid all
the scary ghouls along the way!

Answer on page 276

Computers and Games

Computers Through the Years

Learn about the evolution of the electronic machine that has become a big part of our everyday lives.

1890

American inventor Herman Hollerith designs a punch card machine to help calculate the 1890 census, introducing the world to data processing. He finishes the task in just two years, saving the U.S. government $5 million. He starts a company that will become part of IBM.

1936

British mathematician Alan Turing publishes a paper that is recognized as the foundation for computer science. He proposes the idea of a universal machine that is capable of decoding and performing sets of instructions.

1941

J.V. Atanasoff, an Iowa State University professor, and his graduate student, Clifford Berry, design a computer that can solve 29 equations at the same time. It is considered to be the first electronic digital computer.

1952

Grace Hopper, a computer scientist and U.S. Navy rear admiral, creates a common language that computers can understand. This leads to the creation of the common business oriented language, or COBOL. It's a programming language that is still used today.

1958

Americans Jack Kilby and Robert Noyce independently invent the integrated circuit, or the computer chip. Kilby will win the Nobel Prize in Physics in 2000. Noyce dies in 1990, before he can be honored with the award.

1974-1977

A number of personal computers go on sale. They include Scelbi & Mark-8 Altair, IBM 5100, RadioShack's TRS-80, and the Commodore PET.

1975

Childhood friends Paul Allen and Bill Gates form a software company they name Microsoft. They hope to put a computer in every home.

1976-1977

Steve Jobs and Steve Wozniak start Apple Computers. They roll out the Apple I, the first computer with a single-circuit board. In 1977, they debut the Apple II.

This prototype of a microchip was created by Jack Kilby.

Apple II

1981

The first IBM personal computer is introduced. It uses Microsoft's MS-DOS operating system, has an Intel chip, two floppy disks, and an optional color monitor. It popularizes the term *PC*.

1989

British scientist Tim Berners-Lee develops Hyper-Text Markup Language, or HTML, making the World Wide Web possible. The first website was dedicated to the World Wide Web project.

1990

Dutch researcher Vic Hayes, known as the Father of Wi-Fi, becomes chair of the Institute of Electrical & Electronics Engineers. The committee develops international standards for Wi-Fi technology, the first of which is established in 1997.

1996

Sergey Brin and Larry Page develop the Google search engine at Stanford University.

Apple Watch

IBM's personal computer used floppy disks and an Intel chip.

2004

In February, Mark Zuckerberg launches Facebook from his Harvard dorm room. The site has 1 million users by the end of 2004. Also, Mozilla's Firefox 1.0 challenges Microsoft's Internet Explorer (IE), the dominant web browser of the time. A few years before, IE had defeated the once-popular Netscape Navigator in the first "browser wars."

2005

Chad Hurley, Steve Chen, and Jawed Karim launch a video-sharing website called YouTube. It revolutionizes the way people view videos and connect on the Internet. Google acquires Android, a mobile operating system.

2007-2010

Steve Jobs introduces the Apple iPhone to the world. The smartphone features functions normally on a computer and fits into people's palms. Three years later, Apple unveils the iPad tablet.

2015

Apple releases the Apple Watch, the first wearable tech from the company. Microsoft releases Windows 10.

Former Apple CEO Steve Jobs

FROM TIME FOR KIDS MAGAZINE

Cracking the Code

What role should computer science play in the classroom?

Code Hour
Students at a school in Renton, Washington, learn to write code.

It is not big news that we live in a digital world. Whether at home or in the classroom, most kids are connected to some form of technology. But do students need to know how to create that technology?

Yes, say computer experts. "Learning how technology works and how you can harness it are as important as reading and writing," Srini Mandyam told TFK. He is a cofounder of Tynker, a company that creates programs to teach kids how to write code, or the instructions that tell a computer what to do.

Getting into Schools

Every app, game, and computer program starts with a code. According to the College Board and the Computer Science Teachers Association, only one out of 10 schools in the United States offers computer-science classes. The organization Code.org aims to change that, so every student in every school has the opportunity to learn computer programming. The group wants U.S. schools to follow the examples set by China, Vietnam, and Britain, where coding classes are offered as early as elementary school. Mandyam says one of Tynker's goals is to integrate coding into STEM (science, technology, engineering, and math) lessons.

Back to Basics

But not everyone is ready to devote elementary school hours to coding. "Students in K through 6 need to cultivate both sides of the brain, trying not to focus on one or the other," says Melanie Reiser, the leader of programs and activities at the Association of Waldorf Schools of North America.

Mandyam and other coding supporters argue that kids need to be ready for the future. "Technology is at the heart of every major change that's happening in the world," says Mandyam. "Kids need to feel empowered and know they can be a part of it."

—By Cameron Keady, with reporting by Eliana Dockterman for TIME

Game On!

From a galaxy far, far away to center stage of a rock concert, these cool games transport you to many exciting places.

Star Wars Battlefront (EA, Console, Rated T)

In a galaxy far, far away, an epic war between the forces of light and the forces of dark is raging on. The question is, which side are you on? *Star Wars Battlefront* gives gamers a choice. Armed with blasters, lightsabers, and starships, you'll battle opponents against the backdrop of planets from the Star Wars universe. May the Force be with you!

Minecraft: Story Mode
(Telltale Games, Mobile & Console, E10+)

Terror has been unleashed on the world. In order to save it, you and your friends must find a legendary group of warriors called the Order of the Stone. It's a dangerous journey that will take you across the Overworld, through the Nether, to the End, and beyond.

Guitar Hero Live
(Activision, Console, Rated T)

This popular franchise gets two new gameplay modes and an all-new guitar controller in *Guitar Hero Live*. Players can rock out in GH Live mode, which puts you center stage before a crowd. Or, switch over to GHTV. It's a playable music video network where you can challenge friends around the world.

Shadowmatic
(Triada Studio Games, Mobile)

In this game of shadow puppets, players rotate odd shapes in a spotlight. The goal? To create silhouettes of familiar objects that fit the theme of the room. The levels are divided into chambers, and each room's background gives clues about a type of shadow you need to cast.

Monument Valley
(ustwo, Mobile)

In the dreamlike Monument Valley, you're tasked with guiding the silent princess Ida through a mysterious maze of monuments. The challenge lies in getting the princess to the top of each structure, and the route is not always clear in this topsy-turvy world.

Framed
(Loveshack Entertainment, Mobile)

This puzzle game plays out like an animated comic book thriller—but you get to decide the fate of the characters. Each "page" of the story presents players with a series of panels that show an important event or action. You can change the overall outcome of the tale by changing the order of the panels.

App Happy
Check out these six fun apps.

Dreamify
This dreamy app allows users to create bizarre versions of their smartphone snaps. Select from a dozen preset options to create a whimsical work of art out of any image. Then share it with friends.

Periscope
Twitter's live-stream app makes sure that you will never have a moment of FOMO (fear of missing out) again! It lets you broadcast events in real-time from your mobile device to your followers.

Elementary Minute
This award-winning quiz app presents statements about math, people, and places. You must decide if they are true or false. You'll be a trivia whiz before you know it!

The Foos
Learning how to code has never been easier. The residents of Foosville need your help solving puzzles. As you play, you'll use a unique coding language to build programs that will help the Foos.

Inventioneers
In this fun puzzle app, players are presented with a wacky, incomplete machine. Using problem-solving skills and lots of imagination, players can create crazy inventions.

Nito+
It's time to get animated with Nito+! The app's special technology tracks your face as you talk. Your voice, expressions, and movements are then mirrored perfectly by an animated avatar.

More Than a Game?

Video-game designers work hard to create games that hold your attention and leave you wanting more.

Jaden Darnell, of Southbridge, Massachusetts, has an Xbox 360 and a PlayStation 3. Like many other kids, the fourth grader also plays games on his phone. At times, it can be hard to tear himself away from a device. "Sometimes, I just don't want to stop," Jaden told TFK.

What makes some video games so engaging? Game developers are focused on that question.

With both kids and adults shifting more of their game play to phones and tablets, the makers of mobile games, especially, are focused on keeping players hooked.

Tricks of the Trade

Raph Koster, an expert on game design, says game makers employ a great deal of knowledge about what keeps people playing. He says that players like getting feedback that they can see or hear. The game Peggle, for example, plays the song "Ode to Joy" every time you succeed at beating a level. "It gives you this amazing amount of celebration," says Koster, "and as a result, you feel awesome."

Game makers also know that once players have put in the time and effort to achieve a goal, they don't like to give up. So some games are easy at first and become more challenging. At that point, the player may be offered a resource that makes winning easier.

When players are connected to the Internet, developers can observe what they do. By keeping tabs on players' choices, game companies can find out what keeps people plugged in. "With everything being connected, it's very easy for us to get data on users and build a picture of what is working," says Koster.

Brain-Building Games

Game developers are not the only people interested in what keeps players glued to their devices. Scientists are also recognizing the power of games.

Adam Gazzaley, a scientist at the University of California, San Francisco, has developed games that improve attention and memory in older adults. Now Gazzaley and his team are designing brain-building games for kids. "We think that how video games really pull you in and demand your attention can be used to help improve how the brain processes information," he says.

To test the games' effects on the mind, Gazzaley records brain activity while people play. He says that one day, doctors might prescribe video games to boost a patient's mental abilities. Now that's a game you wouldn't feel guilty playing!

—By Suzanne Zimbler

Goal Oriented Game makers are always working to give players the best experience.

Can You Compute?

Complete this crossword to see how well you know your computer terms.

Across

3. The screen that displays images and accompanies a desktop computer
5. This device allows you to type
7. You can carry this kind of computer around
8. A popular game that centers around placing and breaking blocks
11. One of the original computer companies that also shares a name with a fruit
12. More than a billion users go to this website to post and watch videos
14. You use this device to point and click
17. Portable, as in a phone
18. To make accessible to other users

Down

1. Send a quick note from your phone
2. The World Wide Web
4. The amount of storage space on a computer
6. Hitting Control-S will do this to your document
9. An iPad is this kind of device
10. Short for application
13. Pictures and characters used in electronic messages
15. A well-known search engine and creator of fun doodles
16. The game Angry _____

Answers on page 276

69

The Great Wall of China

Countries

Big Ben in London, England

Amazing Places Around the World

Niagara Falls,
Canada

Statue of Liberty,
United States

Chichen Itza,
Mexico

Perito Moreno
Glacier,
Argentina

Machu Picchu,
Peru

Top 5 Most-Photographed Places

Researchers studied 35 million Flickr photos. They discovered the places that people most visited and photographed. Here are the top-five city sites.

Empire State Building,
NEW YORK, NEW YORK

Trafalgar Square,
LONDON, ENGLAND

Amazing Places Around the World

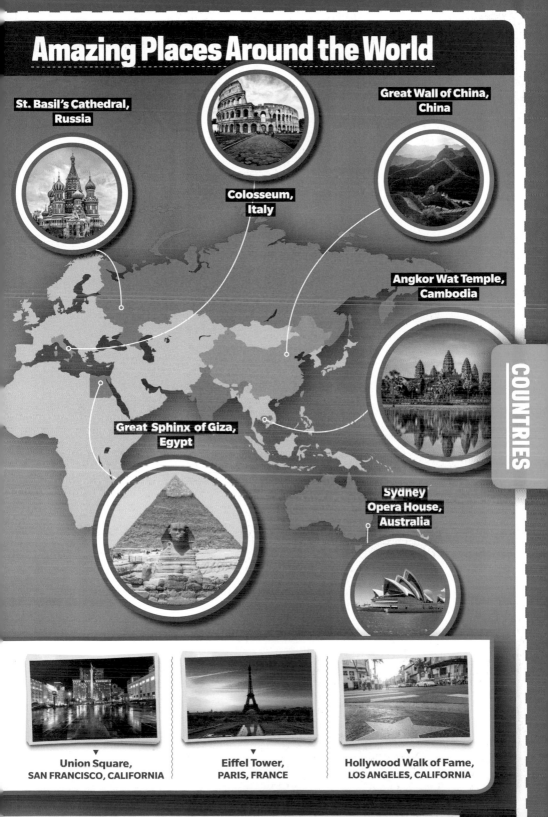

St. Basil's Cathedral, Russia

Colosseum, Italy

Great Wall of China, China

Angkor Wat Temple, Cambodia

Great Sphinx of Giza, Egypt

Sydney Opera House, Australia

COUNTRIES

▼ Union Square, SAN FRANCISCO, CALIFORNIA

▼ Eiffel Tower, PARIS, FRANCE

▼ Hollywood Walk of Fame, LOS ANGELES, CALIFORNIA

73

One Wild Place to Stay

A hotel in Kenya is helping to save a rare species of giraffe.

Giraffes roam freely around the hotel's grounds. Guests await their arrival.

Guests at a hotel in Nairobi, Kenya, have some unusual breakfast companions. Every morning, giraffes poke their heads through the dining room windows. The gentle giants eat right off the guests' plates.

"It is such a magical place," says Tanya Carr-Hartley, who owns the hotel with her husband. "Nowhere in the world can you interact with wild animals like this."

The hotel, called Giraffe Manor, is located outside Kenya's capital city, Nairobi. The 12 long-necked creatures living on the property are Rothschild's giraffes, the most endangered species of the animals. Threats to these animals include habitat loss and illegal hunting.

Saving a Species

Giraffe Manor's first owners wanted to save the Rothschild's giraffe from extinction. They started the African Fund for Endangered Wildlife, also known as the Giraffe Center, in order to breed the animals and release them into the wild.

When the Giraffe Center opened on the hotel's property, in 1974, there were only 100 Rothschild's giraffes in the world. Today, there are more than 700.

Schoolchildren are regular visitors to the Giraffe Center. The center's aim is to teach them how to protect Africa's wild animals. "Children are the future of Africa," says Carr-Hartley. "They must understand and love its animals."

Guests at Giraffe Manor are helping the Rothschild's giraffe, too. A one-night stay costs more than $600, part of which goes to the Giraffe Center. That should help keep these creatures walking tall.

—By Brenda Iasevoli

The United Nations

After World War II ended in 1945, representatives from 51 nations met to set up an international organization that would try to maintain peace worldwide and promote friendly relations between countries. It would make the world a better place for everyone by spreading knowledge and opportunities from the wealthier nations to those that were still developing. This is how the United Nations (U.N.) started. Today, the United Nations has 193 member countries and a strong record of preventing wars, fighting terrorism, and slowing the development of deadly weapons. Its main headquarters are in New York City.

In addition to promoting international peace efforts, the U.N. has many other functions and goals. One branch, the World Health Organization (WHO), brings modern medicine and disease prevention to countries all over the world. UNESCO (United Nations Educational, Scientific, and Cultural Organization) conducts studies and spreads knowledge and cooperation. UNICEF (United Nations Children's Fund) looks after the needs of the youngest citizens of the world. The U.N. also leads the fight to prevent diseases like malaria and diabetes and to stop climate change.

Here are a few of the projects the U.N. currently oversees.

1. Providing aid and protection to more than 34 million refugees and others fleeing war, famine, or persecution.

2. Bringing food to about 90 million hungry people in 80 countries every year through the World Food Programme (WFP).

3. Vaccinating 40% of the world's children through UNICEF, which saves 2 million lives a year.

4. Supporting more than 100,000 U.N. peacekeepers in 16 peace operations.

Main Bodies of the United Nations

The General Assembly refers to the main body of the U.N. It is made up of all 193 members.

Made up of 15 member countries, the U.N. Security Council works to maintain peace in the world.

The Economic and Social Council promotes the well-being of all nations, especially after conflicts or natural disasters.

The International Court of Justice, based in the Hague, settles legal disputes between nations, based on international law.

The Secretariat runs the day-to-day business of the U.N. The chief officer is the Secretary-General.

The United Nations headquarters

Afghanistan

Location: Asia

Capital: Kabul

Area: 251,827 sq mi (652,230 sq km)

Population Estimate (July 2014): 31,822,848

Government: Islamic republic

Languages: Afghan Persian (Dari) and Pashto (both official), Uzbek, Turkmen

Money: Afghani

Life Expectancy: 50

Literacy Rate: 38%

GUESS WHAT? Kite-fighting and kite-running are popular sports in Afghanistan that involve flying kites, cutting them loose with glass-coated wire strings, and racing to retrieve them.

Albania

Location: Europe

Capital: Tirana

Area: 11,100 sq mi (28,748 sq km)

Population Estimate (July 2014): 3,020,209

Government: Parliamentary democracy

Languages: Albanian (Tosk is the official dialect), Greek, others

Money: Lek

Life Expectancy: 78

Literacy Rate: 98%

GUESS WHAT? Traditionally in Albania, if you nod your head up and down, it means no. And if you shake your head side to side, it means yes.

Algeria

Location: Africa

Capital: Algiers

Area: 919,595 sq mi (2,381,741 sq km)

Population Estimate (July 2014): 38,813,722

Government: Republic

Languages: Arabic (official), French, Berber dialects

Money: Dinar

Life Expectancy: 76

Literacy Rate: 80%

GUESS WHAT? The Sahara desert covers four-fifths of Algeria, and it includes some of the world's biggest sand dunes.

Andorra

Location: Europe

Capital: Andorra la Vella

Area: 181 sq mi (468 sq km)

Population Estimate (July 2014): 85,458

Government: Parliamentary democracy

Languages: Catalan (official), French, Castilian, Portuguese

Money: Euro (formerly French franc and Spanish peseta)

Life Expectancy: 83

Literacy Rate: 100%

GUESS WHAT? At an elevation of 3,356 feet (1,023 m) above sea level, Andorra la Vella is the highest capital city in Europe.

Angola

Location: Africa

Capital: Luanda

Area: 481,354 sq mi (1,246,700 sq km)

Population Estimate (July 2014): 19,088,106

Government: Republic

Languages: Portuguese (official), Bantu, other African languages

Money: Kwanza

Life Expectancy: 55

Literacy Rate: 71%

GUESS WHAT? Angola is one of the world's most geographically diverse countries. It has tropical jungles, deserts, savannas, mountains, rivers, and waterfalls.

Antigua and Barbuda

Location: Caribbean

Capital: Saint John's

Area: 171 sq mi (443 sq km)

Population Estimate (July 2014): 91,295

Government: Constitutional monarchy with a parliamentary system of government

Languages: English (official), Antiguan creole

Money: East Caribbean dollar

Life Expectancy: 76

Literacy Rate: 99%

GUESS WHAT? Every year, Antiguans celebrate Carnival, a festival commemorating the end of slavery in Antigua. Slavery ended in 1834, the earliest of any colony in the British Caribbean.

Argentina

Location: South America

Capital: Buenos Aires

Area: 1,073,518 sq mi
(2,780,400 sq km)

**Population Estimate
(July 2014):** 43,024,374

Government: Republic

Languages: Spanish (official),
Italian, English, German,
French, native languages

Money: Argentine peso

Life Expectancy: 78

Literacy Rate: 98%

GUESS WHAT? The city of Ushuaia, located in the Tierra del Fuego Province of Argentina, is the southernmost city with at least 50,000 inhabitants in the world.

Armenia

Location: Asia

Capital: Yerevan

Area: 11,484 sq mi
(29,743 sq km)

**Population Estimate
(July 2014):** 3,060,631

Government: Republic

Languages: Armenian
(official), others

Money: Dram

Life Expectancy: 74

Literacy Rate: 100%

GUESS WHAT? The Great Silk Road, an important early trade route, once passed through Armenia, linking it with developing empires in both Asia and Europe.

Australia

Location: Continent of
Australia

Capital: Canberra

Area: 2,988,902 sq mi
(7,741,220 sq km)

**Population Estimate
(July 2014):** 22,507,617

Government: Federal
parliamentary democracy

Languages: English, others

Money: Australian dollar

Life Expectancy: 82

Literacy Rate: 99%

GUESS WHAT? The Great Barrier Reef, located off the coast of Queensland in northeast Australia, is the world's biggest structure made by living organisms and can be seen from outer space.

Austria

Location: Europe

Capital: Vienna

Area: 32,383 sq mi
(83,871 sq km)

**Population Estimate
(July 2014):** 8,223,062

Government:
Federal republic

Languages: German (official),
Croatian and Hungarian (both
official in Burgenland), Slovene (official in South Carin-
thia), Turkish, Serbian, others

Money: Euro
(formerly schilling)

Life Expectancy: 80

Literacy Rate: 98%

GUESS WHAT? The Austrian city of Innsbruck hosted the 1964 and 1976 editions of the Winter Olympics.

Azerbaijan

Location: Asia

Capital: Baku

Area: 33,436 sq mi
(86,600 sq km)

**Population Estimate
(July 2014):** 9,686,210

Government: Republic

Languages: Azerbaijani
(official), others

Money: Azerbaijani manat

Life Expectancy: 72

Literacy Rate: 100%

GUESS WHAT? Azerbaijan is home to nearly 400 mud volcanoes along the Caspian Sea to its east. The region contains more than half of the world's known mud volcanoes.

The Bahamas

Location: Caribbean

Capital: Nassau

Area: 5,359 sq mi
(13,880 sq km)

**Population Estimate
(July 2014):** 321,834

Government: Constitutional
parliamentary democracy

Languages: English
(official), Creole

Money: Bahamian dollar

Life Expectancy: 72

Literacy Rate: 96%

GUESS WHAT? The Bahamas is made up of approximately 700 islands. Only 30 of the islands are inhabited.

Bahrain

Location: Middle East

Capital: Manama

Area: 293 sq mi (760 sq km)

Population Estimate (July 2014): 1,314,089

Government: Constitutional monarchy

Languages: Arabic (official), English, Farsi, Urdu

Money: Bahraini dinar

Life Expectancy: 79

Literacy Rate: 96%

GUESS WHAT? Bahrain is a small archipelago, or chain of islands, in the Persian Gulf. Its name means "two seas" in Arabic.

Bangladesh

Location: Asia

Capital: Dhaka

Area: 55,598 sq mi (143,998 sq km)

Population Estimate (July 2014): 166,280,712

Government: Parliamentary democracy

Languages: Bangla (official), English

Money: Taka

Life Expectancy: 71

Literacy Rate: 62%

GUESS WHAT? The Sunderbans, a cluster of islands in the southwestern part of Bangladesh, is one of the largest unspoiled mangrove forests in the world, and home to the endangered Bengal tiger.

Barbados

Location: Caribbean

Capital: Bridgetown

Area: 166 sq mi (430 sq km)

Population Estimate (July 2014): 289,680

Government: Parliamentary democracy

Language: English (official)

Money: Barbadian dollar

Life Expectancy: 75

Literacy Rate: 100%

GUESS WHAT? The town of St. Andrew in Barbados was once believed to have healing properties. Many people traveled there and covered themselves in the sands of Cattlewash Beach in hopes of curing their health problems.

Belarus

Location: Europe

Capital: Minsk

Area: 80,155 sq mi (207,600 sq km)

Population Estimate (July 2014): 9,608,058

Government: Republic with authoritarian presidential rule

Languages: Belarusian and Russian (both official), others

Money: Belarusian ruble

Life Expectancy: 72

Literacy Rate: 100%

GUESS WHAT? The movement of glaciers in Belarus has helped create many bodies of water. There are about 11,000 lakes and 20,000 rivers and creeks in the country.

Belgium

Location: Europe

Capital: Brussels

Area: 11,787 sq mi (30,528 sq km)

Population Estimate (July 2014): 10,449,361

Government: Federal parliamentary democracy under a constitutional monarchy

Languages: Dutch, French, and German (all official)

Money: Euro (formerly Belgian franc)

Life Expectancy: 80

Literacy Rate: 99%

GUESS WHAT? Belgium has more castles per square mile than any other country in the world.

Belize

Location: Central America

Capital: Belmopan

Area: 8,867 sq mi (22,966 sq km)

Population Estimate (July 2014): 340,844

Government: Parliamentary democracy

Languages: English (official), Spanish, Creole, Mayan dialects, others

Money: Belizean dollar

Life Expectancy: 68

Literacy Rate: 77%

GUESS WHAT? The Cockscomb Basin Wildlife Sanctuary in the Stann Creek District of Belize was founded in 1990 and was the first wilderness sanctuary for the jaguar.

Benin

Location: Africa

Capital: Porto-Novo

Area: 43,484 sq mi
(112,622 sq km)

**Population Estimate
(July 2014):** 10,160,556

Government: Republic

Languages: French (official),
Fon, Yoruba, tribal languages

Money: CFA franc

Life Expectancy: 61

Literacy Rate: 38%

GUESS WHAT? Benin was known as the Kingdom of Dahomey until 1975.

Bhutan

Location: Asia

Capital: Thimphu

Area: 14,824 sq mi
(38,394 sq km)

**Population Estimate
(July 2014):** 733,643

Government:
Constitutional monarchy

Languages: Dzongkha
(official), Sharchhopka,
Lhotshamkha, others

Money: Ngultrum

Life Expectancy: 69

Literacy Rate: 65%

GUESS WHAT? In 2004, Bhutan became the first country in the world to ban the sale of tobacco.

Bolivia

Location: South America

Capitals: La Paz (seat
of government), Sucre
(legislative capital)

Area: 424,164 sq mi
(1,098,581 sq km)

**Population Estimate
(July 2014):** 10,631,486

Government: Republic

Languages: Spanish,
Quechua, Aymara, and
Guarani (all official), others

Money: Boliviano

Life Expectancy: 69

Literacy Rate: 96%

GUESS WHAT? At an elevation of 12,507 feet (3,812 m), Bolivia's Lake Titicaca is the highest commercially navigable lake in the world.

Bosnia and Herzegovina

Location: Europe

Capital: Sarajevo

Area: 19,767 sq mi
(51,197 sq km)

**Population Estimate
(July 2014):** 3,871,643

Government: Federal
democratic republic

Languages: Bosnian,
Croatian, Serbian (all official)

Money: Convertible mark

Life Expectancy: 76

Literacy Rate: 99%

GUESS WHAT? Bosnia and Herzegovina declared independence from Yugoslavia in 1991.

Botswana

Location: Africa

Capital: Gaborone

Area: 224,607 sq mi
(581,730 sq km)

**Population Estimate
(July 2014):** 2,155,784

Government:
Parliamentary republic

Languages: English
(official), Setswana, Kalanga,
Sekgalagadi, others

Money: Pula

Life Expectancy: 54

Literacy Rate: 89%

GUESS WHAT? Botswana is home to the largest elephant population in Africa.

Brazil

Location: South America

Capital: Brasília

Area: 3,287,612 sq mi
(8,514,877 sq km)

**Population Estimate
(July 2014):** 202,656,788

Government:
Federal republic

Languages: Portuguese
(official), Spanish,
German, Italian, Japanese,
English, various
Amerindian languages

Money: Real

Life Expectancy: 73

Literacy Rate: 93%

GUESS WHAT? More species of primates live in Brazil than in any other country in the world.

Brunei

Location: Asia

Capital: Bandar Seri Begawan

Area: 2,226 sq mi
(5,765 sq km)

**Population Estimate
(July 2014):** 422,675

Government:
Constitutional sultanate

Languages: Malay (official),
English, Chinese dialects

Money: Bruneian dollar

Life Expectancy: 77

Literacy Rate: 96%

GUESS WHAT? The same family has ruled Brunei for six centuries.

Bulgaria

Location: Europe

Capital: Sofia

Area: 42,811 sq mi
(110,879 sq km)

**Population Estimate
(July 2014):** 6,924,716

Government:
Parliamentary democracy

Languages: Bulgarian
(official), Turkish, Roma,
others

Money: Lev

Life Expectancy: 74

Literacy Rate: 98%

GUESS WHAT? The Bulgarian town of Kazanluk exports rose oil, an important and rare ingredient in many perfumes.

Burkina Faso

Location: Asia

Capital: Kabul

Area: 251,827 sq mi
(652,230 sq km)

**Population Estimate
(July 2014):** 31,822,848

Government:
Islamic republic

Languages: Afghan Persian
(Dari) and Pashto (both
official), Uzbek, Turkmen

Money: Afghani

Life Expectancy: 50

Literacy Rate: 38%

GUESS WHAT? Burkina Faso means "land of honest people."

Burundi

Location: Africa

Capital: Bujumbura

Area: 10,745 sq mi
(27,830 sq km)

**Population Estimate
(July 2014):** 10,395,931

Government: Republic

Languages: Kirundi and
French (both official), Swahili

Money: Burundi franc

Life Expectancy: 60

Literacy Rate: 86%

GUESS WHAT? One of the world's largest crocodiles, named Gustave, haunts the waters of Burundi. He is estimated to be 20 feet (6.1 m) long and to weigh 1 ton (907.2 kg).

Cambodia

Location: Asia

Capital: Phnom Penh

Area: 69,898 sq mi
(181,035 sq km)

**Population Estimate
(July 2014):** 15,458,332

Government: Multiparty
democracy under a
constitutional monarchy

Languages: Khmer
(official), French, English

Money: Riel

Life Expectancy: 64

Literacy rate: 77%

GUESS WHAT? Angkor Wat, an ancient temple in Cambodia, is the largest religious monument in the world.

Cameroon

Location: Africa

Capital: Yaoundé

Area: 183,568 sq mi
(475,440 sq km)

**Population Estimate
(July 2014):** 23,130,708

Government: Republic

Languages: French and
English (both official),
various African languages

Money: CFA franc

Life Expectancy: 57

Literacy Rate: 75%

GUESS WHAT? In 1990, Cameroon became the first African nation to reach the quarterfinals of the FIFA World Cup.

Canada

Location: North America

Capital: Ottawa

Area: 3,855,103 sq mi
(9,984,670 sq km)

Population Estimate
(July 2014): 34,834,841

Government: Parliamentary
democracy, federation, and
constitutional monarchy

Languages: English and
French (both official), others

Money: Canadian dollar

Life Expectancy: 82

Literacy Rate: 99%

GUESS WHAT? Canada has the
world's longest
coastline at 125,567 miles
(202,080 km).

Cabo Verde (Cape Verde)

Location: Africa

Capital: Praia

Area: 1,557 sq mi
(4,033 sq km)

Population Estimate
(July 2014): 538,535

Government: Republic

Languages: Portuguese
(official), Crioulo

Money: Cape Verdean escudo

Life Expectancy: 72

Literacy Rate: 88%

GUESS WHAT? The only mammal
native to Cabo Verde
is the grey long-eared bat.

Central African Republic

Location: Africa

Capital: Bangui

Area: 240,535 sq mi
(622,984 sq km)

Population Estimate
(July 2014): 5,277,959

Government: Republic

Languages: French (official),
Sangho, tribal languages

Money: CFA franc

Life Expectancy: 51

Literacy Rate: 37%

GUESS WHAT? The Central African
Republic has more
than 80 ethnic groups, each
with its
own language.

Chad

Location: Africa

Capital: N'Djamena

Area: 495,755 mi
(1,284,000 sq km)

Population Estimate
(July 2014): 11,412,107

Government: Republic

Languages: French and
Arabic (both official),
Sara, others

Money: CFA franc

Life Expectancy: 49

Literacy Rate: 40%

GUESS WHAT? With an approximate
span of 250 feet
(77 m), Chad's Alobi Arch,
located in the Ennedi
Plateau, is the longest
natural arch outside of the
United States.

Chile

Location: South America

Capital: Santiago

Area: 291,933 sq mi
(756,102 sq km)

Population Estimate
(July 2014): 17,363,894

Government: Republic

Languages: Spanish (official),
English, native languages

Money: Chilean peso

Life Expectancy: 78

Literacy Rate: 98%

GUESS WHAT? The world's largest
outdoor swimming
pool is at Chile's San Alfonso
del Mar Resort. It is over half
a mile (1,013 m) long,
115 feet (35 m) deep, and
holds 66 million gallons
(250 million L) of water.

China

Location: Asia

Capital: Beijing

Area: 3,705,407 sq mi
(9,596,960 sq km)

Population Estimate
(July 2014): 1,355,692,576

Government:
Communist state

Languages: Chinese
(Mandarin; official), Yue
(Cantonese), local dialects

Money: Renminbi yuan

Life Expectancy: 75

Literacy Rate: 96%

GUESS WHAT? Kites were invented
in China 3,000 years
ago and were primarily used
for frightening opponents
in battle.

Colombia

Location: South America
Capital: Bogotá
Area: 439,736 sq mi (1,138,910 sq km)
Population Estimate (July 2014): 46,245,297
Government: Republic
Language: Spanish (official)
Money: Colombian peso
Life Expectancy: 75
Literacy Rate: 95%

GUESS WHAT? Colombia is the only country in South America that has a coastline on the Pacific Ocean and the Caribbean Sea.

Comoros

Location: Africa
Capital: Moroni
Area: 863 sq mi (2,235 sq km)
Population Estimate (July 2014): 766,865
Government: Republic
Languages: French, Arabic, and Shikomoro (all official)
Money: Comoran franc
Life Expectancy: 63
Literacy Rate: 78%

GUESS WHAT? The name "Comoros" derives from the Arabic word for moon.

Congo, Democratic Republic of

Location: Africa
Capital: Kinshasa
Area: 905,355 sq mi (2,344,858 sq km)
Population Estimate (July 2014): 77,433,744
Government: Republic
Languages: French (official), Lingala, Kingwana, Kikongo, Tshiluba
Money: Congolese franc
Life Expectancy: 57
Literacy Rate: 64%

GUESS WHAT? The Democratic Republic of the Congo has the highest frequency of lightning on Earth.

Congo, Republic of

Location: Africa
Capital: Brazzaville
Area: 132,047 sq mi (342,000 sq km)
Population Estimate (July 2014): 4,662,446
Government: Republic
Languages: French (official), Lingala, Monokutuba, Kikongo, others
Money: CFA franc
Life Expectancy: 59
Literacy Rate: 79%

GUESS WHAT? The Republic of the Congo is home to one of the world's largest populations of chimpanzees.

Costa Rica

Location: Central America
Capital: San José
Area: 19,730 sq mi (51,100 sq km)
Population Estimate (July 2014): 4,755,234
Government: Democratic republic
Languages: Spanish (official), English
Money: Costa Rican colón
Life Expectancy: 78
Literacy Rate: 98%

GUESS WHAT? "Pura vida," which in English means "pure life," is a phrase commonly used in Costa Rica. It can be used as a greeting, as a farewell, as a way to say how you are doing, and as a way to say thanks.

Cote d'Ivoire (Ivory Coast)

Location: Africa
Capital: Yamoussoukro
Area: 124,504 sq mi (322,463 sq km)
Population Estimate (July 2014): 22,848,945
Government: Republic
Languages: French (official), Dioula and many other native dialects
Money: CFA franc
Life Expectancy: 58
Literacy Rate: 43%

GUESS WHAT? Côte d'Ivoire is the world's largest exporter of cocoa beans. Cocoa beans are used to make chocolate.

Croatia

Location: Europe
Capital: Zagreb
Area: 21,851 sq mi
(56,594 sq km)
Population Estimate
(July 2014): 4,470,534
Government:
Parliamentary democracy
Languages: Croatian
(official), Serbian, others
Money: Kuna
Life Expectancy: 76
Literacy Rate: 99%

GUESS WHAT? The Dalmatian dog breed is named after Croatia's mountainous Dalmatian Coast, which runs along the Adriatic Sea.

Cuba

Location: Caribbean
Capital: Havana
Area: 42,803 sq mi
(110,860 sq km)
Population Estimate
(July 2014): 11,047,251
Government:
Communist state
Language: Spanish (official)
Money: Cuban peso
Life Expectancy: 78
Literacy Rate: 100%

GUESS WHAT? With an area of 40,852 square miles (105,806 square km), the main island of Cuba is the largest island in the Caribbean.

Cyprus

Location: Middle East
Capital: Nicosia
Area: 3,572 sq mi
(9,251 sq km)
Population Estimate
(July 2014): 1,172,458
Government: Republic
Languages: Greek and
Turkish (both official),
English, others
Money: Euro
(formerly Cyprus pound)
Life Expectancy: 78
Literacy Rate: 99%

GUESS WHAT? Cyprus, an island nation in the Mediterranean Sea, has two mountain ranges: the Kyrenia Mountains in the north and the Trodoros Mountains in the south.

Czech Republic

Location: Europe
Capital: Prague
Area: 30,451 sq mi
(78,867 sq km)
Population Estimate
(July 2014): 10,627,448
Government:
Parliamentary democracy
Languages: Czech (official),
Slovak, others
Money: Koruna
Life Expectancy: 78
Literacy Rate: 99%

GUESS WHAT? Prague Castle, located in the Czech Republic's capital city, is the largest ancient castle in the world.

Denmark

Location: Europe
Capital: Copenhagen
Area: 16,639 sq mi
(43,094 sq km)
Population Estimate
(July 2014): 5,569,077
Government:
Constitutional monarchy
Languages: Danish, Faroese,
Greenlandic, German
Money: Krone
Life Expectancy: 79
Literacy Rate: 99%

GUESS WHAT? Lego bricks are made in Denmark. In 1939, the first Lego factory had only 10 employees. Today, the toy company employs about 10,000 people.

Djibouti

Location: Africa
Capital: Djibouti
Area: 8,958 sq mi
(23,200 sq km)
Population Estimate
(July 2014): 810,179
Government: Republic
Languages: Arabic and
French (both official),
Somali, Afar
Money: Djiboutian franc
Life Expectancy: 62
Literacy Rate: 68%

GUESS WHAT? The blue on Djibouti's flag represents the Somali Issa people and the green represents the Muslim Afar people. The red star and white triangle represent peace and unity between the two groups.

Dominica

Location: Caribbean

Capital: Roseau

Area: 290 sq mi (751 sq km)

Population Estimate (July 2014): 73,449

Government: Parliamentary democracy

Languages: English (official), French patois

Money: East Caribbean dollar

Life Expectancy: 77

Literacy Rate: 94%

GUESS WHAT? A boiling lake in Dominica's Morne Troit Pitons (Mountain of Three Peaks) National Park is the largest in the Western Hemisphere. The boiling is caused by steam and gases emitted from a crack in the Earth's crust.

Dominican Republic

Location: Caribbean

Capital: Santo Domingo

Area: 18,792 sq mi (48,670 sq km)

Population Estimate (July 2014): 10,349,741

Government: Democratic republic

Language: Spanish (official)

Money: Dominican peso

Life Expectancy: 78

Literacy Rate: 92%

GUESS WHAT? Five Dominican-born players have won Major League Baseball MVP awards (George Bell, Sammy Sosa, Miguel Tejada, Vladimir Guerrero, and Albert Pujols), more than any other foreign country.

East Timor (Timor Leste)

Location: Asia

Capital: Dili

Area: 5,743 sq mi (14,874 sq km)

Population Estimate (July 2014): 1,201,542

Government: Republic

Languages: Tetum and Portuguese (both official), Indonesian, English, other native languages

Money: U.S. dollar

Life Expectancy: 67

Literacy Rate: 68%

GUESS WHAT? East Timor takes up the eastern half of the island of Timor. The western half is part of Indonesia.

Ecuador

Location: South America

Capital: Quito

Area: 109,484 sq mi (283,561 sq km)

Population Estimate (July 2014): 15,654,411

Government: Republic

Languages: Spanish (official), Quechua, other Amerindian languages

Money: U.S. dollar

Life Expectancy: 76

Literacy Rate: 95%

GUESS WHAT? At the festival called Año Viejo (or "old year"), Ecuadorans make puppets that represent the bad things of the past year, then burn them to welcome the new year.

Egypt

Location: Africa

Capital: Cairo

Area: 386,662 sq mi (1,001,450 sq km)

Population Estimate (July 2014): 86,895,099

Government: Republic

Language: Arabic (official)

Money: Egyptian pound

Life Expectancy: 73

Literacy Rate: 74%

GUESS WHAT? Of the Seven Wonders of the Ancient World, the Great Pyramid of Giza, built over 4,000 years ago, is the oldest and only one still intact.

El Salvador

Location: Central America

Capital: San Salvador

Area: 8,124 sq mi (21,041 sq km)

Population Estimate (July 2014): 6,125,512

Government: Republic

Languages: Spanish (official), Nahua

Money: U.S. dollar

Life Expectancy: 74

Literacy Rate: 88%

GUESS WHAT? El Salvador is the smallest Central American country, and it's the only one that has no Atlantic Ocean coastline.

Equatorial Guinea

Location: Africa

Capital: Malabo

Area: 10,831 sq mi (28,051 sq km)

Population Estimate (July 2014): 722,254

Government: Republic

Languages: Spanish and French (both official), Fang, Bubi

Money: CFA franc

Life Expectancy: 63

Literacy Rate: 95%

GUESS WHAT? Gaining its independence from Spain in 1968, Equatorial Guinea is the only African country with Spanish as an official language.

Eritrea

Location: Africa

Capital: Asmara

Area: 45,406 sq mi (117,600 sq km)

Population Estimate (July 2014): 6,380,803

Government: Transitional

Languages: Tigrinya, Arabic, and English (all official), Tigre, Kunama, Afar, others

Money: Nakfa

Life Expectancy: 64

Literacy Rate: 74%

GUESS WHAT? The Danakil Depression in Eritrea, Ethiopia, and Djibouti is one of the hottest places on Earth. Temperatures reach as high as 145°F (63°C).

Estonia

Location: Europe

Capital: Tallinn

Area: 17,463 sq mi (45,228 sq km)

Population Estimate (July 2014): 1,257,921

Government: Parliamentary republic

Languages: Estonian (official), Russian, others

Money: Euro (formerly kroon)

Life Expectancy: 74

Literacy Rate: 100%

GUESS WHAT? Estonia is one of the most wired countries in the world. About 95% of government services are online and wireless internet access is readily available for free.

Ethiopia

Location: Africa

Capital: Addis Ababa

Area: 426,373 sq mi (1,104,300 sq km)

Population Estimate (July 2014): 96,633,458

Government: Federal republic

Languages: Amharic (official), Oromo, Somali, Tigrigna, Afar (all regional official), others

Money: Birr

Life Expectancy: 61

Literacy Rate: 49%

GUESS WHAT? Because the Ethiopian calendar has more days than the Gregorian calendar (used by most nations worldwide), Ethiopian dates are about seven-and-a-half years "behind" most of the world.

Fiji

Location: Oceania

Capital: Suva

Area: 7,056 sq mi (18,274 sq km)

Population Estimate (July 2014): 903,207

Government: Republic

Languages: English and Fijian (both official), Hindustani

Money: Fijian dollar

Life Expectancy: 72

Literacy Rate: 94%

GUESS WHAT? In Fijian villages, only the chief can wear a hat or sunglasses.

Finland

Location: Europe

Capital: Helsinki

Area: 130,559 sq mi (338,145 sq km)

Population Estimate (July 2014): 5,268,799

Government: Republic

Languages: Finnish and Swedish (both official), others

Money: Euro (formerly markka)

Life Expectancy: 80

Literacy Rate: 100%

GUESS WHAT? Finland has won the most medals per capita (compared to their population) in Olympic history.

France

Location: Europe

Capital: Paris

Area: 248,573 sq mi (643,801 sq km)

Population Estimate (July 2014): 66,259,012

Government: Republic

Language: French (official)

Money: Euro (formerly franc)

Life Expectancy: 82

Literacy Rate: 99%

GUESS WHAT? When Paris hosted the 1900 Olympic Games, winning athletes received valuable pieces of art instead of gold medals.

Gabon

Location: Africa

Capital: Libreville

Area: 103,347 sq mi (267,667 sq km)

Population Estimate (July 2014): 1,672,597

Government: Republic

Languages: French (official), Fang, Myene, Nzebi, Bapounou/Eschira, Bandjabi

Money: CFA franc

Life Expectancy: 52

Literacy Rate: 83%

GUESS WHAT? Gabon is one of 13 countries situated on the Equator. Its average temperature is 79°F (26°C) with high humidity year-round.

The Gambia

Location: Africa

Capital: Banjul

Area: 4,361 sq mi (11,295 sq km)

Population Estimate (July 2014): 1,925,527

Government: Republic

Languages: English (official), Mandinka, Wolof, Fula, others

Money: Dalasi

Life Expectancy: 64

Literacy Rate: 56%

GUESS WHAT? The Gambia hosts a project every year called Wide Open Walls, in which street artists from around the world spend two weeks painting murals on walls in villages around the country.

Georgia

Location: Asia

Capital: Tbilisi

Area: 26,911 sq mi (69,700 sq km)

Population Estimate (July 2014): 4,935,880

Government: Republic

Languages: Georgian (official), Russian, Armenian, Azeri, others

Money: Lari

Life Expectancy: 76

Literacy Rate: 100%

GUESS WHAT? Krubera Cave in Georgia is the deepest known cave on Earth, stretching 7,208 feet (2,197m) below the surface.

Germany

Location: Europe

Capital: Berlin

Area: 137,847 sq mi (357,022 sq km)

Population Estimate (July 2014): 80,996,685

Government: Federal republic

Language: German (official)

Money: Euro (formerly deutsche mark)

Life Expectancy: 80

Literacy Rate: 99%

GUESS WHAT? Ulmer Münster, a church in the southern German city Ulm, is the tallest church in the world. Construction began in 1377 and subsequent additions have resulted in a height of 530 feet (161.5 m).

Ghana

Location: Africa

Capital: Accra

Area: 92,098 sq mi (238,533 sq km)

Population Estimate (July 2014): 25,758,108

Government: Constitutional democracy

Languages: English (official), Asante, Ewe, Fante, Boron, others

Money: Cedi

Life Expectancy: 66

Literacy Rate: 77%

GUESS WHAT? The word *ghana* means "warrior king" in the Ashanti language.

Greece

Location: Europe

Capital: Athens

Area: 50,949 sq mi (131,957 sq km)

Population Estimate (July 2014): 10,775,557

Government: Parliamentary republic

Language: Greek (official)

Money: Euro (formerly drachma)

Life Expectancy: 80

Literacy Rate: 98%

GUESS WHAT? There are more than 2,000 Greek islands. Fewer than 200 are inhabited.

Grenada

Location: Caribbean

Capital: Saint George's

Area: 133 sq mi (344 sq km)

Population Estimate (July 2014): 110,152

Government: Parliamentary democracy

Languages: English (official), French patois

Money: East Caribbean dollar

Life Expectancy: 74

Literacy Rate: 96%

GUESS WHAT? Grenada's national bird is the Grenada dove, an endangered species estimated to have a population of under 200.

Guatemala

Location: Central America

Capital: Guatemala City

Area: 42,042 sq mi (108,889 sq km)

Population Estimate (July 2014): 14,647,083

Government: Constitutional democratic republic

Languages: Spanish (official), Amerindian languages

Money: Quetzal

Life Expectancy: 72

Literacy Rate: 82%

GUESS WHAT? Guatemala's national bird, the quetzal, appears on its flag. The quetzal's bright coloration and long tail, which is usually longer than its body, are emphasized.

Guinea

Location: Africa

Capital: Conakry

Area: 94,926 sq mi (245,857 sq km)

Population Estimate (July 2014): 11,474,383

Government: Republic

Languages: French (official), native languages

Money: Guinean franc

Life Expectancy: 60

Literacy Rate: 30%

GUESS WHAT? Guinea is one of the wettest places on Earth. Conakry gets about 169 inches (429 cm) of rain per year.

Guinea-Bissau

Location: Africa

Capital: Bissau

Area: 13,948 sq mi (36,125 sq km)

Population Estimate (July 2014): 1,693,398

Government: Republic

Languages: Portuguese (official), Crioulo, French, English, others

Money: CFA franc

Life Expectancy: 50

Literacy Rate: 60%

GUESS WHAT? Over 90% of Guinea-Bissau's exports are nuts (if coconuts, not technically nuts, are included).

Guyana

Location: South America

Capital: Georgetown

Area: 83,000 sq mi (214,969 sq km)

Population Estimate (July 2014): 735,554

Government: Republic

Languages: English (official), Guyanese Creole, Amerindian dialects, Caribbean Hindustani

Money: Guyanese dollar

Life Expectancy: 68

Literacy Rate: 89%

GUESS WHAT? On Guyana's flag, red represents the people's passion for reform and nation-building, the yellow stands for its mineral wealth, and green symbolizes Guyana's vast forests.

Haiti

Location: Caribbean

Capital: Port-au-Prince

Area: 10,714 sq mi (27,750 sq km)

Population Estimate (July 2014): 9,996,731

Government: Republic

Languages: French and Creole (both official)

Money: Gourde

Life Expectancy: 63

Literacy Rate: 61%

GUESS WHAT? Haiti was founded in 1804 after the only fully successful slave revolt in history. It was the first black-led republic in the world.

Honduras

Location: Central America

Capital: Tegucigalpa

Area: 43,278 sq mi (112,090 sq km)

Population Estimate (July 2014): 8,598,561

Government: Democratic constitutional republic

Languages: Spanish (official), Amerindian dialects

Money: Lempira

Life Expectancy: 71

Literacy Rate: 89%

GUESS WHAT? Lluvia de Peces (Rain of Fish) is a phenomenon that occurs in the town of Yoro. During a massive rainstorm in May or June, small fish supposedly fall from the sky.

Hungary

Location: Europe

Capital: Budapest

Area: 35,918 sq mi (93,028 sq km)

Population Estimate (July 2014): 9,919,128

Government: Parliamentary democracy

Languages: Hungarian (official), others

Money: Forint

Life Expectancy: 75

Literacy Rate: 99%

GUESS WHAT? Budapest's Dohány Street Synagogue is the largest synagogue in Europe. It was constructed between 1854 and 1859 and seats 3,000.

Iceland

Location: Europe

Capital: Reykjavík

Area: 39,769 sq mi (103,000 sq km)

Population Estimate (July 2014): 317,351

Government: Constitutional republic

Languages: Icelandic, English, Nordic languages, German

Money: Icelandic krona

Life Expectancy: 81

Literacy Rate: 99%

GUESS WHAT? The oldest individual animal ever discovered was a 507-year-old clam found off Iceland's north coast in 2006.

India

Location: Asia

Capital: New Delhi

Area: 1,269,219 sq mi (3,287,263 sq km)

Population Estimate (July 2014): 1,236,344,631

Government: Federal republic

Languages: Hindi, Bengali, Telugu, Marathi, Tamil, Urdu, Gujarati, Malayalam, Kannada, Oriya, Punjabi, Assamese, Kashmiri, Sindhi, and Sanskrit (all official), English, others

Money: Indian rupee

Life Expectancy: 68

Literacy Rate: 71%

GUESS WHAT? An unprecedented 540 million citizens voted in India's last Prime Minister election.

Indonesia

Location: Asia

Capital: Jakarta

Area: 735,358 sq mi (1,904,569 sq km)

Population Estimate (July 2014): 253,609,643

Government: Republic

Languages: Bahasa Indonesia (official), English, Dutch, many local dialects

Money: Indonesian rupiah

Life Expectancy: 72

Literacy Rate: 94%

GUESS WHAT? Indonesia's 76 active volcanoes are more than any other country. The eruption of Mt. Tambora on the Indonesian island of Sumbawa in 1815 is the largest volcanic eruption in recorded history.

Iran

Location: Middle East

Capital: Tehran

Area: 636,372 sq mi (1,648,195 sq km)

Population Estimate (July 2014): 80,840,713

Government: Theocratic republic

Languages: Persian (official), Turkic, Kurdish, others

Money: Rial

Life Expectancy: 71

Literacy Rate: 87%

GUESS WHAT? The hottest temperature ever recorded on Earth was found in Iran's Lut Desert. NASA satellite's measured a 159°F (70.7°C) temperature in 2005.

Iraq

Location: Middle East

Capital: Baghdad

Area: 169,235 sq mi (438,317 sq km)

Population Estimate (July 2014): 32,585,692

Government: Parliamentary democracy

Languages: Arabic and Kurdish (official), Turkmen, Assyrian

Money: Iraqi dinar

Life Expectancy: 71

Literacy Rate: 80%

GUESS WHAT? The first written language, the first city and the invention of the wheel are all traced back to Mesopotamia, an ancient civilization in modern-day Iraq.

Ireland

Location: Europe

Capital: Dublin

Area: 27,133 sq mi (70,273 sq km)

Population Estimate (July 2014): 4,832,765

Government: Republic, parliamentary democracy

Languages: English and Irish (Gaelic) (both official)

Money: Euro (formerly Irish pound, or punt)

Life Expectancy: 81

Literacy Rate: 99%

GUESS WHAT? Halloween traces its origins back to the Irish festival of Samhain, which marked the end of the harvest season and the beginning of winter.

Israel

Location: Middle East

Capital: Jerusalem

Area: 8,019 sq mi (20,770 sq km)

Population Estimate (July 2014): 7,821,850

Government: Parliamentary democracy

Languages: Hebrew (official), Arabic, English

Money: New Israeli shekel

Life Expectancy: 81

Literacy Rate: 98%

GUESS WHAT? Paper currency in Israel has Braille printed on it in order to allow blind people to identify different amounts of money.

Italy

Location: Europe

Capital: Rome

Area: 116,348 sq mi (301,340 sq km)

Population Estimate (July 2014): 61,680,122

Government: Republic

Languages: Italian (official), German, French, Slovene

Money: Euro (formerly lira)

Life Expectancy: 82

Literacy Rate: 99%

GUESS WHAT? Violins, violas, and cellos were first made in Italy in the early 1500s.

Jamaica

Location: Caribbean

Capital: Kingston

Area: 4,244 sq mi (10,991 sq km)

Population Estimate (July 2014): 2,930,050

Government: Constitutional parliamentary democracy

Languages: English, English patois

Money: Jamaican dollar

Life Expectancy: 73

Literacy Rate: 89%

GUESS WHAT? Jamaica's national bird is the "doctor bird," a hummingbird whose green and black coloration matches Jamaica's flag.

Japan

Location: Asia

Capital: Tokyo

Area: 145,914 sq mi (377,915 sq km)

Population Estimate (July 2014): 127,103,388

Government: Parliamentary government with a constitutional monarchy

Language: Japanese

Money: Yen

Life Expectancy: 84

Literacy Rate: 99%

GUESS WHAT? Japan is made up of more than 3,000 islands. It does not share a land border with any other country.

Jordan

Location: Middle East

Capital: Amman

Area: 34,495 sq mi (89,342 sq km)

Population Estimate (July 2014): 7,930,491

Government: Constitutional monarchy

Languages: Arabic (official), English

Money: Jordanian dinar

Life Expectancy: 74

Literacy Rate: 95%

GUESS WHAT? Petra is an ancient city in southwestern Jordan. It was carved into stone mountains 2,000 years ago.

Kazakhstan

Location: Asia

Capital: Astana

Area: 1,052,090 sq mi (2,724,900 sq km)

Population Estimate (July 2014): 17,948,816

Government: Republic with authoritarian presidential rule

Languages: Kazakh and Russian (both official)

Money: Tenge

Life Expectancy: 70

Literacy Rate: 100%

GUESS WHAT? Kazakhstan is the largest landlocked country in the world.

Kenya

Location: Africa

Capital: Nairobi

Area: 224,081 sq mi (580,367 sq km)

Population Estimate (July 2014): 45,010,056

Government: Republic

Languages: English and Kiswahili (both official), others

Money: Kenyan shilling

Life Expectancy: 64

Literacy Rate: 78%

GUESS WHAT? The tallest recorded land animal was a Kenyan-born giraffe named George. George lived in the 1960s at the Chester Zoo in the United Kingdom and was estimated to be about 20 feet (6 m) tall.

Kirbati

Location: Oceania

Capital: Tarawa

Area: 313 sq mi (811 sq km)

Population Estimate (July 2014): 104,488

Government: Republic

Languages: English (official), I-Kiribati (Gilbertese)

Money: Australian dollar

Life Expectancy: 65

Literacy Rate: Not available

GUESS WHAT? Consisting of 33 islands, Kiribati is the only country that spans all four hemispheres (northern, southern, eastern, and western.)

Korea, North

Location: Asia

Capital: Pyongyang

Area: 46,540 sq mi (120,538 sq km)

Population Estimate (July 2014): 24,851,627

Government: Communist state and one-man dictatorship

Language: Korean

Money: North Korean won

Life Expectancy: 70

Literacy Rate: 100%

GUESS WHAT? With capacity for 150,000 people, Pyongyang's Rungrado 1st of May Stadium is the largest stadium in the world. It hosts soccer matches, festivals, and dictatorial celebrations.

Korea, South

Location: Asia

Capital: Seoul

Area: 38,502 sq mi
(99,720 sq km)

Population Estimate
(July 2014): 49,039,986

Government: Republic

Languages: Korean, English

Money: South Korean won

Life Expectancy: 80

Literacy Rate: 98%

GUESS WHAT? South Korea has the highest average internet connection speed of any country.

Kosovo

Location: Europe

Capital: Pristina

Area: 4,203 sq mi
(10,887 sq km)

Population Estimate
(July 2014): 1,859,203

Government: Republic

Languages: Albanian and Serbian (both official), Bosnian, Turkish, others

Money: Euro (formerly deutsche mark)

Life Expectancy: 71

Literacy Rate: 92%

GUESS WHAT? For his aid in helping Kosovo establish independence from Yugoslavia, former U.S. president Bill Clinton has an 11-foot (3.4 m) statue of his likeness in Pristina.

Kuwait

Location: Middle East

Capital: Kuwait City

Area: 6,880 sq mi
(17,818 sq km)

Population Estimate
(July 2014): 2,742,711

Government:
Constitutional emirate

Languages: Arabic (official), English

Money: Kuwaiti dinar

Life Expectancy: 78

Literacy Rate: 96%

GUESS WHAT? On average, there are only about eight rainy days a year in Kuwait.

Kyrgyzstan

Location: Asia

Capital: Bishkek

Area: 77,202 sq mi
(199,951 sq km)

Population Estimate
(July 2014): 5,604,212

Government: Republic

Languages: Kyrgyz and Russian (both official), Uzbek, others

Money: Som

Life Expectancy: 70

Literacy Rate: 100%

GUESS WHAT? More than 90% of Kyrgyzstan is mountainous, with the Tian Shan ("Heavenly Mountains") range dominating the landscape.

Laos

Location: Asia

Capital: Vientiane

Area: 91,429 sq mi
(236,800 sq km)

Population Estimate
(July 2014): 6,803,699

Government:
Communist state

Languages: Lao (official), French, English, others

Money: Kip

Life Expectancy: 64

Literacy Rate: 80%

GUESS WHAT? From the 14th to 18th centuries, Laos was known as Lan Xang, which translates to "a million elephants." Thousands of elephants still live in Laos.

Latvia

Location: Europe

Capital: Riga

Area: 24,938 sq mi
(64,589 sq km)

Population Estimate
(July 2014): 2,165,165

Government:
Parliamentary democracy

Languages: Latvian (official), Russian, others

Money: Euro (formerly lats)

Life Expectancy: 73

Literacy Rate: 100%

GUESS WHAT? Riga Castle, on the banks of the Daugava River, was first built in 1330. It is now the official residence of Latvian presidents.

Lebanon

Location: Middle East

Capital: Beirut

Area: 4,015 sq mi (10,400 sq km)

Population Estimate (July 2014): 5,882,562

Government: Republic

Languages: Arabic (official), French, English, Armenian

Money: Lebanese pound

Life Expectancy: 77

Literacy Rate: 94%

GUESS WHAT? The cedar tree, which appears on the flag, is a national symbol. Cedars have been in the region since Biblical times and recent efforts have been made to preserve its dwindling population.

Lesotho

Location: Africa

Capital: Maseru

Area: 11,720 sq mi (30,355 sq km)

Population Estimate (July 2014): 1,942,008

Government: Parliamentary constitutional monarchy

Languages: Sesotho and English (official), Zulu, Xhosa

Money: Loti

Life Expectancy: 53

Literacy Rate: 79%

GUESS WHAT? Lesotho is one of three countries completely surrounded by one other country (South Africa). San Marino and Vatican City, both surrounded by Italy, are the others.

Liberia

Location: Africa

Capital: Monrovia

Area: 43,000 sq mi (111,369 sq km)

Population Estimate (July 2014): 4,092,310

Government: Republic

Languages: English (official), ethnic dialects

Money: Liberian dollar

Life Expectancy: 58

Literacy Rate: 48%

GUESS WHAT? Liberia was founded in 1821 as an American colony aimed at establishing a homeland for freed slaves.

Libya

Location: Africa

Capital: Tripoli

Area: 679,362 sq mi (1,759,540 sq km)

Population Estimate (July 2014): 6,244,174

Government: Transitional

Languages: Arabic (official), Italian, English, Berber

Money: Libyan dinar

Life Expectancy: 76

Literacy Rate: 91%

GUESS WHAT? *The Guinness Book of World Records* lists Libyan Suleiman Ali Nashnush as the tallest basketball player ever. The Libyan legend, who was 8 feet (2.45 m) tall, never played in the NBA.

Liechtenstein

Location: Europe

Capital: Vaduz

Area: 62 sq mi (160 sq km)

Population Estimate (July 2014): 37,313

Government: Constitutional monarchy

Languages: German (Alemannic dialect) (official)

Money: Swiss franc

Life Expectancy: 82

Literacy Rate: 100%

GUESS WHAT? Liechtenstein is the world's largest producer of false teeth.

Lithuania

Location: Europe

Capital: Vilnius

Area: 25,212 sq mi (65,300 sq km)

Population Estimate (July 2014): 3,505,738

Government: Parliamentary democracy

Languages: Lithuanian (official), Russian, Polish, others

Money: Euro (formerly litas)

Life Expectancy: 76

Literacy Rate: 100%

GUESS WHAT? In 1989, two million people in Estonia, Latvia, and Lithuania joined hands and formed a chain 420 miles (676 km) long to protest the Soviet occupation of those countries.

Luxembourg

Location: Europe
Capital: Luxembourg
Area: 998 sq mi (2,586 sq km)
Population Estimate (July 2014): 520,672
Government: Constitutional monarchy
Languages: Luxembourgish, French, and German (all official), Portuguese
Money: Euro (formerly Luxembourg franc)
Life Expectancy: 80
Literacy Rate: 100%

GUESS WHAT? Luxembourg is the only country led by a grand duke, a monarchial role lower than that of a king or queen.

Macedonia

Location: Europe
Capital: Skopje
Area: 9,928 sq mi (25,713 sq km)
Population Estimate (July 2014): 2,091,719
Government: Parliamentary democracy
Languages: Macedonian and Albanian (both official), Turkish, others
Money: Macedonian denar
Life Expectancy: 76
Literacy Rate: 98%

GUESS WHAT? Mother Teresa, a charitable nun who won the 1979 Nobel Peace Prize, was born in Skopje in 1910. At that time, it was part of the Ottoman Empire.

Madagascar

Location: Africa
Capital: Antananarivo
Area: 226,658 sq mi (587,041 sq km)
Population Estimate (July 2014): 23,201,926
Government: Republic
Languages: French and Malagasy (both official), English
Money: Malagasy ariary
Life Expectancy: 65
Literacy Rate: 65%

GUESS WHAT? About 80% of the plants and animals found in Madagascar are endemic, meaning they don't exist naturally anywhere else.

Malawi

Location: Africa
Capital: Lilongwe
Area: 45,747 sq mi (118,484 sq km)
Population Estimate (July 2014): 17,377,468
Government: Multiparty democracy
Languages: English (official), Chichewa, others
Money: Malawian kwacha
Life Expectancy: 60
Literacy Rate: 66%

GUESS WHAT? Dance is a very important part of Malawi culture. The country has more than 80 traditional dances performed at different special occasions and ceremonies.

Malaysia

Location: Asia
Capital: Kuala Lumpur
Area: 127,355 sq mi (329,847 sq km)
Population Estimate (July 2014): 30,073,353
Government: Constitutional monarchy
Languages: Bahasa Malay (official), English, Chinese, Tamil, others
Money: Ringgit
Life Expectancy: 75
Literacy Rate: 95%

GUESS WHAT? The Sarawak Chamber, on the island of Borneo, is the largest cave chamber in the world. Discovered in 1981, it covers 1,770,220 square feet. (164,459 sq m)

Maldives

Location: Asia
Capital: Malé
Area: 115 sq mi (298 sq km)
Population Estimate (July 2014): 393,595
Government: Republic
Languages: Dhivehi (official), English
Money: Rufiyaa
Life Expectancy: 75
Literacy Rate: 99%

GUESS WHAT? The highest elevation in the Maldives is only 17 feet (5 m) above sea level.

Mali

Location: Africa

Capital: Bamako

Area: 478,841 sq mi (1,240,192 sq km)

Population Estimate (July 2014): 16,455,903

Government: Republic

Languages: French (official), Bambara, African languages

Money: CFA franc

Life Expectancy: 55

Literacy Rate: 39%

GUESS WHAT? Mali's Great Mosque of Djenné is believed to be the largest mud-built structure in the world. It is 33 feet (10 m) high and covers more than 60,000 square feet (5,600 sq m).

Malta

Location: Europe

Capital: Valletta

Area: 122 sq mi (316 sq km)

Population Estimate (July 2014): 412,655

Government: Republic

Languages: Maltese and English (both official), others

Money: Euro (formerly Maltese lira)

Life Expectancy: 80

Literacy Rate: 94%

GUESS WHAT? The Maltese Islands are home to a unique sub-species of bees. The name "Malta" most likely derives from similar words in Albanian and Greek meaning "honey."

Marshall Islands

Location: Oceania

Capital: Majuro

Area: 70 sq mi (181 sq km)

Population Estimate (July 2014): 70,983

Government: Constitutional government

Languages: Marshallese and English (both official), others

Money: U.S. dollar

Life Expectancy: 73

Literacy Rate: 94%

GUESS WHAT? In 2011, the Marshall Islands established the world's largest shark sanctuary, banning commercial fishing of sharks in 768,547 square miles (1,990,530 sq km) of the Pacific Ocean.

Mauritania

Location: Africa

Capital: Nouakchott

Area: 397,955 sq mi (1,030,700 sq km)

Population Estimate (July 2014): 3,516,806

Government: Presidential republic

Languages: Arabic (official), Pulaar, Soninke, Wolof, French, Hassaniya

Money: Ouguiya

Life Expectancy: 62

Literacy Rate: 52%

GUESS WHAT? Mauritania is one of two countries that does not use decimals as part of money transactions. Madagascar is the other.

Mauritius

Location: Africa

Capital: Port Louis

Area: 788 sq mi (2,040 sq km)

Population Estimate (July 2014): 1,331,155

Government: Parliamentary democracy

Languages: English (official), Creole, Bhojpuri, French, others

Money: Mauritian rupee

Life Expectancy: 75

Literacy Rate: 91%

GUESS WHAT? The 2015 Global Peace Index ranked Mauritius as the most peaceful country in Africa.

Mexico

Location: North America

Capital: Mexico City

Area: 758,449 sq mi (1,964,375 sq km)

Population Estimate (July 2014): 120,286,655

Government: Federal republic

Languages: Spanish, native languages

Money: Mexican peso

Life Expectancy: 75

Literacy Rate: 95%

GUESS WHAT? The gila monster lives in the desert areas of northwestern Mexico. The large, slow-moving lizard stores fat in its thick tail, so it can go for months between meals.

Micronesia, Federated States of

Location: Oceania

Capital: Palikir

Area: 271 sq mi (702 sq km)

Population Estimate (July 2014): 105,681

Government: Constitutional government

Languages: English (official), Chuukese, Kosraean, Pohnpeian, Yapese, Ulithian, others

Money: U.S. dollar

Life Expectancy: 72

Literacy Rate: 89%

GUESS WHAT? Micronesia's Chuuk Lagoon was a Japanese base in World War II. More than 100 wrecked ships, submarines, and planes still litter the lagoon.

Moldova

Location: Europe

Capital: Chisinau

Area: 13,070 sq mi (33,851 sq km)

Population Estimate (July 2014): 3,583,288

Government: Republic

Languages: Moldovan (official), Romanian, Russian, Ukrainian, Gagauz, others

Money: Leu

Life Expectancy: 70

Literacy Rate: 99%

GUESS WHAT? Moldova was one of 15 states established when the Soviet Union was dissolved. The country declared independence in 1991.

Monaco

Location: Europe

Capital: Monaco

Area: 0.77 sq mi (2 sq km)

Population Estimate (July 2014): 30,508

Government: Constitutional monarchy

Languages: French (official), English, Italian, Monégasque

Money: Euro (formerly French franc)

Life Expectancy: 90

Literacy Rate: 99%

GUESS WHAT? With 30,508 people in just 0.77 square miles, Monaco is the most densely populated nation in the world.

Mongolia

Location: Asia

Capital: Ulaanbaatar

Area: 603,909 sq mi (1,564,116 sq km)

Population Estimate (July 2014): 2,953,190

Government: Parliamentary

Languages: Khalkha Mongol (official), Turkic, Russian

Money: Togrog/tugrik

Life Expectancy: 69

Literacy Rate: 98%

GUESS WHAT? With only 2,953,190 people in 603,909 square miles, Mongolia is the least densely populated nation in the world.

Montenegro

Location: Europe

Capital: Podgorica

Area: 5,333 sq mi (13,812 sq km)

Population Estimate (July 2014): 650,036

Government: Republic

Languages: Montenegrin (official), Serbian, Bosnian, Albanian, others

Money: Euro (formerly deutsche mark)

Life Expectancy: 75

Literacy Rate: 99%

GUESS WHAT? Montenegro's Tara River Canyon is the deepest river canyon in Europe. It stretches as far down as 4,300 feet (1,300 m) deep.

Morocco

Location: Africa

Capital: Rabat

Area: 172,414 sq mi (446,550 sq km)

Population Estimate (July 2014): 32,987,206

Government: Constitutional monarchy

Languages: Arabic and Tamazight (both official), Berber dialects, French

Money: Dirham

Life Expectancy: 77

Literacy Rate: 69%

GUESS WHAT? Morocco grows more peppermint than any other nation.

Mozambique

Location: Africa

Capital: Maputo

Area: 308,642 sq mi (799,380 sq km)

Population Estimate (July 2014): 24,692,144

Government: Republic

Languages: Portuguese (official), Emakhuwa, Xichangana, others

Money: Metical

Life Expectancy: 53

Literacy Rate: 59%

GUESS WHAT? Mozambique celebrates Heroes' Day on February 3. The date marks the death of Eduardo Mondlane, a Mozambican-born activist who founded the country's liberation movement in the 1960s.

Myanmar (Burma)

Location: Asia

Capital: Nay Pyi Taw

Area: 261,228 sq mi (676,578 sq km)

Population Estimate (July 2014): 55,746,253

Government: Parliamentary government

Languages: Burmese (official), minority languages

Money: Kyat

Life Expectancy: 66

Literacy Rate: 93%

GUESS WHAT? The Burmese python is one of the largest snakes on Earth. It can grow to be more than 22 feet long.

Namibia

Location: Africa

Capital: Windhoek

Area: 318,261 sq mi (824,292 sq km)

Population Estimate (July 2014): 2,198,406

Government: Republic

Languages: English (official), Afrikaans, native languages

Money: Namibian dollar

Life Expectancy: 52

Literacy Rate: 82%

GUESS WHAT? Namibia was the first African country to put land protection into its constitution. Keeping its land and animals safe remains a top priority.

Nauru

Location: Oceania

Capital: Yaren District (unofficial)

Area: 8.11 sq mi (21 sq km)

Population Estimate (July 2014): 9,488

Government: Republic

Languages: Nauruan (official), English, others

Money: Australian dollar

Life Expectancy: 66

Literacy Rate: 97%

GUESS WHAT? British ship captain John Fearn was the first European to discover Nauru in 1798. He received such a friendly greeting from the native Nauruans, he named the land "Pleasant Island."

Nepal

Location: Asia

Capital: Kathmandu

Area: 56,827 sq mi (147,181 sq km)

Population Estimate (July 2014): 30,986,975

Government: Federal democratic republic

Languages: Nepali (official), Maithali, Bhojpuri, Tharu, Tamang, others

Money: Nepalese rupee

Life Expectancy: 67

Literacy Rate: 64%

GUESS WHAT? Nepal is the only country whose flag doesn't have four sides. The moon and sun on the flag symbolize the desire for Nepal to last as long as these permanent celestial bodies.

Netherlands

Location: Europe

Capital: Amsterdam

Area: 16,040 sq mi (41,543 sq km)

Population Estimate (July 2014): 16,877,351

Government: Constitutional monarchy

Languages: Dutch (official), Frisian (official in Friesland)

Money: Euro (formerly guilder)

Life Expectancy: 81

Literacy Rate: 99%

GUESS WHAT? There are twice as many bicycles as cars in the Netherlands.

New Zealand

Location: Oceania

Capital: Wellington

Area: 103,363 sq mi (267,710 sq km)

Population Estimate (July 2014): 4,401,916

Government: Parliamentary democracy

Languages: English, Maori, and sign language (all official), others

Money: New Zealand dollar

Life Expectancy: 81

Literacy rate: 99%

GUESS WHAT? In New Zealand, sheep outnumber people five to one.

Nicaragua

Location: Central America

Capital: Managua

Area: 50,336 sq mi (130,370 sq km)

Population Estimate (July 2014): 5,848,641

Government: Republic

Language: Spanish (official), Amerindian languages

Money: Córdoba

Life Expectancy: 73

Literacy Rate: 83%

GUESS WHAT? Lake Nicaragua, sometimes called the freshwater sea, is more than twice the size of Rhode Island. It is one of the few places on Earth were freshwater sharks are found.

Niger

Location: Africa

Capital: Niamey

Area: 489,191 sq mi (1,267,000 sq km)

Population Estimate (July 2014): 17,466,172

Government: Republic

Languages: French (official), Hausa, Djerma

Money: CFA franc

Life Expectancy: 55

Literacy Rate: 19%

GUESS WHAT? Niger's nickname is the Frying Pan of the World because temperatures range from 85°F (24°C) to 105°F (40°C) year-round.

Nigeria

Location: Africa

Capital: Abuja

Area: 356,669 sq mi (923,768 sq km)

Population Estimate (July 2014): 177,155,754

Government: Federal republic

Languages: English (official), Hausa, Yoruba, Igbo, Fulani, and 500+ native languages

Money: Naira

Life Expectancy: 53

Literacy Rate: 60%

GUESS WHAT? The Yoruba, one ethnic group in Nigeria, has the highest known rate of twin births in the world. About one out of every 21 Yoruba births will result in twins.

Norway

Location: Europe

Capital: Oslo

Area: 125,021 sq mi (323,802 sq km)

Population Estimate (July 2014): 5,147,792

Government: Constitutional monarchy

Languages: Bokmal and Nynorsk (both official), Sami (regional official)

Money: Krone

Life Expectancy: 82

Literacy Rate: 100%

GUESS WHAT? The town of Longyearbyen is so far north that residents don't see the sun set for four months in the summer and see no direct sunlight for three-and-a-half months in the winter.

Oman

Location: Middle East

Capital: Muscat

Area: 119,499 sq mi (309,500 sq km)

Population Estimate (July 2014): 3,219,775

Government: Monarchy

Languages: Arabic (official), English, Baluchi, Urdu, Indian dialects

Money: Omani rial

Life Expectancy: 75

Literacy Rate: 91%

GUESS WHAT? Camel racing is a popular sport in Oman. Camels can reach speeds of 40 miles per hour (64 kpm).

Pakistan

Location: Asia

Capital: Islamabad

Area: 307,374 sq mi (796,095 sq km)

Population Estimate (July 2014): 196,174,380

Government: Federal republic

Languages: Urdu and English (official), Punjabi, Sindhi, Siraiki, Pashto, others

Money: Pakistani rupee

Life Expectancy: 67

Literacy Rate: 58%

GUESS WHAT? Pakistan produces some of the world's most beautiful fabrics. Each area of the country has its own style of embroidery, or design, sewn into the fabric.

Palau

Location: Oceania

Capital: Ngerulmud

Area: 177 sq mi (459 sq km)

Population Estimate (July 2014): 21,186

Government: Constitutional government

Languages: Palauan (official on most islands), English (official), Filipino, Chinese, others

Money: U.S. dollar

Life Expectancy: 73

Literacy Rate: 100%

GUESS WHAT? Ngerulmud was home to an estimated 391 people in 2006, when it became Palau's capital. At the time, it was the least populated national capital in the world.

Panama

Location: Central America

Capital: Panama City

Area: 29,120 sq mi (75,420 sq km)

Population Estimate (July 2014): 3,608,431

Government: Constitutional democracy

Languages: Spanish (official), Amerindian languages

Money: Balboa, U.S. dollar

Life Expectancy: 78

Literacy Rate: 95%

GUESS WHAT? You can see both the Atlantic and Pacific Oceans from the top of Panama's Barú volcano.

Papua New Guinea

Location: Oceania

Capital: Port Moresby

Area: 178,704 sq mi (462,840 sq km)

Population Estimate (July 2014): 6,552,730

Government: Constitutional parliamentary democracy

Languages: Tok Pisin, English, and Hiri Motu (all official), about 836 native languages

Money: Kina

Life Expectancy: 67

Literacy Rate: 64%

GUESS WHAT? More languages are spoken in Papua New Guinea than anywhere else in the world.

Paraguay

Location: South America

Capital: Asunción

Area: 157,048 sq mi (406,752 sq km)

Population Estimate (July 2014): 6,703,860

Government: Constitutional republic

Languages: Spanish and Guaraní (both official)

Money: Guaraní

Life Expectancy: 77

Literacy Rate: 94%

GUESS WHAT? The 643-foot (196 m) high Itaupi ("Sounding Stone") Dam on the border of Paraguay and Brazil produces more hydroelectricity than any other dam in the Western Hemisphere.

Peru

Location: South America

Capital: Lima

Area: 496,225 sq mi (1,285,216 sq km)

Population Estimate (July 2014): 30,147,935

Government: Constitutional republic

Languages: Spanish, Quechua, and Aymara (all official), Aymara, others

Money: Nuevo sol

Life Expectancy: 73

Literacy Rate: 95%

GUESS WHAT? La Rinconada, a city in Peru, is more than three miles above sea level, making it the highest inhabited place on Earth.

Philippines

Location: Asia

Capital: Manila

Area: 115,831 sq mi (300,000 sq km)

Population Estimate (July 2014): 107,668,231

Government: Republic

Languages: Filipino (based on Tagalog) and English (both official), regional languages

Money: Philippine peso

Life Expectancy: 72

Literacy Rate: 96%

GUESS WHAT? Mount Mayon rises to 8,077 feet on the island of Luzon. Mayon, which is called the world's most perfect cone, frequently blows its top—it is one of the world's most active volcanoes.

Poland

Location: Europe

Capital: Warsaw

Area: 120,728 sq mi (312,685 sq km)

Population Estimate (July 2014): 38,346,279

Government: Republic

Language: Polish (official)

Money: Zloty

Life Expectancy: 77

Literacy Rate: 100%

GUESS WHAT? Born in modern-day Poland in 1473, Nicolaus Copernicus was the first scientist to calculate that the Earth rotates around the Sun, not the other way around.

Portugal

Location: Europe

Capital: Lisbon

Area: 35,556 sq mi (92,090 sq km)

Population Estimate (July 2014): 10,813,834

Government: Republic; parliamentary democracy

Languages: Portuguese and Mirandese (both official)

Money: Euro (formerly escudo)

Life Expectancy: 79

Literacy Rate: 96%

GUESS WHAT? Vasco da Gama Bridge in Lisbon is the longest bridge in Europe. It spans the Tagus River and extends for 10.7 miles (17.2 km).

Qatar

Location: Middle East

Capital: Doha

Area: 4,473 sq mi (11,586 sq km)

Population Estimate (July 2014): 2,123,160

Government: Constitutional monarchy

Languages: Arabic (official), English

Money: Qatari riyal

Life Expectancy: 78

Literacy Rate: 97%

GUESS WHAT? Qatar will host the 2022 FIFA World Cup soccer tournament. Because of the scorching summer temperatures in Qatar, the tournament will be held in November and December instead of June and July.

Romania

Location: Europe

Capital: Bucharest

Area: 92,043 sq mi (238,391 sq km)

Population Estimate (July 2014): 21,729,871

Government: Republic

Languages: Romanian (official), Hungarian, Romany, other

Money: Leu

Life Expectancy: 75

Literacy Rate: 99%

GUESS WHAT? Spiru Haret University in Bucharest is the largest university in Europe, with an enrollment of more than 310,000 students.

Russia

Location: Europe and Asia

Capital: Moscow

Area: 6,601,668 sq mi (17,098,242 sq km)

Population Estimate (July 2014): 142,470,272

Government: Federation

Languages: Russian (official), many minority languages

Money: Russian ruble

Life Expectancy: 70

Literacy Rate: 100%

GUESS WHAT? Russia is the largest country in the world. It is nearly double the size of the United States, and covers one-eighth of the world's surface. The country is so huge that is has 11 different time zones, compared with four in the continental U.S.

Rwanda

Location: Africa

Capital: Kigali

Area: 10,169 sq mi (26,338 sq km)

Population Estimate (July 2014): 12,337,138

Government: Republic

Languages: Kinyarwanda, French, and English (all official), others

Money: Rwandan franc

Life Expectancy: 59

Literacy Rate: 71%

GUESS WHAT? Rwanda is Africa's most densely populated country.

Saint Kitts and Nevis

Location: Caribbean

Capital: Basseterre

Area: 101 sq mi (261 sq km)

Population Estimate (July 2014): 51,538

Government: Parliamentary democracy

Language: English (official)

Money: East Caribbean dollar

Life Expectancy: 75

Literacy Rate: 98%

GUESS WHAT? Christopher Columbus originally named the larger island after the patron saint of travelers, St. Christopher. The name was later shortened to St. Kitts.

Saint Lucia

Location: Caribbean

Capital: Castries

Area: 238 sq mi (616 sq km)

Population Estimate (July 2014): 163,362

Government: Parliamentary democracy

Languages: English (official), French patois

Money: East Caribbean dollar

Life Expectancy: 77

Literacy Rate: 90%

GUESS WHAT? St. Lucia was formed by volcanic activity. The town of Soufrière offers tourists a chance to drive into a volcano.

Saint Vincent and the Grenadines

Location: Caribbean

Capital: Kingstown

Area: 150 sq mi (389 sq km)

Population Estimate (July 2014): 102,918

Government: Parliamentary democracy

Languages: English, French patois

Money: East Caribbean dollar

Life Expectancy: 75

Literacy Rate: 96%

GUESS WHAT? Bananas make up more than half of St. Vincent and the Grenadines' exports.

Samoa

Location: Oceania

Capital: Apia

Area: 1,093 sq mi (2,831 sq km)

Population Estimate (July 2014): 196,628

Government: Parliamentary democracy

Languages: Samoan (official), English

Money: Tala

Life Expectancy: 73

Literacy Rate: 99%

GUESS WHAT? Robert Louis Stevenson, the Scottish author who penned *Treasure Island* and *Dr. Jekyll and Mr. Hyde*, spent his last years in Samoa. He is buried on Mount Vaea.

San Marino

Location: Europe

Capital: San Marino

Area: 24 sq mi (61 sq km)

Population Estimate (July 2014): 32,742

Government: Republic

Language: Italian

Money: Euro (formerly Italian lira)

Life Expectancy: 83

Literacy Rate: 96%

GUESS WHAT? San Marino, founded around 301 A.D., is the world's oldest republic.

Sao Tome and Principe

Location: Africa

Capital: São Tomé

Area: 372 sq mi (964 sq km)

Population Estimate (July 2014): 190,428

Government: Republic

Languages: Portuguese (official), Forro, Cabo Verdian, French, Angolan, English, others

Money: Dobra

Life Expectancy: 64

Literacy Rate: 75%

GUESS WHAT? Sao Tome and Principe's largest export is cocoa, a main ingredient in chocolate.

Saudi Arabia

Location: Middle East

Capital: Riyadh

Area: 830,000 sq mi (2,149,690 sq km)

Population Estimate (July 2014): 27,345,986

Government: Monarchy

Language: Arabic (official)

Money: Saudi riyal

Life Expectancy: 75

Literacy Rate: 95%

GUESS WHAT? The Kingdom Tower, currently under construction in the Saudi city of Jeddah, is on track to become the world's tallest building. The structure is planned to be 3,307 feet (1,008 m) high and completed in 2019.

Senegal

Location: Africa

Capital: Dakar

Area: 75,955 sq mi (196,722 sq km)

Population Estimate (July 2014): 13,635,927

Government: Republic

Languages: French (official), Wolof, Pulaar, Jola, Mandinka

Money: CFA franc

Life Expectancy: 61

Literacy Rate: 58%

GUESS WHAT? Senegal's Pink Lake is actually pink because of its high level of salt and the types of algae that live in it.

Serbia

Location: Europe

Capital: Belgrade

Area: 29,913 sq mi (77,474 sq km)

Population Estimate (July 2014): 7,209,764

Government: Republic

Languages: Serbian (official), Hungarian, others

Money: Serbian dinar

Life Expectancy: 75

Literacy Rate: 98%

GUESS WHAT? A Serbian monk named Lazar built the first mechanical public clock in 1404.

Seychelles

Location: Africa

Capital: Victoria

Area: 176 sq mi (455 sq km)

Population Estimate (July 2014): 91,650

Government: Republic

Languages: Seychellois Creole, English, and French (all official), others

Money: Seychelles rupee

Life Expectancy: 74

Literacy Rate: 92%

GUESS WHAT? The motto of Seychelles is Finis coronat opus, which is Latin for "The end crowns the work."

Sierra Leone

Location: Africa

Capital: Freetown

Area: 27,699 sq mi (71,740 sq km)

Population Estimate (July 2014): 5,743,725

Government: Constitutional democracy

Languages: English (official), Mende, Temne, Krio

Money: Leone

Life Expectancy: 57

Literacy Rate: 48%

GUESS WHAT? Serra da Leoa, the Portuguese name for Sierra Leone, means "Mountain of the Lion."

Singapore

Location: Asia

Capital: Singapore

Area: 269 sq mi
(697 sq km)

Population Estimate
(July 2014): 5,567,301

Government:
Parliamentary republic

Languages: Chinese
(Mandarin), English, Malay,
and Tamil (all official);
Hokkien, Cantonese,
Teochew, others

Money: Singapore dollar

Life Expectancy: 84

Literacy Rate: 97%

GUESS WHAT? Singapore has one of the world's best zoos. Many animals roam freely in a lush, natural environment.

Slovakia

Location: Europe

Capital: Bratislava

Area: 18,933 sq mi
(49,035 sq km)

Population Estimate
(July 2014): 5,443,583

Government:
Parliamentary democracy

Languages: Slovak
(official), Hungarian, Roma,
Ruthenian, others

Money: Euro
(formerly koruna)

Life Expectancy: 77

Literacy Rate: 100%

GUESS WHAT? With Austria to its west and Hungary to its south, Bratislava is the only world capital that borders two other countries.

Slovenia

Location: Europe

Capital: Ljubljana

Area: 7,827 sq mi
(20,273 sq km)

Population Estimate
(July 2014): 1,988,292

Government:
Parliamentary republic

Languages: Slovenian
(official), Serbo-Croatian,
Italian, Hungarian, others

Money: Euro
(formerly Slovenian tolar)

Life expectancy: 78

Literacy Rate: 100%

GUESS WHAT? More than half of Slovenia's land is protected, meaning it is used for places like scientific reserves, national parks, and wildlife sanctuaries.

Solomon Islands

Location: Oceania

Capital: Honiara

Area: 11,157 sq mi
(28,896 sq km)

Population Estimate
(July 2014): 609,883

Government:
Parliamentary democracy

Languages: English (official),
Melanesian pidgin, more
than 120 local languages

Money: Solomon
Islands dollar

Life Expectancy: 75

Literacy Rate: 84%

GUESS WHAT? Located in the New Georgia Islands in the Western Province, Marovo Lagoon is the world's largest saltwater lagoon. It is home to bottlenose dolphins.

Somalia

Location: Africa

Capital: Mogadishu

Area: 246,201 sq mi
(637,657 sq km)

Population Estimate
(July 2014): 10,428,043

Government:
Transitional; parliamentary
federal republic

Languages: Somali
and Arabic (both official),
Italian, English

Money: Somali shilling

Life Expectancy: 52

Literacy Rate: 38%

GUESS WHAT? Sheep are a major export for Somalia. Somali sheep have black hair on their heads and white hair on their bodies.

South Africa

Location: Africa

Capitals: Pretoria (administrative), Cape Town (legislative), Bloemfontein (judicial)

Area: 470,693 sq mi
(1,219,090 sq km)

Population Estimate
(July 2014): 48,375,645

Government: Republic

Languages: Zulu, Xhosa,
Afrikaans, English, Sepedi,
Setswana, Sesotho, Tsonga,
Swati, Tshivenda, Ndebele
(all official), others

Money: Rand

Life Expectancy: 50

Literacy Rate: 94%

GUESS WHAT? At 2.5 miles below ground, South Africa's Mponeng gold mine is the deepest in the world.

Spain

Location: Europe

Capital: Madrid

Area: 195,124 sq mi (505,370 sq km)

Population Estimate (July 2014): 47,737,941

Government: Parliamentary monarchy

Languages: Castilian Spanish (official), Catalan, Galician, Basque

Money: Euro (formerly peseta)

Life Expectancy: 81

Literacy Rate: 98%

GUESS WHAT? Instead of the Tooth Fairy, a mouse named Ratoncito Pérez visits Spanish children to leave them treasures in exchange for their lost teeth.

Sri Lanka

Location: Asia

Capital: Colombo (executive and judicial), Sri Jayewardenepura Kotte (legislative)

Area: 25,332 sq mi (65,610 sq km)

Population Estimate (July 2014): 21,866,445

Government: Republic

Languages: Sinhala (official), Tamil, English, others

Money: Sri Lankan rupee

Life Expectancy: 76

Literacy Rate: 93%

GUESS WHAT? More than 80% of the world's *C. verum* cinnamon, also known as "true cinnamon," is produced in Sri Lanka.

Sudan

Location: Africa

Capital: Khartoum

Area: 718,723 sq mi (1,861,484 sq km)

Population Estimate (July 2014): 35,482,233

Government: Federal republic

Languages: Arabic and English (both official), Nubian, Ta Bedawie, Fur

Money: Sudanese pound

Life Expectancy: 63

Literacy Rate: 76%

GUESS WHAT? Sudan is home to the world's largest swamp. Formed by a tributary of the Nile River, the Sudd can cover more than 50,000 square miles (130,000 sq km) in the rainy season.

Sudan, South

Location: Africa

Capital: Juba

Area: 284,777 sq mi (644,329 sq km)

Population Estimate (July 2014): 11,562,695

Government: Republic

Languages: English (official), Arabic, others

Money: South Sudanese pound

Life Expectancy: 55

Literacy Rate: 27%

GUESS WHAT? South Sudan's national anthem, "South Sudan Oyee [Hurray]," was written by a group of students from the University of Juba. Their lyrics were chosen during a competition held in 2010.

Suriname

Location: South America

Capital: Paramaribo

Area: 63,251 sq mi (163,820 sq km)

Population Estimate (July 2014): 573,311

Government: Constitutional democracy

Languages: Dutch (official), English, Surinamese, Caribbean Hindustani, Javanese

Money: Surinamese dollar

Life Expectancy: 72

Literacy Rate: 96%

GUESS WHAT? Ninety percent of Suriname's land is covered in forests, the highest percentage of any country.

Swaziland

Location: Africa

Capital: Mbabane

Area: 6,704 sq mi (17,364 sq km)

Population Estimate (July 2014): 1,419,623

Government: Monarchy

Languages: English and Swati (both official)

Money: Lilangeni

Life Expectancy: 51

Literacy Rate: 88%

GUESS WHAT? Swaziland is one of just four countries that lies entirely to the south of the Tropic of Capricorn, the imaginary line which marks the southernmost point on Earth at which the sun can be directly overhead.

COUNTRIES

Sweden

Location: Europe

Capital: Stockholm

Area: 173,860 sq mi (450,295 sq km)

Population Estimate (July 2014): 9,723,809

Government: Constitutional monarchy

Languages: Swedish (official), Sami, Finnish

Money: Krona

Life Expectancy: 82

Literacy Rate: 99%

GUESS WHAT? A hotel made entirely of snow and ice has been built in Jukkasjärvi, Sweden, every winter since 1989. The design varies from year to year and covers almost 60,000 square feet (5,500 sq m).

Switzerland

Location: Europe

Capital: Bern

Area: 15,937 sq mi (41,277 sq km)

Population Estimate (July 2014): 8,061,516

Government: Federal republic

Languages: German, French, Italian, and Romansh (all official), others

Money: Swiss franc

Life Expectancy: 82

Literacy Rate: 99%

GUESS WHAT? Of the four national languages, only about 1% of the population speaks Romansh. It is a language developed from Latin and spoken in southeastern Switzerland.

Syria

Location: Middle East

Capital: Damascus

Area: 71,498 sq mi (185,180 sq km)

Population Estimate (July 2014): 17,951,639

Government: Republic under an authoritarian regime

Languages: Arabic (official), Kurdish, Armenian, Aramaic, Circassian, others

Money: Syrian pound

Life Expectancy: 68

Literacy Rate: 86%

GUESS WHAT? Damascus is one of the oldest cities in the world, dating back at least 4,000 years. Some settlements on the outskirts of the region are more than 10,000 years old.

Taiwan

Location: Asia

Capital: Taipei

Area: 13,892 sq mi (35,980 sq km)

Population Estimate (July 2014): 23,359,928

Government: Multiparty democracy

Languages: Chinese (Mandarin; official), Taiwanese, Hakka dialects

Money: New Taiwan dollar

Life Expectancy: 80

Literacy Rate: 99%

GUESS WHAT? Because of an ongoing dispute with China over its independence and legitimacy, Taiwanese athletes compete in Olympic and FIFA events as the country of "Chinese Taipei."

Tajikistan

Location: Asia

Capital: Dushanbe

Area: 55,251 sq mi (143,100 sq km)

Population Estimate (July 2014): 8,051,512

Government: Republic

Languages: Tajik (official), Russian

Money: Somoni

Life Expectancy: 67

Literacy Rate: 100%

GUESS WHAT? Nurek Dam, on the Vakhsh River in Tajikistan, was the tallest man-made dam in the world when it was completed in 1980. At 984 feet (300 m) tall, it is still the second tallest dam, trailing only China's Jinping-I Dam.

Tanzania

Location: Africa

Capitals: Dar es Salaam (commercial), Dodoma (political)

Area: 365,755 sq mi (947,300 sq km)

Population Estimate (July 2014): 49,639,138

Government: Republic

Languages: Swahili and English (both official), Arabic, others

Money: Tanzanian shilling

Life Expectancy: 61

Literacy Rate: 71%

GUESS WHAT? Tanzania is believed to have the largest lion population in the world.

Thailand

Location: Asia

Capital: Bangkok

Area: 198,117 sq mi
(513,120 sq km)

Population Estimate
(July 2014): 67,741,401

Government:
Constitutional monarchy

Languages: Thai (Siamese)
(official), English, regional
dialects

Money: Baht

Life Expectancy: 74

Literacy Rate: 97%

GUESS WHAT? Phra Phuttha Maha Suwan Patimakon (the Golden Buddha) is the world's largest solid gold statue. It is 9.8 feet (3 m) tall and weighs more than 12,000 pounds (5,500 kg).

Togo

Location: Africa

Capital: Lomé

Area: 21,925 sq mi
(56,785 sq km)

Population Estimate
(July 2014): 7,351,374

Government: Republic,
under transition to
multiparty democratic rule

Languages: French (official),
Ewe, Mina, Kabye, Dagomba

Money: CFA franc

Life Expectancy: 64

Literacy Rate: 67%

GUESS WHAT? Togo celebrates its Independence Day on April 27, marking its peaceful separation from France in 1960.

Tonga

Location: Oceania

Capital: Nuku'alofa

Area: 288 sq mi (747 sq km)

Population Estimate
(July 2014): 106,440

Government:
Constitutional monarchy

Languages: Tongan and
English (both official), others

Money: Pa'anga

Life Expectancy: 76

Literacy Rate: 99%

GUESS WHAT? In the Tongan language, "Tonga" means "south."

Trinidad and Tobago

Location: Caribbean

Capital: Port-of-Spain

Area: 1,980 sq mi
(5,128 sq km)

Population Estimate
(July 2014): 1,223,916

Government:
Parliamentary democracy

Languages: English (official),
Caribbean Hindustani,
French, Spanish, Chinese

Money: Trinidad and
Tobago dollar

Life Expectancy: 72

Literacy Rate: 99%

GUESS WHAT? The steel pan, a popular Caribbean percussion instrument, originated in Trinidad in the 1930s.

Tunisia

Location: Africa

Capital: Tunis

Area: 63,170 sq mi
(163,610 sq km)

Population Estimate
(July 2014): 10,937,521

Government: Republic

Languages: Arabic (official),
French, Berber

Money: Tunisian dinar

Life Expectancy: 76

Literacy Rate: 82%

GUESS WHAT? Tunisia's Jasmine Revolution (2010–11) was a series of protests that led to democracy in Tunisia. It was the first of a wave of demonstrations in the Middle East and North Africa that became known as the Arab Spring.

Turkey

Location: Europe and Asia

Capital: Ankara

Area: 302,535 sq mi
(783,562 sq km)

Population Estimate
(July 2014): 81,619,392

Government: Republican
parliamentary democracy

Languages: Turkish (official),
Kurdish, others

Money: Turkish lira

Life Expectancy: 73

Literacy Rate: 95%

GUESS WHAT? Turkey is the world's largest producer of cherries, apricots, and figs.

Turkmenistan

Location: Asia

Capital: Ashgabat

Area: 188,456 sq mi (488,100 sq km)

Population Estimate (July 2014): 5,171,943

Government: Republic with authoritarian presidential rule

Languages: Turkmen (official), Russian, Uzbek, others

Money: Turkmen manat

Life Expectancy: 69

Literacy Rate: 100%

GUESS WHAT? Scientists have found thousands of preserved dinosaur footprints at The Plateau of the Dinosaurs in the eastern region of Turkmenistan.

Tuvalu

Location: Oceania

Capital: Funafuti

Area: 10 sq mi (26 sq km)

Population Estimate (July 2014): 10,782

Government: Parliamentary democracy

Languages: Tuvaluan and English (both official), Samoan, Kiribati

Money: Australian dollar, Tuvaluan dollar

Life Expectancy: 66

Literacy Rate: 99%

GUESS WHAT? Tuvalu's main export is copra, the dried insides of coconuts, from which coconut oil is extracted.

Uganda

Location: Africa

Capital: Kampala

Area: 93,065 sq mi (241,038 sq km)

Population Estimate (July 2014): 35,918,915

Government: Republic

Languages: English (official), Luganda, other Niger-Congo languages, Nilo-Saharan languages, Swahili, Arabic

Money: Ugandan shilling

Life Expectancy: 54

Literacy Rate: 78%

GUESS WHAT? On the Ugandan flag, the red color symbolizes the brotherhood of man, black represents the African people, and yellow stands for the sun.

Ukraine

Location: Europe

Capital: Kiev

Area: 233,032 sq mi (603,550 sq km)

Population Estimate (July 2014): 44,291,413

Government: Republic

Languages: Ukrainian (official), Russian, others

Money: Hryvnia

Life Expectancy: 69

Literacy Rate: 100%

GUESS WHAT? The world's largest aircraft is the Ukranian-built Antonov An-225 Mriya. First flown in 1988, the Mriya (Ukranian for "dream") carried a world-record 279.8-ton (253,820 kg) payload on a flight in 2001.

United Arab Emirates

Location: Middle East

Capital: Abu Dhabi

Area: 32,278 sq mi (83,600 sq km)

Population Estimate (July 2014): 5,628,805

Government: Federation

Languages: Arabic (official), Persian, English, Hindi, Urdu

Money: U.A.E. dirham

Life Expectancy: 77

Literacy Rate: 94%

GUESS WHAT? The Mall of the Emirates, in Dubai, features an indoor ski slope. The slope, which is more than 1,300 feet (396 m) tall, requires 6,000 tons (5,443 metric tons) of snow.

United Kingdom

Location: Europe

Capital: London

Area: 94,058 sq mi (243,610 sq km)

Population Estimate (July 2014): 63,742,977

Government: Constitutional monarchy

Languages: English, Scots, Scottish Gaelic, Welsh, Irish, Cornish

Money: British pound

Life Expectancy: 80

Literacy Rate: 99%

GUESS WHAT? The first dinosaur fossils ever identified were in the U.K., and it was British scientist Richard Owen who came up with the term "dinosaur" (Greek for monstrous lizard) in 1842.

United States

Location: North America

Capital: Washington, D.C.

Area: 3,794,100 sq mi (9,826,675 sq km)

Population Estimate (July 2014): 318,892,103

Government: Constitution-based federal republic

Languages: English, Spanish (spoken by a sizable minority), others

Money: U.S. dollar

Life Expectancy: 80

Literacy Rate: 99%

GUESS WHAT? In 1777, America's first official flag had 13 stripes and 13 stars, one of each for each state in the union. Congress passed acts to add more stars over time.

Uruguay

Location: South America

Capital: Montevideo

Area: 68,037 sq mi (176,215 sq km)

Population Estimate (July 2014): 3,332,972

Government: Constitutional republic

Languages: Spanish (official), Portuñol, Brazilero

Money: Uruguayan peso

Life Expectancy: 77

Literacy Rate: 99%

GUESS WHAT? Uruguay's northernmost point is farther south than any other country's.

Uzbekistan

Location: Asia

Capital: Tashkent

Area: 172,742 sq mi (447,400 sq km)

Population Estimate (July 2014): 28,929,716

Government: Republic with authoritarian presidential rule

Languages: Uzbek (official), Russian, Tajik, others

Money: Uzbekistani som

Life Expectancy: 73

Literacy Rate: 100%

GUESS WHAT? Uzbekistan is one of the two doubly landlocked countries in the world. (Liechtenstein is the other.) It is bordered only by countries that are also landlocked.

Vanuatu

Location: Oceania

Capital: Port-Vila

Area: 4,706 sq mi (12,189 sq km)

Population Estimate (July 2014): 266,937

Government: Parliamentary republic

Languages: Bislama, English, and French (all official); most people speak one of more than 100 local languages

Money: Vatu

Life Expectancy: 72

Literacy Rate: 85%

GUESS WHAT? The sideways yellow Y on Vanuatu's flag roughly matches the configuration of its approximately 82 islands.

Vatican City (Holy See)

Location: Europe

Capital: Vatican City

Area: 0.17 sq mi (0.44 sq km)

Population Estimate (July 2014): 842

Government: Ecclesiastical

Languages: Italian, Latin, French, others

Money: Euro

Life Expectancy: Not available

Literacy Rate: 100%

GUESS WHAT? Vatican City, where the Pope lives, is located inside Rome, Italy. It is the smallest country in the world.

Venezuela

Location: South America

Capital: Caracas

Area: 352,144 sq mi (912,050 sq km)

Population Estimate (July 2014): 28,868,486

Government: Federal republic

Languages: Spanish (official), native languages

Money: Bolívar

Life Expectancy: 74

Literacy Rate: 96%

GUESS WHAT? At 3,212 feet (979 m), Salto Ángel ("Angel Falls") in Venezuela is the world's tallest waterfall.

COUNTRIES

Vietnam

Location: Asia

Capital: Hanoi

Area: 127,881 sq mi (331,210 sq km)

Population Estimate (July 2014): 93,421,835

Government: Communist state

Languages: Vietnamese (official), English, French, Chinese, Khmer

Money: Dong

Life Expectancy: 73

Literacy Rate: 93%

 Centuries ago, when the rice fields would flood, farmers in Vietnam entertained themselves by putting on puppet shows in the water. The tradition lives on to this day.

Yemen

Location: Middle East

Capital: Sanaa

Area: 203,850 sq mi (527,968 sq km)

Population Estimate (July 2014): 26,052,966

Government: Republic

Language: Arabic (official)

Money: Yemeni rial

Life Expectancy: 65

Literacy Rate: 70%

 In 2011, Tawakkol Karman became the first Yemeni and the first Arab woman to win the Nobel Prize. Karman, a journalist, won for her work fighting for human rights and freedom of expression in Yemen, in the Middle East.

Zambia

Location: Africa

Capital: Lusaka

Area: 290,587 sq mi (752,618 sq km)

Population Estimate (July 2014): 14,638,505

Government: Republic

Languages: English (official), Bembe, Nyanja, Tonga, others

Money: Zambian kwacha

Life Expectancy: 52

Literacy Rate: 63%

Hippopotamuses are easy to spot in Zambia's lakes and rivers. The country has the largest hippo population in the world.

Zimbabwe

Location: Africa

Capital: Harare

Area: 150,872 sq mi (390,757 sq km)

Population Estimate (July 2014): 13,771,721

Government: Parliamentary democracy

Languages: Shona, Ndebele, English, 13 minority languages (all official)

Money: U.S. dollar, South African rand, and six other currencies

Life Expectancy: 56

Literacy Rate: 87%

Victoria Falls, the world's largest waterfall, is located on the border between Zimbabwe and Zambia.

Where in the World?

Get ready to take a trip around the globe.
See if you can match these recognizable landmarks with
the city in which they're located.

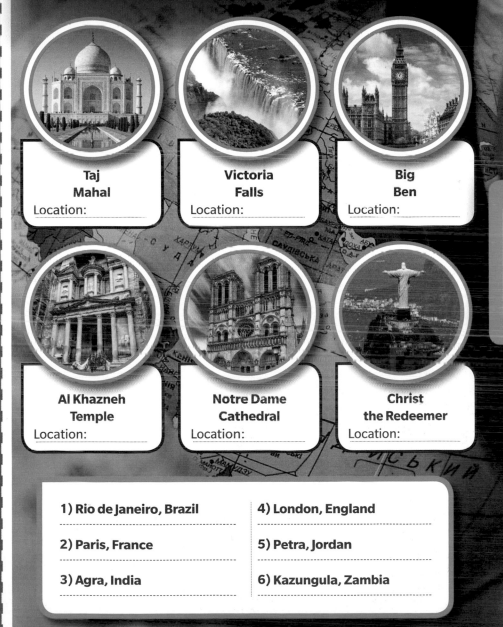

Taj Mahal
Location:

Victoria Falls
Location:

Big Ben
Location:

Al Khazneh Temple
Location:

Notre Dame Cathedral
Location:

Christ the Redeemer
Location:

1) Rio de Janeiro, Brazil

2) Paris, France

3) Agra, India

4) London, England

5) Petra, Jordan

6) Kazungula, Zambia

Answers on page 276

Energy and the Environment

Sources of Energy

Nonrenewable Sources

Most of the energy we use comes from fossil fuels. Fossil fuels include coal, oil, and natural gas. All of these resources come out of the ground. The problem is that these fuels cannot be replaced. Once we use them up, they are gone for good. Fossil fuels also cause harmful pollution that can add to climate change.

Nuclear Energy

In a process known as nuclear fission, the nucleus of a uranium-235 atom is hit with an atomic particle called a neutron. The uranium atom splits and gives off a lot of heat. Nuclear energy relies on this heat to boil water and create steam to power electrical generators. The waste created during nuclear fission can be harmful to people and the environment. It must be stored away from people for thousands of years.

Nuclear power plants turn water into steam to power generators.

Natural Gas

Natural gas is the odorless by-product of decaying plant and animal matter that has been buried under many layers of earth. The gas pockets are trapped underground and can be piped to the surface. Natural gas is used to cook and heat homes.

The energy used to heat homes, manufacture goods, grow and harvest food, transport products, and more comes from two kinds of sources. Nonrenewable sources are in limited supply. Renewable energy sources are not in danger of running out.

Petroleum

Found deep within the Earth, petroleum has to be drilled and piped to the surface. Like natural gas and coal, it was formed from pressure and heat over many millions of years and made of decaying plant and animal remains. In its "crude" state, before it is refined, it is known as petroleum. Petroleum can be refined into oil, gasoline, or diesel fuel.

Coal

Coal is a hard rock made of carbon. Like natural gas, it started out as decaying matter covered by many layers of dirt. Over the course of millions of years, the pressure of all this dirt, as well as Earth's heat, transformed the matter into coal. Because coal takes so long to form, it cannot be manufactured. Coal is the largest source of fossil fuel in the United States.

Petroleum Plant

Renewable Sources

Renewable energy is made from natural resources that can be replaced. They include sunlight, wind, water, and the earth's heat. Renewable energy is also known as clean energy or green energy. Unlike fossil fuels, most renewable energy sources do not create pollution.

Hoover Dam

Solar Collectors

Solar energy comes from the sun and can be used to heat water, homes, and large buildings. Solar heat collectors, such as solar boxes, trap the sun's rays to generate heat. (Some solar boxes are designed to cook food.) There are also solar cells, which change sunlight directly into electricity. These cells can be found in devices as small as calculators. When they are grouped together in large panels, they can power entire buildings.

Solar panels absorb sunlight to heat and power a building.

Hydroelectric Power Plants

Hydropower is power created by moving water. Fast-flowing rivers and large waterfalls create a lot of power. We can harness that energy using hydroelectric power plants.

There are several types of hydroelectric power plants. One design uses the natural flow of a river to turn the blades of a turbine, which spins a generator to make electricity. Another design uses a dam, which slows a river's flow and stores up water in a lake. The water flowing through the dam turns the turbine to power an electric generator.

Wind Turbines

People have been using wind power for thousands of years. Wind moved boats along Egypt's Nile River as early as 5,000 B.C. Windmills on farms were used to harness the wind's energy to power machines to pump water and grind grain. Wind turbines are modern windmills that help generate electricity.

Many wind turbines look like giant fans. They are most effective on top of a hill or on open land. The wind turns the blades and causes a generator to spin. This is what creates electricity.

Geothermal Heat

The earth's core is as hot as the surface of the sun. This heat is called geothermal energy.

Geothermal heat pumps use pipes buried underground to access the earth's heat. These pipes carry water, which absorbs the heat. A device then takes the heat from the water and uses it to warm the air inside buildings. (The system can also work in reverse to cool buildings. The same device takes the heat from the air and moves it back underground.)

Geothermal power plants use extremely hot water within the earth to create steam. The steam then drives a generator, which produces power.

Biomass Fuels

Have you ever made s'mores by a campfire? If so, you've used biomass energy! Biomass is natural material from animals or plants. It contains stored energy from the sun.

Burning biomass is one way to release its energy. That heat can be used to produce steam and make electricity. Crops like corn and sugarcane can be turned into biofuels to power vehicles. Also, when biomass rots, such as in a landfill, it releases methane gas, a natural gas that can be turned into electricity.

Wood Chips

FROM TIME FOR KIDS MAGAZINE

Greening Africa

Countries in Africa have come together to plant trees, protect resources, and fight poverty.

Across northern Africa, the desert is steadily growing. Parched lands are spreading. But a bold project known as the Great Green Wall aims to help protect and maintain resources and fight poverty.

Farmers are learning to care for their land and use water wisely. They are also planting millions of trees and crops. The Great Green Wall would cover an area more than 4,000 miles long—from Senegal to Djibouti (see map).

The Great Green Wall was first approved by the African Union, a group of 53 nations, in 2007. The program receives support from the United Nations, the World Bank, and other groups.

According to the U.N. Food and Agriculture Organization (FAO), about two-thirds of Africa is desert or dry land. Climate change has led to long periods of drought. Some areas that once had crops are no longer fertile, or able to produce crops, because the land was not properly taken care of.

The Great Green Wall's trees provide a barrier against desert winds and help hold moisture in the air and soil, allowing crops to grow. In time, the richer soil will provide more land for animals to graze on. More resources will bring more jobs. "The goal is to create sustainable land management," Nora Berrahmouni, a forestry

officer with the FAO, told TFK.

Trees and crops have been planted in Senegal and Niger. An added benefit of the Great Green Wall is that countries in the region are sharing information about which programs work and which don't. Now, along with trees, ideas are taking root.

—By Melanie Kletter

These women are tending potato plants in Senegal.

Take Charge!

Here are 10 things you and your family can do everyday to live a green life and help the environment.

1. Replace your incandescent light bulbs. Use more energy efficient options, which cut back on your energy use.

2. Carpool or ride the bus. When possible, ask your family if you can walk, bike, or use public transportation, such as the subway or bus. Or, see if your friends and neighbors want to start a carpool to school.

3. Plant more trees.

A single tree will absorb one ton of carbon dioxide (CO_2) over its lifetime! Imagine how much cleaner the air would be if every person on earth planted a tree.

4. Adjust your thermostat. Moving your thermostat down two degrees in wintertime and up two degrees in summertime can save a lot of energy. You can also ask your parents if your local utility company offers alternative power.

5. Avoid products with lots of packaging. Buy products that are better for the environment. Look for items that are made from recycled materials, and have less or no packaging. And when it comes to food, support local farmers markets.

6. Use less hot water. Install a low-flowing shower head and use cold water to wash a full load of clothes.

7. In fact, use less water overall! Save water by taking shorter showers. Also, remember to turn off the faucet while you're brushing your teeth.

8. Recycle
Think before you throw something in the trash. Glass, paper, and many plastics can be recycled. And be sure to take e-waste, like computers and cell phones, to a special recycling facility.

9. Turn off and unplug devices. When you're not watching TV, turn it off—and unplug it. Unplugging your appliances and chargers when not in use can keep thousands of pounds of CO_2 from entering the atmosphere every year.

10. Spread the word! Talk to your friends and family about going green, too. Tell them what you've learned and think of ways to raise awareness and educate others, like creating fundraisers for green causes.

ENERGY AND THE ENVIRONMENT

Water Worries

Facing a drought, California issued a tough order to cut water use.

California has survived many droughts. But the most recent dry spell is one of the most severe the state has ever experienced. A shortage of precipitation has left lakes, reservoirs, and other sources of water at historic lows. In 2015, Governor Jerry Brown issued an executive order requiring towns and cities to cut back water usage by 25%.

The move marks the first time California has ordered mandatory cuts. "It's something we're going to have to live with," said Brown at a press conference. "For how long, we're not sure." In January 2014, he asked Californians to voluntarily reduce their water use by 20%. But they fell short of that goal.

The dry banks of Don Pedro Lake, in La Grange, California, are a visible reminder of the drought.

Under the executive order, the state can fine water agencies $10,000 a day if they do not meet guidelines. People face fines of up to $500 a day. They may water lawns only two days per week. Colleges, golf courses, and other places with large grassy areas must curb their water use. Half the water used in the state's cities and suburbs goes to landscaping. Californians use more than twice as much water per person as Australians, who have a similar climate and economy.

The strictest measures do not apply to water used on farms. Some critics say farmers should not have been spared. But farmers argue that the drought has already hurt them. California farms produce nearly half of the fruit, nuts, and vegetables grown in the U.S. The industry has seen a loss of $1.5 billion from the lack of water.

Brown is challenging Californians to change their ways. The drought, he says, calls for "action and changes in behavior from the Oregon border all the way to the Mexican border."

—*By Glenn Greenberg, with TIME and AP reporting*

California governor Jerry Brown required state residents to cut back on water use.

Save the Planet

The 12 words below all relate to helping the Earth.
See if you can find them in the grid. They may read up, down,
across, diagonal, or backward.

N	J	G	S	O	L	A	R	L	D	A	E
A	O	B	U	T	H	T	A	I	B	E	G
T	R	I	S	H	Y	L	R	R	N	F	L
U	E	G	T	U	R	B	I	N	E	F	M
R	C	P	A	A	Y	O	A	E	L	I	K
A	Y	Z	I	H	V	X	N	V	Y	C	E
L	C	I	N	B	G	R	E	E	N	I	T
E	L	B	A	W	E	N	E	R	K	E	A
R	E	N	B	A	C	L	I	S	O	N	M
P	B	F	L	T	W	S	O	L	N	T	I
A	L	B	E	R	S	U	S	Q	B	O	L
E	N	V	I	R	O	N	M	E	N	T	C

- Conservation
- Solar
- Turbine
- Renewable
- Green
- Climate
- Efficient
- Environment
- Sustainable
- Recycle
- Hybrid
- Natural

Ed Sheeran

Entertainment

Taylor Swift

Emma Stone

Star Wars' BB-8

Academy Award for Best Picture

2011: *The King's Speech*

2012: *The Artist*

2013: *Argo*

2014: *12 Years a Slave*

2015: *Birdman or (The Unexpected Virtue of Ignorance)*

2016: *Spotlight*

Academy Award for Best Actor in a Leading Role

2011: Colin Firth

2012: Jean Dujardin

2013: Daniel Day-Lewis

2014: Matthew McConaughey

2015: Eddie Redmayne

2016: Leonardo DiCaprio

Academy Award for Best Actress in a Leading Role

2011: Natalie Portman

2012: Meryl Streep

2013: Jennifer Lawrence

2014: Cate Blanchett

2015: Julianne Moore

2016: Brie Larson

abc

Kids' Choice Award for Favorite Movie Actor

2010: Taylor Lautner

2011: Johnny Depp

2012: Adam Sandler

2013: Johnny Depp

2014: Adam Sandler

2015: Ben Stiller

Kids' Choice Award for Favorite Movie

2010: *Alvin and the Chipmunks: The Squeakquel*

2011: *The Karate Kid*

2012: *Alvin and the Chipmunks: Chipwrecked*

2013: *The Hunger Games*

2014: *The Hunger Games: Catching Fire*

2015: *The Hunger Games: Mockingjay Part 1*

Kids' Choice Award for Favorite Movie Actress

2010: Miley Cyrus

2011: Miley Cyrus

2012: Kristen Stewart

2013: Kristen Stewart

2014: Jennifer Lawrence

2015: Emma Stone

MYSTERY PERSON

I was born in Paris, France, in 1990, to English parents. My big break came when I landed the role of Hermione Granger for the Harry Potter movie series. In the 2017 film *Beauty and the Beast*, I play Belle. I graduated from Brown University and serve as a Goodwill Ambassador for UN Women.

◀ **Who am I?** Answer on page 276

123

Kids' Choice Award for Favorite TV Show

2010: *iCarly*

2011: *iCarly*

2012: *Victorious*

2013: *Victorious*

2014: *Sam and Cat*

2015: *Austin & Ally*

Kids' Choice Award for Favorite TV Actor

2010: Dylan Sprouse

2011: Dylan Sprouse

2012: Jake Short

2013: Ross Lynch

2014: Ross Lynch

2015: Ross Lynch

Kids' Choice Award for Favorite Cartoon

2010: *SpongeBob SquarePants*

2011: *SpongeBob SquarePants*

2012: *SpongeBob SquarePants*

2013: *SpongeBob SquarePants*

2014: *SpongeBob SquarePants*

2015: *SpongeBob SquarePants*

Emmy Award for Outstanding Reality-Competition Program

2010: *Top Chef*

2011: *The Amazing Race*

2012: *The Amazing Race*

2013: *The Voice*

2014: *The Amazing Race*

2015: *The Voice*

Emmy Award for Outstanding Comedy Series

2010: *Modern Family*

2011: *Modern Family*

2012: *Modern Family*

2013: *Modern Family*

2014: *Modern Family*

2015: *VEEP*

Kids' Choice Award for Favorite TV Actress

2010: Selena Gomez

2011: Selena Gomez

2012: Selena Gomez

2013: Selena Gomez

2014: Ariana Grande

2015: Laura Marano

Grammy Award for Album of the Year

2011: *The Suburbs*, Arcade Fire

2012: *21*, Adele

2013: *Babel*, Mumford & Sons

2014: *Random Access Memories*, Daft Punk

2015: *Morning Phase*, Beck

2016: *1989*, Taylor Swift

Grammy Award for Record of the Year

2011: "Need You Now," Lady Antebellum

2012: "Rolling in the Deep," Adele

2013: "Somebody That I Used to Know," Gotye feat. Kimbra

2014: "Get Lucky," Daft Punk feat. Pharrell Williams and Nile Rodgers

2015: "Stay with Me," Sam Smith

2016: "Uptown Funk," Mark Ronson feat. Bruno Mars

Grammy Award for Song of the Year

2011: "Need You Now," Lady Antebellum

2012: "Rolling in the Deep," Adele

2013: "We Are Young," Fun.

2014: "Royals," Lorde

2015: "Stay with Me," Sam Smith

2016: "Thinking Out Loud," Ed Sheeran

Kids' Choice Award for Favorite Music Group

2010: Black Eyed Peas

2011: Black Eyed Peas

2012: Big Time Rush

2013: One Direction

2014: One Direction

2015: One Direction

Kids' Choice Award for Favorite Female Singer

2010: Taylor Swift

2011: Katy Perry

2012: Selena Gomez

2013: Katy Perry

2014: Selena Gomez

2015: Selena Gomez

Kids' Choice Award for Favorite Male Singer

2010: Jay-Z

2011: Justin Bieber

2012: Justin Bieber

2013: Justin Bieber

2014: Justin Timberlake

2015: Nick Jonas

A Taylor-Made Star

Taylor Swift is one of the most powerful people in the entertainment industry. How did a small-town girl become the queen of the music?

Taylor Swift is no stranger to success. But even by her standards, 2014 was a great year. Her album *1989* sold almost 1.3 million copies the week it was released. It was music's biggest sales week of the year. *Billboard* named her its Woman of the Year for the second time in the award's eight-year history. Her Red Tour made $150 million—the most ever in country music. And she has 72.1 million followers on Twitter, among the most of anyone in the world. How does someone who just turned 25 handle all this success?

The Two Taylors

Swift likes to tell a story about how she came to be named Taylor. Well, she likes to tell two. The first is that she was named for the

singer James Taylor, whom her parents adored. And the other: "My mom named me Taylor because she thought that I would probably end up in business—my parents are both finance people—and she didn't want any kind of executive, boss, or manager to see if I was a girl or a boy if they got my résumé."

Swift was born in Reading, Pennsylvania. As a child, she wrote and performed whenever she could. She won a nationwide poetry contest in fourth grade. But her true love was country songwriting, so she went to Nashville, Tennessee, at age 11 to get noticed. She struck out. But she met with more success when she tried again at 13.

In eighth grade, Swift persuaded her parents and her younger brother, Austin, to move near Nashville. She would write song lyrics for a few hours each week after school. While performing, she got noticed by a music executive. Her first album came out the next year and was an immediate hit.

A Little Help from Her Fans

After years of fame, Swift has adjusted to life in the spotlight. But it can still be hard on the small-town

girl. "If I'm not interested in [reading about] how I'm walking, whether I look tired, how my makeup is right, what's that mark on my knee, did I hurt myself?—I just don't go out," Swift says. But her fans make it all worthwhile. She says they give her "extreme, unconditional, wonderful loyalty that I never thought I'd receive in my life, not from a best friend, not from a boyfriend, not from a husband, not from a dog."

Swift recalls a rainy concert in 2011. "In the middle of the show, a torrential downpour starts. In my head, the first thing I'm thinking is, Everyone's going to leave. . . . It's going to look just like my nightmares look," she recalls. "But instead of leaving, they just danced."
—*By Jack Dickey for TIME*

Swift sings in Nashville, her hometown, while on the Red Tour.

Album sales have been weak worldwide. But Swift still shows significant selling power. The amounts below are her first-week sales, in millions.

T.S. 1989

1.29
1989
Swift's 2014 album was named for the year in which she was born.

RED
TAYLOR SWIFT

1.21
RED
The Red Tour made the most money in country-music history.

Speak Now

1.05
SPEAK NOW
This 2010 album was praised for its songs in many different styles.

Top-Selling Artists of All Time

1. The Beatles
2. Garth Brooks
3. Elvis Presley
4. Led Zeppelin
5. The Eagles
6. Billy Joel
7. Michael Jackson
8. Pink Floyd
9. Elton John
10. Barbra Streisand

Song that Spent the Most Weeks at No. 1 on Billboard's Hot 100

16 weeks: *One Sweet Day*, Mariah Carey & Boyz II Men (1995–96)

14 weeks: *Uptown Funk*, Mark Ronson featuring Bruno Mars (2015)

14 weeks: *I Gotta Feeling*, Black Eyed Peas (2009)

14 weeks: *We Belong Together*, Mariah Carey (2005)

14 weeks: *Candle in the Wind/ Something About the Way You Look Tonight*, Elton John (1997)

14 weeks: *Macarena*, Los Del Rio (1996)

14 weeks: *I'll Make Love to You*, Boyz II Men (1994)

14 weeks: *I Will Always Love You*, Whitney Houston (1992-1993)

Top-Selling Albums of All Time

1. Michael Jackson, *Thriller*
2. The Eagles, *Their Greatest Hits 1971-1975*
3. Pink Floyd, *The Wall*
4. Led Zeppelin, *Led Zeppelin IV*
5. Billy Joel, *Greatest Hits Volume I & Volume II*
6. AC/DC, *Back in Black*
7. Garth Brooks, *Double Live*
8. Shania Twain, *Come on Over*
9. Fleetwood Mac, *Rumours*
10. The Beatles, *The Beatles*

Movies that Spent the Most Weeks as Box Office No. 1

16 weeks: *E.T.: The Extra-Terrestrial* (1982)

15 weeks: *Titanic* (1997)

14 weeks: *Beverly Hills Cop* (1984)

14 weeks: *Tootsie* (1982)

12 weeks: *Home Alone* (1990)

11 weeks: *Back to the Future* (1985)

10 weeks: *Ghostbusters* (1984)

Highest-Grossing Films of All Time

1. *Avatar* (2009), $2.79 billion
2. *Titanic* (1997), $2.19 billion
3. *Star Wars: The Force Awakens* (2015), $2.15 billion
4. *Jurassic World* (2015), $1.67 billion
5. *The Avengers* (2012), $1.52 billion
6. *Furious 7* (2015), $1.52 billion
7. *Avengers: Age of Ultron* (2015), $1.41 billion
8. *Harry Potter and the Deathly Hallows Part 2* (2011), $1.34 billion
9. *Frozen* (2013), $1.28 billion
10. *Iron Man 3* (2013), $1.22 billion

Most-Watched TV Programs in the U.S.

2009–2010: *American Idol*

2010–2011: *American Idol*

2011–2012: *Sunday Night Football*

2012–2013: *NCIS*

2013–2014: *Sunday Night Football*

2014–2015: *The Big Bang Theory*

Longest-Running TV Programs in the U.S.

News program:
Meet the Press (1947–present)

Talk show:
The Tonight Show (1954–present)

Dramatic series:
Guiding Light (1952–2009)

Children's show:
Sesame Street (1969–present)

Game show:
The Price is Right (1972–present)

Variety show:
Saturday Night Live (1975–present)

Animated series and sitcom:
The Simpsons (1989–present)

American Film Institute's Greatest Animated Movies of All Time

1. *Snow White and the Seven Dwarfs* (1937)

2. *Pinocchio* (1940)

3. *Bambi* (1942)

4. *The Lion King* (1994)

5. *Fantasia* (1940)

6. *Toy Story* (1995)

7. *Beauty and the Beast* (1991)

8. *Shrek* (2001)

9. *Cinderella* (1950)

10. *Finding Nemo* (2003)

Double Take

These photos of the cast of *Modern Family* getting slimed may look similar—but look closely and you'll find that not everything is quite the same. Can you find all 10 changes?

Answers on page 277

Geography

The Seven Continents

North America
(INCLUDING CENTRAL AMERICA AND THE CARIBBEAN)
How big is it? 9,449,460 square miles (24,474,000 sq km)
Highest point Denali in the U.S., 20,322 feet (6,194 m)
Lowest point **Death Valley** in the U.S., 282 feet (86 m) below sea level

Europe
How big is it?
3,837,000 square miles (9,938,000 sq km)
Highest point Mount Elbrus in Russia, 18,481 feet (5,642 m)
Lowest point Caspian Sea in Kazakhstan, Russia, Azerbaijan, Iran and Turkmenistan, 92 feet (28 m) below sea level

South America
How big is it? 6,879,000 square miles (17,819,000 sq km)
Highest point **Mount Aconcagua** in Argentina, 22,834 feet (6,960 m)
Lowest point Valdes Peninsula in Argentina, 131 feet (40 m) below sea level

Africa
How big is it? 11,608,000 square miles (30,065,000 sq km)
Highest point Mount Kilimanjaro in Tanzania, 19,340 feet (5,895 m)
Lowest point Lake Assal in Djibouti, 512 feet (156 m) below sea level

Antarctica
How big is it? 5,100,000 square miles (13,209,000 sq km)
Highest point Vinson Massif, 16,066 feet (4,897 m)
Lowest point Bentley Subglacial Trench, 8,383 feet (2,555 m) below sea level

2

5

Asia

(INCLUDING THE MIDDLE EAST)

How big is it? 17,212,000 square miles (44,579,000 sq km)

Highest point Mount Everest in Nepal and Tibet, 29,035 feet (8,850 m)

Lowest point Dead Sea in Israel and Jordan, 1,286 feet (392 m) below sea level

Australia/ Oceania

How big is it? 3,132,000 square miles (8,112,000 sq km)

Highest point Mount Wilhelm in Papua New Guinea, 14,794 feet (4,509 m)

Lowest point Lake Eyre in Australia, 52 feet (16 m) below sea level

The Five Oceans

1. Arctic Ocean

Area: 5,427,000 square miles (14,056,000 sq km)
Average depth: 3,953 feet (1,205 m)

2. Atlantic Ocean

Area: 29,637,900 square miles (76,762,000 sq km)
Average depth: 12,880 feet (3,926 m)

3. Indian Ocean

Area: 24,469,500 square miles (68,556,000 sq km)
Average depth: 13,002 feet (3,963 m)

4. Pacific Ocean

Area: 60,060,700 square miles (155,557,000 sq km)
Average depth: 15,215 feet (4,638 m)

5. Southern Ocean

Area: 7,848,300 square miles (20,327,000 sq km)
Average depth: 13,100 to 16,400 feet (4,000 to 5,000 m)

GEOGRAPHY

Our Changing Planet

Earth is approximately 4.5 billion years old. In that time, it has changed a lot. The ground that we walk on is the outer layer of the Earth, or the Earth's crust. On the continents, the crust averages about 20 miles (32 km) thick, but beneath the oceans, it may be only a few miles thick. Beneath the crust is the mantle, a rocky layer that makes up about two-thirds of the weight of the planet. The center, or the core, of the Earth consists of a liquid layer of molten rock and lava and a solid ball of mostly iron and nickel. Although we do not feel the land shifting beneath our feet, it is moving. Sometimes, events like erupting volcanoes and earthquakes quickly change the face of the planet, but most of the time, the changes happen very slowly.

Plate Tectonics

The Earth's crust is broken up into seven major plates: the African, North American, South American, Eurasian, Australian, Antarctic, and Pacific plates. **Volcanoes** form where plates meet—both above ground and deep underwater. In areas where plates frequently move alongside one another, earthquakes occur more often. The San Andreas Fault, in California, is one of these plates.

Tungurahua volcano in Ecuador erupts.

Pangaea

Many scientists believe that the seven continents we have today were once part of a **single gigantic supercontinent**, which they call Pangaea. According to this theory, Pangaea began to break apart about 200 million to 225 million years ago, and the continents have been slowly drifting ever since. Valleys and rifts were formed by plates moving away from one another, and mountains were formed when plates crashed together. Due to the slow movement of two of Earth's plates, the Atlantic Ocean actually becomes about 1 inch (2.5 cm) wider each year.

Antarctic Adventure

TFK writer David Bjerklie traveled to Antarctica. Here, he shares some of his experiences.

David Bjerklie stands at the South Pole. In 1911, Roald Amundsen was the first to reach the pole.

Antarctica is the coldest, windiest, and emptiest place on Earth. Along the coast, it is also home to millions of waddling penguins. The black-and-white birds are just the tip of the iceberg when it comes to the breathtaking sights and experiences Antarctica offers visitors.

The National Science Foundation (NSF) invited TFK to go on an adventure. The U.S. agency funds polar research in the Arctic and the Antarctic. During my time in Antarctica, I traveled to the South Pole, tagged along with researchers in the field, and interviewed scientists.

My first stop on the continent was McMurdo Station. It is the largest of the three U.S. research stations in Antarctica. During the summer months (November to February), McMurdo has a population of around 800 people. In winter, the population is less than 200. McMurdo is a small town. Many of its residents are scientists. But McMurdo is also home to carpenters, cooks, plumbers, pilots, and other people who help the station run smoothly.

In Antarctica, you learn not to take anything for granted. The only plants that grow there are mosses and tiny algae. Food, water, and fuel all have to be shipped or flown in. Then, every bit of garbage must be taken out.

No country owns Antarctica. It is governed by the Antarctic Treaty System. The agreements call for the continent to be set aside for peaceful purposes and scientific exploration. There are researchers who study things that may surprise you. Did you know Antarctica has an active volcano? Scientists are studying a bubbling lava lake on Mount Erebus.

I had an amazing adventure. I left Antarctica with deep respect for the modern explorers who work and live in an environment that is both extreme and extraordinary.

GEOGRAPHY

Africa

ATLANTIC OCEAN

EUROPE

ASIA

MEDITERRANEAN SEA

RED SEA

FRANCE
SPAIN
PORTUGAL
Majorca
Corsica
Sardinia
Sicily
MALTA
ITALY
BOSNIA AND HERZEGOVINA
MONTENEGRO · KOSOVO
SERBIA
MACEDONIA
ALBANIA
GREECE
Crete
BULGARIA
ROMANIA
CYPRUS
LEBANON
ISRAEL
JORDAN
SYRIA
IRAQ
IRAN
GEORGIA
ARMENIA
SAUDI ARABIA
YEMEN
Madeira Islands
Canary Islands (Spain)

Tangier
Casablanca
Marrakech
Fès
Rabat
MOROCCO
Oran
Algiers
Constantine
ALGERIA
Tunis
TUNISIA
Tripoli
Banghazi
LIBYA
Alexandria
Cairo
Suez
EGYPT
Luxor
Aswan

Nile R.

SAHARA

Al Jawf

Laayoune
WESTERN SAHARA (Occupied by Morocco)
Nouakchott
MAURITANIA
Timbuktu
MALI
Mopti
Ségou
Bamako
Bobo-Dioulasso
Ouagadougou
BURKINA FASO
Niamey
Agadez
NIGER
Zinder
CHAD
N'Djamena
Khartoum
SUDAN
Port Sudan
ERITREA
Asmara
DJIBOUTI
Djibouti
Hargeysa
SOMALIA
Mogadishu
Addis Ababa
Dire Dawa
ETHIOPIA
SOUTH SUDAN
Juba
UGANDA
Kampala
KENYA
Congo R.
CENTRAL AFRICAN REPUBLIC
Bangui
OF THE
CAMEROON
Yaoundé
Douala
Malabo
EQUATORIAL GUINEA
SÃO TOME
GULF OF GUINEA
Benue R.
NIGERIA
Kano
Abuja
Ibadan
Lagos
Niger R.
BENIN
Porto-Novo
TOGO
Lomé
GHANA
Accra
Abidjan
CÔTE D'IVOIRE
Yamoussoukro
LIBERIA
Monrovia
SIERRA LEONE
Freetown
GUINEA
Conakry
GUINEA-BISSAU
Bissau
THE GAMBIA
Banjul
Dakar
SENEGAL

Niger R.

N E W S

140

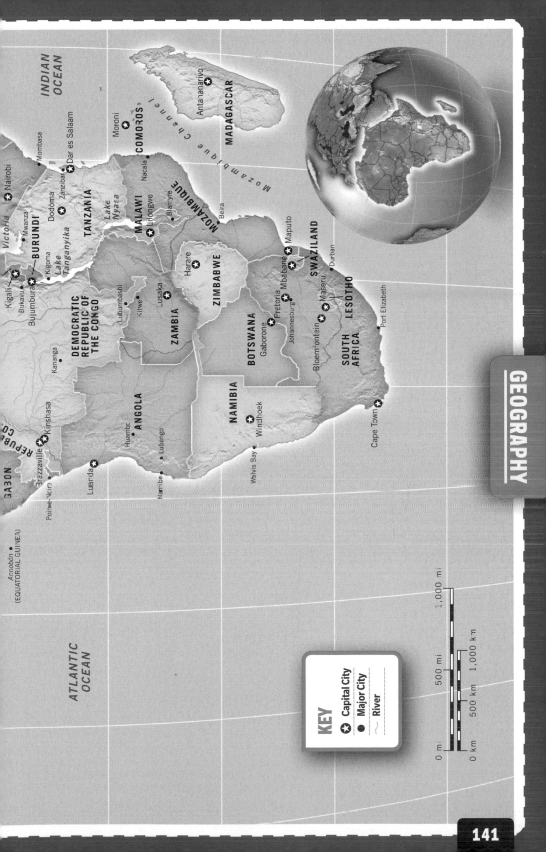

INDIAN OCEAN

Antananarivo

MADAGASCAR

Moroni

COMOROS

Mombasa
Dar es Salaam
Zanzibar
Nacala

Nairobi

Dodoma

Mwanza

TANZANIA

Lake Nyasa

MALAWI

MOZAMBIQUE

Lilongwe

Blantyre

Beira

BURUNDI

Kigoma

Lake Tanganyika

Kigali

Bukavu

Bujumbura

Lubumbashi

Harare

ZIMBABWE

Maputo

SWAZILAND

Mbabane

Durban

Kitwe

Lusaka

DEMOCRATIC REPUBLIC OF THE CONGO

ZAMBIA

BOTSWANA

Pretoria

Maseru

LESOTHO

Port Elizabeth

Kananga

Gaborone

Johannesburg

Bloemfontain

SOUTH AFRICA

Kinshasa

ANGOLA

NAMIBIA

REPUBLIC...

Brazzaville

GABON

Huambo

Windhoek

Cape Town

Pointe-Noire

Luanda

Lobito

Lubango

Walvis Bay

Annobón (EQUATORIAL GUINEA)

ATLANTIC OCEAN

Mozambique Channel

Lake Victoria

KEY

⭐ Capital City
● Major City
〜 River

0 mi   500 mi   1,000 mi

0 km   500 km   1,000 km

Asia and the Middle East

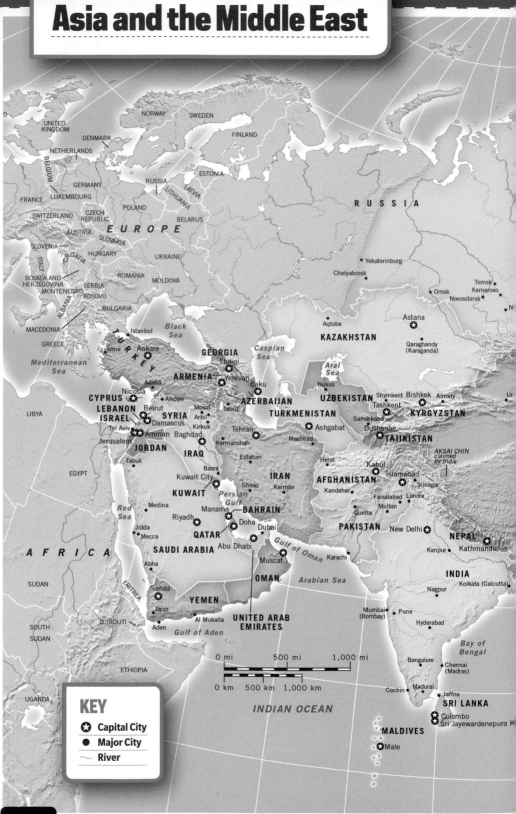

UNITED KINGDOM
NETHERLANDS
BELGIUM
DENMARK
NORWAY
SWEDEN
FINLAND
ESTONIA
LATVIA
LITHUANIA
RUSSIA
FRANCE
LUXEMBOURG
GERMANY
POLAND
BELARUS
SWITZERLAND
CZECH REPUBLIC
AUSTRIA
SLOVAKIA
UKRAINE
E U R O P E
SLOVENIA
CROATIA
HUNGARY
ITALY
BOSNIA AND HERZEGOVINA
MONTENEGRO
SERBIA
KOSOVO
ROMANIA
MOLDOVA
ALBANIA
BULGARIA
MACEDONIA
GREECE

R U S S I A

Yekaterinburg
Chelyabinsk
Omsk
Tomsk
Kemerovo
Novosibirsk
N

Mediterranean Sea

Istanbul
Black Sea
Izmir
Ankara
T U R K E Y
Adana
GEORGIA
Tbilisi
ARMENIA
Yerevan
Baku
Caspian Sea
Aral Sea
Nukus
Aqtobe
KAZAKHSTAN
Astana
Qaraghandy (Karaganda)
CYPRUS
Nicosia
Aleppo
AZERBAIJAN
Tabriz
Shymkent
Bishkek
Almaty
Ur
LEBANON
Beirut
Mosul
Arbil
TURKMENISTAN
UZBEKISTAN
Tashkent
KYRGYZSTAN
ISRAEL
SYRIA
Damascus
Kirkuk
Tehran
Ashgabat
Samarkand
Dushanbe
TAJIKISTAN
Tel Aviv
Jerusalem
Amman
Baghdad
Kermanshah
Mashhad
AKSAI CHIN claimed by India
LIBYA
JORDAN
IRAQ
Esfahan
Herat
Kabūl
AFGHANISTAN
Islamabad
Srinagar
Tabuk
Basra
IRAN
Kermān
Kandahar
Faisalabad
Lahore
EGYPT
Kuwait City
Shiraz
Quetta
Multan
KUWAIT
Persian Gulf
New Delhi
Medina
Manama
BAHRAIN
Dubai
PAKISTAN
NEPAL
Kathmandu
Red Sea
Riyadh
Doha
Abu Dhabi
Karachi
Kanpur
Jidda
Mecca
QATAR
Muscat
INDIA
Nagpur
Kolkata (Calcutta)
A F R I C A
SAUDI ARABIA
Gulf of Oman
OMAN
Arabian Sea
Abha
UNITED ARAB EMIRATES
Mumbai (Bombay)
Pune
Hyderabad
SUDAN
ERITREA
Sanaa
YEMEN
Taizz
Al Mukalla
Bay of Bengal
SOUTH SUDAN
DJIBOUTI
Aden
Gulf of Aden
Bangalore
Chennai (Madras)
ETHIOPIA
Cochin
Madurai
UGANDA
INDIAN OCEAN
Jaffna
SRI LANKA
Colombo
Sri Jayewardenepura K
MALDIVES
Male

0 mi   500 mi   1,000 mi

0 km   500 km   1,000 km

KEY

⭐ Capital City

● Major City

〜 River

ARCTIC OCEAN

United States

Bering
Sea

Cherskiy

Tiksi

Verkhoyansk

Kamchatka
Peninsula

Magadan

Yakutsk

Sea of
Okhotsk

Petropavlovsk-
Kamchatskiy

S I B E R I A

rasnoyarsk

Sakhalin

uznetsk

Khabarovsk

Irkutsk

Sapporo

Harbin

Ulaanbaatar

Changchun

Vladivostok

JAPAN

MONGOLIA

Shenyang

NORTH KOREA

Hohhot

Beijing

P'yongyang

Tokyo

Tianjin

Seoul

Nagoya

Taiyuan

Jinan

SOUTH
KOREA

Taegu
Pusan

Kyoto
Kobe

Osaka

PACIFIC
OCEAN

Lanzhou

Qingdao

Fukuoka

Hiroshima

Xi'an

Nagasaki

CHINA

Chengdu

Hefei

Shanghai

hasa

Chongqing

Wuhan

Naha

BHUTAN

Fuzhou

Taipei

Xiamen

BANGLADESH

Liuzhou

Guangzhou

TAIWAN

Dhaka

Nanning

Macao
(special
admin.
region)

Kao-hsiung

Mandalay

Hong Kong (special admin. region)

Chittagong

MYANMAR
(BURMA)

Hanoi

LAOS

Baguio

Nay Pyi Taw

Chiang Mai

Vientiane

Quezon City

Da Nang

South
China
Sea

Manila

THAILAND

VIETNAM

PHILIPPINES

Bangkok

Cebu

CAMBODIA

Andaman
Sea

Phnom
Penh

Ho Chi Minh City

Davao

Phuket

Songkhla

Bandar Seri Begawan

Ipoh

BRUNEI

Kota Kinabalu

M A L A Y S I A

Manado

Manokwari

Medan

Kuala Lumpur

Kuching

Serong

Jayapura

SINGAPORE

Borneo

Celebes

New Guinea

Singapore

Pontianak

Palu

Sumatra

Samarinda

Palembang

Banjarmasin

I   N   D   O   N   E   S   I   A

Makassar

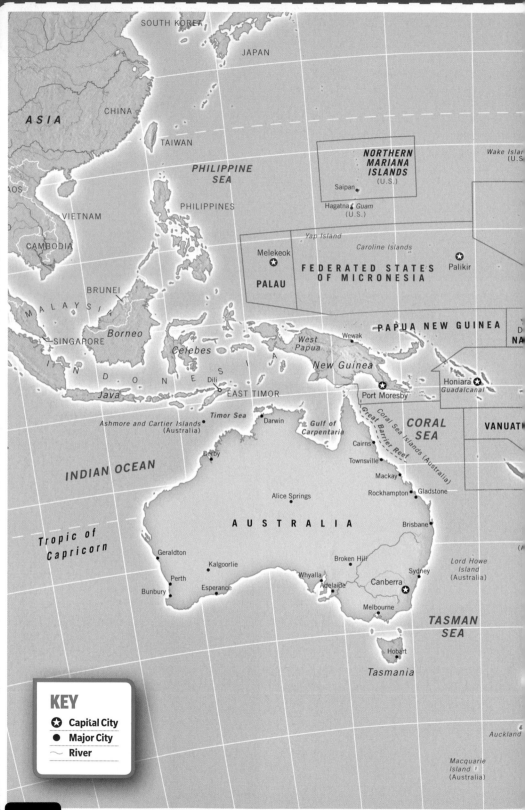

SOUTH KOREA

JAPAN

ASIA

CHINA

TAIWAN

PHILIPPINE
SEA

LAOS

VIETNAM

PHILIPPINES

CAMBODIA

NORTHERN
MARIANA
ISLANDS
(U.S.)

Saipan

Wake Island
(U.S.

Hagatna Guam
(U.S.)

Yap Island

Caroline Islands

BRUNEI

Melekeok

MALAYSIA

SINGAPORE

Borneo

Celebes

PALAU

FEDERATED STATES
OF MICRONESIA

Palikir

I   N   D   O   N   E   S   I   A

West
Papua

Wewak

PAPUA NEW GUINEA

D
NA

Java

Dili

EAST TIMOR

New Guinea

Honiara

Guadalcanal

Port Moresby

Ashmore and Cartier Islands
(Australia)

Timor Sea

Darwin

Gulf of
Carpentaria

Coral Sea Islands (Australia)

Great Barrier Reef

CORAL
SEA

VANUAT

INDIAN OCEAN

Derby

Cairns

Townsville

Mackay

Rockhampton

Gladstone

Alice Springs

AUSTRALIA

Brisbane

Tropic of
Capricorn

Geraldton

Kalgoorlie

Broken Hill

Lord Howe
Island
(Australia)

Perth

Esperance

Whyalla

Sydney

Bunbury

Adelaide

Canberra

Melbourne

TASMAN
SEA

Hobart

Tasmania

KEY

⭐ Capital City
● Major City
~ River

Auckland

Macquarie
Island
(Australia)

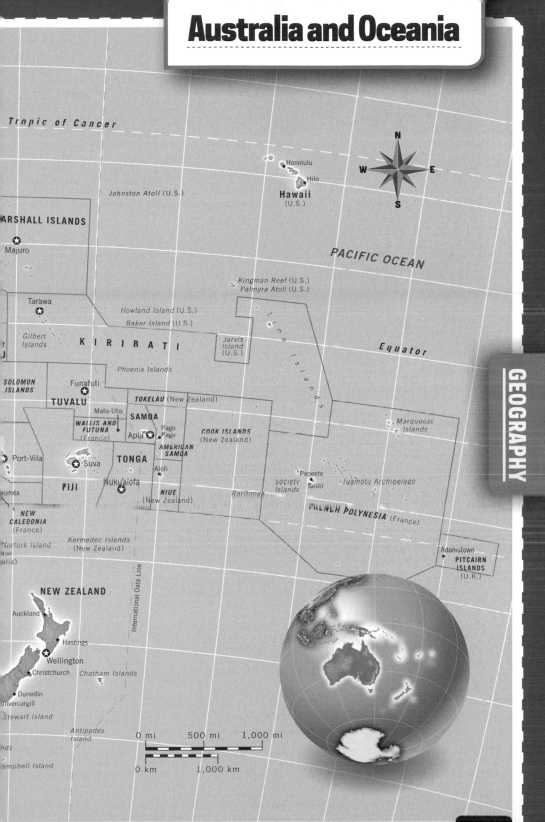

Tropic of Cancer

Honolulu
Hilo
Hawaii
(U.S.)

Johnston Atoll (U.S.)

N
W   E
S

MARSHALL ISLANDS

Majuro

PACIFIC OCEAN

Tarawa

Kingman Reef (U.S.)
Palmyra Atoll (U.S.)

Gilbert
Islands

Howland Island (U.S.)
Baker Island (U.S.)

K I R I B A T I

Jarvis
Island
(U.S.)

Equator

Line Islands

SOLOMON
ISLANDS

Funafuti

Phoenix Islands

TUVALU

TOKELAU (New Zealand)

Mata-Utu

SAMOA

Marquesas
Islands

WALLIS AND
FUTUNA
(France)

Apia
Pago
Pago

COOK ISLANDS
(New Zealand)

Port-Vila

AMERICAN
SAMOA

Suva

TONGA

Alofi

Papeete
Society
Islands

Tuamotu Archipelago

Tahiti

nouméa

FIJI

Nuku'alofa

NIUE
(New Zealand)

Rarotonga

FRENCH POLYNESIA (France)

NEW
CALEDONIA
(France)

Kermadec Islands
(New Zealand)

Norfolk Island
ton
alia)

Adamstown
PITCAIRN
ISLANDS
(U.K.)

NEW ZEALAND

Auckland

Hastings

Wellington

Christchurch
Chatham Islands

Dunedin
Invercargill

International Date Line

Stewart Island

Antipodes
Island

ds

Campbell Island

0 mi   500 mi   1,000 mi

0 km   1,000 km

GEOGRAPHY

Europe

ARCTIC OCEAN

Arctic Circle

ICELAND
Reykjavík

FAROE ISLANDS
(Denmark)
Torshavn

NORWEGIAN
SEA

Trondheim

0 mi   300 mi   600 mi

0 km   300 km   600 km

SHETLAND ISLANDS

ORKNEY
ISLANDS

HEBRIDES

NORWAY

Bergen

Oslo

Gavle

Stavanger

SWEDEN

Aberdeen

Glasgow

Edinburgh

DENMARK

Goteborg

Belfast

**UNITED
KINGDOM**

NORTH
SEA

Alborg

IRELAND

Dublin

Liverpool

Leeds

Copenhagen

Malmo

BALTIC
SEA

Manchester

Sheffield

NETHERLANDS

Birmingham

London

Amsterdam
The Hague
Rotterdam

Hamburg

Gdansk

Bremen

Berlin

Poznan

Calais

Antwerp

Essen

Düsseldorf
Cologne

GERMANY

Wroclaw

GUERNSEY (U.K.)
JERSEY (U.K.)

Lille

BELGIUM

Brussels

Bonn

Frankfurt

Le Havre

Paris

LUXEMBOURG

Luxembourg

Stuttgart

Prague

**CZECH
REPUBLIC**

Brno

Nantes

Strasbourg

Dijon

LIECHTENSTEIN

Munich

Vienna

Bratislava

ATLANTIC OCEAN

BAY OF
BISCAY

FRANCE

Zurich

Vaduz

Bern

Geneva

SWITZERLAND

AUSTRIA

HUNGARY

Bordeaux

Lyon

Ljubljana

SLOVENIA

Trieste

Turin

Milan

Venice

Porto

Bilbao

Toulouse

CROATIA

Zagreb

Genoa

PORTUGAL

Madrid

Andorra
la Vella

Marseille

Monaco

MONACO

Florence

**SAN
MARINO**

**BOSNIA AND
HERZEGOVINA**

Sarajevo

Lisbon

SPAIN

ANDORRA

Bastia

MONTENEGRO

Podgorica

Barcelona

Corsica

ITALY

Faro

Seville

Valencia

Majorca

Palma

**VATICAN
CITY
(HOLY SEE)**

Rome

Bari

Tirana

Málaga

Gibraltar
(U.K.)

MEDITERRANEAN SEA

Sardinia

Naples

ALBANIA

Cagliari

TYRRHENIAN
SEA

Kerkira

MOROCCO

ALGERIA

Palermo

Messina

Sicily

IONIAN
SEA

AFRICA

TUNISIA

Valletta

MALTA

MEDITE

KEY
⭐ Capital City
● Major City
〜 River

Murmansk

Pechora

ASIA

Arkhangel'sk

FINLAND

Oulu

Tampere

Turku

Helsinki

St. Petersburg

Tallinn

ESTONIA

R U S S I A

Izhevsk

Nizhniy Novgorod

Kazan

Riga

LATVIA

Moscow

Samara

LITHUANIA

Vilnius

Smolensk

Minsk

BELARUS

Lipetsk

Saratov

KAZAKHSTAN

Homyel'

Voronezh

POLAND

Brest

Kiev

Kharkiv

Volgograd

Lviv

Luhansk

Derazhnia

UKRAINE

Gorlovka

Makeyevka

Rostov

Chisinau

Iasi

Mariupol

CASPIAN
SEA

Odessa

Mykolayiv

MOLDOVA

Kerch

Grozny

ROMANIA

Simferopol

Bucharest

Constanta

Sevastopol

BLACK SEA

Craiova

Varna

Sofia

BULGARIA

MACEDONIA

Istanbul

Thessaloniki

Skopje

T U R K E Y

Volos

GREECE

AEGEAN
SEA

Athens

Crete

CYPRUS

LEBANON

SYRIA

IRAQ

IRAN

MEDITERRANEAN SEA

KEY
⊛ Capital City
● Major City
～ River

ATLANTIC OCEAN

N E S W

BERMUDA (U.K.)

Hamilton

Halifax

Montreal
Montpelier
Ottawa
Concord
Augusta
Albany
Boston
Hartford
Buffalo
Providence
Toronto
New York
Detroit
Cleveland
Harrisburg
Philadelphia
Milwaukee
Lansing
Pittsburgh
Dover
Chicago
Columbus
Washington, D.C.
Cincinnati
Baltimore
Madison
Indianapolis
Frankfort
Richmond
Springfield
Louisville
Raleigh
St. Paul
Minneapolis
Jefferson City
Nashville
Columbia
Des Moines
Omaha
St. Louis
Charleston
Kansas City
Topeka
Memphis
Atlanta
Savannah
Lincoln
Jackson
Birmingham
Montgomery
Jacksonville
Denver
Little Rock
Tallahassee
Cheyenne
Oklahoma City
Dallas
New Orleans
Miami
Freeport
Nassau

UNITED STATES

Salt Lake City
Santa Fe
Austin
Houston
San Antonio
El Paso
Ciudad Juárez
Phoenix

Los Angeles
San Diego
Tijuana
Hermosillo

GULF OF MEXICO

Tropic of Cancer

Mérida
Cancún
Tampico
Veracruz

MEXICO

Monterrey
León
Guadalajara
Mexico City
Puebla
Oaxaca
Acapulco
Mazatlán
Puerto Vallarta

Gulf of California

La Paz

PACIFIC OCEAN

THE BAHAMAS

CUBA
Havana
Camagüey

TURKS AND CAICOS ISLANDS (U.K.)
Grand Turk

CAYMAN ISLANDS (U.K.)
George Town

JAMAICA
Montego Bay
Kingston

CARIBBEAN SEA

Guantánamo Bay

HAITI
Port-au-Prince

DOMINICAN REPUBLIC
Santiago
Santo Domingo

VIRGIN ISLANDS (U.S.)

PUERTO RICO (U.S.)
San Juan

SAINT MAARTEN/ SAINT MARTIN (Netherlands/France)

SAINT BARTHÉLEMY (France)

ANGUILLA (U.K.)

ANTIGUA AND BARBUDA

SAINT KITTS AND NEVIS
MONTSERRAT (U.K.)
GUADELOUPE (France)
DOMINICA
MARTINIQUE (France)
SAINT LUCIA
SAINT VINCENT AND THE GRENADINES
BARBADOS
GRENADA

BONAIRE (Neth.)
CURAÇAO (Neth.)
ARUBA (Neth.)

TRINIDAD AND TOBAGO

GUYANA

VENEZUELA

COLOMBIA

SOUTH AMERICA

BELIZE
Belize City
Belmopan

GUATEMALA
Guatemala City

HONDURAS
Tegucigalpa

EL SALVADOR
San Salvador

NICARAGUA
Managua

COSTA RICA
San José

PANAMA
Panama City

1,000 mi

500 mi

1,000 km

500 km

0 mi
0 km

South America

MEXICO

BELIZE

HONDURAS

NICARAGUA

COSTA RICA

PANAMA

JAMAICA

HAITI

DOMINICAN REPUBLIC (U.S.)

ANTIGUA AND BARBUDA

SAINT KITTS AND NEVIS

GUADELOUPE

DOMINICA

SAINT LUCIA

BARBADOS

GRENADA

SAINT VINCENT AND THE GRENADINES

TRINIDAD AND TOBAGO

CARIBBEAN SEA

ATLANTIC OCEAN

Barranquilla
Cartagena
Maracaibo
Lake Maracaibo
Caracas

Medellín
Bogotá
Cali

Ciudad Guayana
Georgetown
Paramaribo
Cayenne

Orinoco River

VENEZUELA
GUYANA
SURINAME
FRENCH GUIANA (France)

COLOMBIA

Esmeraldas
Quito
Equator

ECUADOR
Guayaquil

Negro River

Macapá

Amazon River
Belém
São Luís
Parnaíba

Manaus
Santarém

Fortaleza

Natal

Iquitos
Benjamin Constant

A M A Z O N   B A S I N

Amazon River

PERU

Piura

Cruzeiro do Sul

Rain Forest

Pôrto Velho

BRAZIL

Recife
Maceió

Trujillo

Madeira River

Cobija
Riberalta

Cuzco

Lima

Xingu River

Tocantins River

Araguaia River

São Francisco River

Salvador

Lake Titicaca

La Paz

BOLIVIA

Cochabamba

Arequipa

Arica

Santa Cruz
Sucre

Brasília

Iquique

Brazilian Highlands

Belo Horizonte

Antofagasta

PARAGUAY

Paraguay River

São Paulo
Rio de Janeiro

Asunción
Ciudad del Este

Formosa
Encarnación

Curitiba

San Miguel de Tucumán
Resistencia

Paraná River

Pôrto Alegre

CHILE

Córdoba

Salto

Valparaíso
Santiago

Rosario

URUGUAY

ATLANTIC OCEAN

Concepción

ARGENTINA

Buenos Aires
Montevideo

Río de la Plata

Ucayali River

Marañón River

Putumayo River

Magdalena River

Andes Mts.

PACIFIC OCEAN

Bahía Blanca
Mar del Plata

Puerto Montt

Comodoro Rivadavia

Strait of Magellan

Río Gallegos
Stanley

Punta Arenas
Ushuaia

Falkland Islands (Islas Malvinas)
(Administered by U.K., claimed by Argentina)

Cape Horn

N
W   E
S

KEY

⊛ Capital City
● Major City
〜 River

0 mi   500 mi   1,000 mi

0 km   500 km   1,000 km

150

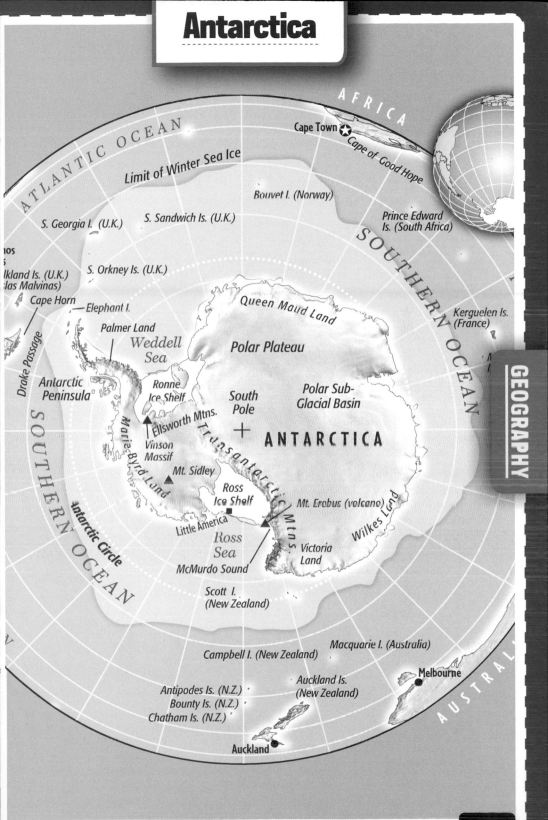

Antarctica

ATLANTIC OCEAN

AFRICA

Cape Town ✪

Cape of Good Hope

Limit of Winter Sea Ice

Bouvet I. (Norway)

S. Georgia I. (U.K.)

S. Sandwich Is. (U.K.)

Prince Edward
Is. (South Africa)

SOUTHERN OCEAN

nos

lkland Is. (U.K.)
las Malvinas)

S. Orkney Is. (U.K.)

Cape Horn

Elephant I.

Queen Maud Land

Kerguelen Is.
(France)

Palmer Land

Weddell
Sea

Polar Plateau

Drake Passage

Antarctic
Peninsula

Ronne
Ice Shelf

South
Pole

Polar Sub-
Glacial Basin

Ellsworth Mtns.

SOUTHERN OCEAN

Marie Byrd Land

Vinson
Massif

Mt. Sidley

Transantarctic Mtns.

+ ANTARCTICA

Ross
Ice Shelf

Mt. Erebus (volcano)

Little America

Wilkes Land

Antarctic Circle

Ross
Sea

McMurdo Sound

Victoria
Land

Scott I.
(New Zealand)

Macquarie I. (Australia)

Campbell I. (New Zealand)

Melbourne

Antipodes Is. (N.Z.)

Auckland Is.
(New Zealand)

Bounty Is. (N.Z.)

Chatham Is. (N.Z.)

AUSTRALIA

Auckland

The Pyramids of Giza and Sphinx in Egypt

History

Prehistory

The period before human beings began keeping records is called prehistory. Scientists examine fossils and rock formations to make educated guesses about what happened on Earth during this time.

PRECAMBRIAN ERA

4.6 BILLION YEARS AGO Earth is formed from the dust and debris thrown off by an exploding star.

3.8 BILLION YEARS AGO The first rocks on Earth—chunks of Earth's crust—appear. There is evidence of bacteria in these rocks.

2.5 BILLION YEARS AGO Single-celled cyanobacteria use the sun's power to create oxygen. The process is similar to the way plants create oxygen in photosynthesis.

PALEOZOIC ERA

Cambrian Period

570 MILLION YEARS AGO Very simple creatures appear. Made of just a few cells, they have shells and can move about. Over the next 20 to 30 million years, early fish, shellfish, and corals are born.

Ordovician Period

440–450 MILLION YEARS AGO A mass extinction occurs during the Ordovician period. Many scientists think Earth may have suddenly cooled, killing off huge amounts of marine life (animals and plants that live in water).

Silurian Period

430 MILLION YEARS AGO The first plants start growing in water. Later, they develop root systems that allow them to live on dry land.

Devonian Period

370 MILLION YEARS AGO Fish leave the water and begin to breathe on land. These early amphibians look a little like crocodiles. Some insects come into existence.

Carboniferous Period

300–360 MILLION YEARS AGO During the Carboniferous period, all the land areas on Earth join into one supercontinent known as Pangaea. The land is mostly marshy swamp, covered with plants. This vegetation absorbs lots of carbon dioxide and creates an oxygen-rich atmosphere.

Permian Period

251–300 MILLION YEARS AGO The first reptiles appear. They evolve slowly into sluggish creatures, some with odd-looking sails on their backs.

Straight-Shelled Nautiloid

Early Amphibian Fossil

245–251 MILLION YEARS AGO The Great Dying occurs. About 95% of marine life and 70% of the plants and animals on land are wiped out. Some scientists think that the climate may have changed because of volcanic eruptions or gases released from the ocean floor.

Albertosaurus

Triassic Period

200–240 MILLION YEARS AGO The first dinosaurs appear. The earliest are about the size of kangaroos and are called prosauropods. Diplodocus, stegosaurus, and brachiosaurus are some of the dinosaurs that lived during this time. During this period, Pangaea breaks into separate continents, with oceans and seas between them.

Jurassic Period

145–200 MILLION YEARS AGO During the Jurassic period, the landscape is lush and green, with palm trees and lots of shrubs. Plant-eating dinosaurs, like the apatosaurus and the seismosaurus, thrive and become gigantic. The seismosaurus is about 148 feet (45 m) long. It has a tiny head and swallows rocks to help process all the leaves it eats. Ferocious meat-eating dinosaurs also roam the Earth.

Cretaceous Period

65–145 MILLION YEARS AGO There are even more dinosaurs in the Cretaceous period than in the Jurassic period. Dinosaurs develop different features that help protect them from predators and kill their prey. For example, the horns on a triceratops's head could gore other dinosaurs. The biggest and most fierce of all Cretaceous meat eaters is the *Tyrannosaurus rex*, or *T. rex*.

CENOZOIC ERA

65 MILLION YEARS AGO About 65 million years ago, something happens that kills all the dinosaurs. Some think that deadly germs were to blame. Others believe that dinosaurs killed and ate each other. There is also a theory that a huge asteroid slammed into Earth and created walls of water and dust that killed the dinosaurs. It's one of the great mysteries of world history.

65 MILLION YEARS AGO–THE PRESENT The continents reach their current positions. New life evolves. Many mammals, including humans, appear in this period. Around 6,000 years ago, humans start leaving records, which marks the end of prehistory and the beginning of history.

Prehistoric Man

Ancient History

The Trojan War

510 B.C. Democracy is established in Athens, Greece.

500 B.C. Carthage, in modern-day Tunisia, becomes an important trading center on the Mediterranean coast. During the Punic Wars (264 to 146 B.C.), Carthage battles with Rome. In 219, Hannibal, Carthage's leader, leads an army of troops and elephants across the Alps into Italy but is eventually defeated.

5000–3500 B.C. Sumer, located in what is now Iraq, becomes the earliest known civilization. Sumerians develop a written alphabet, among other innovations.

3500–2600 B.C. People settle in the Indus River Valley, in what is now India and Pakistan.

2600 B.C. Minoan civilization begins on the island of Crete, in the Mediterranean Sea.

circa 2560 B.C. The Egyptian king Khufu finishes building the Great Pyramid at Giza. The Great Sphinx is completed soon after by Khufu's son Khafre.

2000 B.C. Babylonians develop a system of mathematics.
   The kingdom of Kush, in Africa, becomes a major center of trade and learning.

1792 B.C. Hammurabi becomes the ruler of Babylonia. He creates the first set of laws, now known as Hammurabi's Code.

circa 1600–1050 B.C. The Shang Dynasty is the first Chinese dynasty to leave written records.

1200 B.C. The Trojan War is fought between the Greeks and the Trojans.

814 B.C. The city of Carthage, located in what is now Tunisia, is founded by the Phoenicians.

753 B.C. According to legend, Rome is founded by Romulus.

563 B.C. Siddhartha Gautama, who becomes the Buddha, or Enlightened One, is born. He will become the founder of the Buddhist religion.

551 B.C. Chinese philosopher Confucius is born. His teachings on honesty, humanity, and how people should treat one another are the foundations of Confucianism.

438 B.C. Construction of the Parthenon temple on the Acropolis (the highest hill in Athens) is completed.

431 B.C. The Peloponnesian War breaks out between Sparta and Athens. In 404 B.C., Sparta finally wins the war and takes over Athens.

334 B.C. Macedonian king Alexander the Great invades Persia. He eventually conquers lands from Greece to India. He even crosses into North Africa.

100 B.C. The great city of Teotihuacán flourishes in Mexico.

58 B.C. Julius Caesar leaves Rome for Gaul (France) and spends nine years conquering much of central Europe. He is murdered in 44 B.C.

27 B.C. Octavian becomes the first Roman emperor, ushering in a long period of peace. He is also known by the title Augustus.

HISTORY

79 Mount Vesuvius erupts, destroying the city of Pompeii (present-day Italy).

122 Construction on Hadrian's Wall begins. It spans northern England and offers protection from the tribes to the north.

circa 250 The classic period of Mayan civilization begins. It lasts until about 900. The Maya erect impressive stone buildings and temples in areas that are now part of Mexico and Central America.

330 Constantine the Great chooses Byzantium as the capital of the Roman Empire, and the city becomes known as Constantinople.

476 The Roman Empire collapses.

622 Muhammad, the founder of Islam, flees from Mecca to Medina in what is now Saudi Arabia. This journey is called the Hegira. After the death of Muhammad in 632, Muslims conquer much of North Africa and the Middle East. In 711, Muslims also conquer Spain.

700—800 Ghana is the major empire in Africa south of the Sahara desert. The kingdom, which controls the gold trade, reaches its peak in the 11th century before being defeated by Almoravids of Morocco.

800 Charlemagne is crowned the first Holy Roman Emperor by Pope Leo III.

960 The Song Dynasty begins in China. This dynasty is known for its advances in art, poetry, and philosophy.

circa 1000—1300 During the classic period of their culture, Anasazi people build homes and other structures in the sides of cliffs in what is now the southwestern United States.

1066 At the Battle of Hastings, the Norman king William the Conqueror invades England and defeats English king Harold II.

1095 Pope Urban II delivers a speech urging Christians to capture the Holy Land from the Muslims. The fighting between 1096 and 1291 is known as the Crusades.

Mayan Statue

circa 1200 The Inca Empire begins, and elaborate stone structures are eventually built in Cuzco and Machu Picchu, Peru. The Incas flourish until Francisco Pizarro, a Spaniard, conquers them in 1533.

1206 A Mongolian warrior named Temujin is proclaimed Genghis Khan. He expands his empire so that it includes most of Asia.

1215 A group of barons in England force King John to sign the Magna Carta, a document limiting the power of the king.

1271—1295 Marco Polo, a Venetian merchant, travels throughout Asia. His book, Il Milione (The Million), is a major European source of information about Asia.

1273 The Habsburg Dynasty begins in Eastern Europe. It remains a powerful force in the region until World War I.

1325 Aztecs begin building Tenochtitlán on the site of modern Mexico City.

1337 The Hundred Years' War starts between the English and French. France finally wins in 1453.

1347 The Black Death, or bubonic plague, breaks out in Europe. It spreads quickly, killing more than one-third of Europe's population.

1368 The Ming Dynasty is founded in China by Buddhist monk Zhu Yuanzhang (or Chu Yuan-Chang).

World History

1434 Portuguese explorer Gil Eannes sails past Cape Bojador, in western Africa, which was thought to be the edge of the world.

1453 Constantinople falls to the Ottoman Turks, ending the Byzantine Empire.

1455 Johannes Gutenberg invents the printing press. The Gutenberg Bible is the first book printed on the press.

1464–1591 Based in what is now Mali, Songhai is an important empire in Africa. When it is destroyed by armies from Morocco, the great culture of Timbuktu is lost.

1478 The Spanish Inquisition begins.

1487–1488 Bartolomeu Dias of Portugal leads the first European expedition around the Cape of Good Hope, at the southern tip of Africa, opening up a sea route to Asia.

1492 Christopher Columbus leaves Spain, hoping to sail to the East Indies. Instead, he and his crew land in the Bahamas and visit Cuba, Hispaniola (which is now Haiti and the Dominican Republic), and other small islands.

1497–1499 Portuguese explorer Vasco da Gama leads the first European expedition to India by sea via the Cape of Good Hope.

1517 Martin Luther protests the abuses of the Catholic Church, which leads to a religious split and the rise of the Protestant faith.

1519 While exploring Mexico, Spanish adventurer Hernán Cortés conquers the Aztec Empire.

1519–1522 Portuguese explorer Ferdinand Magellan's expedition circumnavigates, or sails around, the globe.

1532–1533 Spanish explorer Francisco Pizarro conquers the Inca Empire in South America.

1543 Polish astronomer Copernicus shares his theory that the sun, not the Earth, is the center of the universe.

1547 Ivan the Terrible becomes the first czar, or ruler, of Russia.

1588 The English defeat the Spanish Armada, or fleet of warships, when Spain attempts to invade England.

1618 The Thirty Years' War breaks out between Protestants and Catholics in Europe.

1620 English Pilgrims aboard the Mayflower land at Plymouth Rock, in present-day Massachusetts.

1632 Italian astronomer Galileo, the first person to use a telescope to look into space, confirms Copernicus's theory that Earth revolves around the sun.

1642 The English Civil War, sometimes called the Puritan Revolution, begins in Britain.

1688 The Glorious Revolution, or Bloodless Revolution, takes place in England. James II is removed from the throne, and William and Mary become the heads of the country.

1721 Peter the Great becomes czar of Russia.

1789 An angry mob storms the Bastille, a prison in Paris, setting off the French Revolution.

1803 Denmark becomes the first country in Europe to ban slave trading. Four years later, Britain does the same. The U.S. bans the slave trade in 1808.

1819 Simón Bolívar crosses the Andes to launch a surprise attack against the Spanish, liberating New Granada (now Colombia, Venezuela, Panama, and Ecuador) from Spain.

Fabergé egg made for a Russian czar

1824 Mexico becomes independent from Spain.

1845 A blight ruins the potato crop in Ireland. More than 1 million Irish starve to death, and an additional million leave for the United States to escape the Irish potato famine.

1848 Known as the year of revolutions in Europe, there is upheaval in France, Italy, Germany, Hungary, and elsewhere.

1859 Charles Darwin publishes *On the Origin of Species*, which introduces the scientific theory of evolution.

1871 A group of independent states unifies, creating the German Empire.

1876 Alexander Graham Bell invents the telephone.

1884–1885 During the Berlin Conference, European leaders divide up Africa into areas of control.

1892 The diesel engine is invented by Parisian Rudolf Diesel.

1893 New Zealand becomes the first country to give women the right to vote.
   The Columbian Exposition, also known as the Chicago World's Fair, is held.

1894 The Sino-Japanese War breaks out between China and Japan, who are fighting for control of Korea. An 1895 treaty declares Korea independent.

The Boxer Rebellion

1898 The Spanish-American War begins.

1899 During the Boxer Rebellion, the Chinese fight against Christian and foreign influences in their country. American, Japanese, and European forces help stop the fighting by 1901.

1904 Japan declares war on Russia, beginning the Russo-Japanese War. The countries clash over influence in Manchuria and Korea. Japan wins the conflict and becomes a world power.

1909 Robert Peary is credited as being the first to reach the North Pole, although recent evidence suggests he might have reached only as far as 30 to 60 miles (48 to 97 km) away.

1911 Roald Amundsen, the first man to travel the Northwest Passage, reaches the South Pole.

1914 Austro-Hungarian archduke Franz Ferdinand is assassinated, setting off the chain of events that starts World War I.

1917 The United States enters World War I.
   Led by socialist Vladimir Lenin, the Russian Revolution begins. The czarist government is overthrown, and in 1922, the Soviet Union is formed.

1918 A flu epidemic spreads quickly around the world, killing more than 20 million people.

1919 The Treaty of Versailles ends World War I.

1927 Philo Farnsworth invents the television.

1928 Alexander Fleming discovers penicillin accidentally, after leaving a dish of staphylococcus bacteria uncovered and finding mold.

1929 The U.S. stock market collapses, beginning the Great Depression.

1933 Adolf Hitler becomes chancellor of Germany.
Frequency modulation, or FM, radio is developed by Edwin Armstrong.

1936 The Spanish Civil War breaks out.

1939 World War II begins when Germany invades Poland. Britain responds by declaring war on Germany. The Nazis, Germany's leaders during WWII, torture and kill nearly 6 million Jews in Europe during the war. This persecution is known as the Holocaust.

1941 The Japanese launch a surprise attack on the United States, bombing U.S. ships docked in Hawaii's Pearl Harbor. In response, the United States declares war on Japan, and both Germany and Italy declare war on the U.S.

1945 Germany surrenders on May 7, ending the war in Europe. In August, the United States drops two atomic bombs on the Japanese cities Hiroshima and Nagasaki. Japan surrenders, ending World War II.

1947 India and Pakistan become free of British colonial rule.

1948 Israel becomes a nation.

1949 Following China's civil war, Mao Zedong sets up the Communist People's Republic of China.
South Africa enacts apartheid laws, which make discrimination against non-white people part of public policy.

1950 North Korean communist forces invade South Korea, beginning the Korean War. U.S. forces support South Korea. China backs North Korea. The war ends three years later.

1952 The hydrogen bomb is developed by Edward Teller and a team at a laboratory in Los Alamos, New Mexico.

1953 Edmund Hillary and Tenzing Norgay climb to the top of Mount Everest.

1955 Jonas Salk's polio vaccine is introduced.

1957 Ghana is the first territory in sub-Saharan Africa to regain its independence from a European power. Over the next 20 years, most African countries also become independent.

1961 A group of Cuban exiles, supported by the United States, invades Cuba at the Bay of Pigs. The invasion fails, and U.S.-Cuban relations worsen.
Aboard the Vostok spacecraft, Yuri Gagarin is the first human in space.

1962 The Cuban Missile Crisis, a conflict between the United States, the Soviet Union, and Cuba, brings the world to the brink of nuclear war.

1963 U.S. President John F. Kennedy is assassinated on November 22, 1963, in Dallas, Texas. Vice President Lyndon B. Johnson is inaugurated.

1965 The United States begins officially sending troops to Vietnam to aid South Vietnam in its civil war with North Vietnam.

1967 The Six-Day War breaks out between Israel and neighboring Arab nations Egypt, Syria, and Jordan. Israel seizes the Golan Heights, the Gaza Strip, the Sinai Peninsula, and part of the West Bank of the Jordan River.

1969 Neil Armstrong is the first person to walk on the surface of the moon.

1973 The Paris Peace Accords end the Vietnam War. North Vietnam later violates the terms of the

HISTORY

MYSTERY PERSON

I was born in 1869 in Porbandar, India. I became known for leading non-violent protests of British Empire rule in India. I was arrested several times for political reasons and fasted in prison as a form of protest. Through peaceful means, I helped India gain independence.

◄ **Who am I?** Answer on page 277

Malala Yousafzai

government falls quickly, resistance and fighting continue. In 2006, Saddam Hussein is executed for crimes against humanity.

2004 A powerful tsunami kills nearly 300,000 people in Indonesia, Sri Lanka, India, Thailand, and other Asian countries.

2006 Ellen Johnson Sirleaf becomes president of Liberia. She is Africa's first elected female leader.

2008 A global economic crisis leads to loss of jobs and homes, and to a downturn in trade.

2011 Protests erupt in the Middle East and North Africa, toppling leaders in Tunisia and Egypt. It leads to what became known as the Arab Spring.

2013 Cardinal Jorge Mario Bergoglio, of Argentina, is elected pope, taking on the name Francis.

2014 Malala Yousafzai wins the Nobel Peace Prize for her work advocating for girls' rights to education.

2015 Facing violence at home, hundreds of thousands of refugees flee Syria for foreign countries, sparking debate in Europe about immigration policies.

2015 A series of terrorist attacks in Paris, France, kill 130 people. The terrorist group known as the Islamic State, sometimes called ISIS, takes responsibility for the attacks.

treaty and, in 1975, takes control of Saigon, the capital of South Vietnam.

1978 U.S. president Jimmy Carter, Israeli president Menachem Begin, and Egyptian president Anwar Sadat sign the Camp David Accords in an attempt to achieve peace in the Middle East.

1989 The Chinese army crushes a demonstration in Tiananmen Square, in Beijing, killing hundreds, possibly thousands, of students and protesters.
   The Berlin Wall is torn down, and the city of Berlin, Germany, is reunified.

1990 Apartheid ends in South Africa. Four years later, Nelson Mandela is elected president in the country's first free, multiracial elections.
   The Persian Gulf War begins when Iraq invades Kuwait.

1991 The Soviet Union dissolves.
   Croatia, Slovenia, and

Macedonia declare independence from Yugoslavia. The next year, the country of Bosnia and Herzegovina also declares independence, but war breaks out and does not end until 1995.
   Tim Berners-Lee develops the World Wide Web.

1994 Tensions between the Hutu majority and the Tutsi minority in Rwanda, Africa, lead to a genocide, or systematic killing of a racial or ethnic group. About 800,000 Tutsis are killed.

1999 Honda releases the two-door Insight, a fuel-efficient hybrid car, the first of its kind marketed to the masses in the U.S.

2001 After the September 11 terrorist attacks, the U.S. declares an international War on Terror, attacking the Taliban government in Afghanistan and searching for Osama bin Laden and al-Qaeda.

2003 With the aid of Britain and other allies, the U.S. invades Iraq. Though the

George Washington

1524 Italian explorer Giovanni da Verrazano is the first European to reach New York Harbor.

1540 In search of gold, Spanish explorer Francisco Vásquez de Coronado travels north from Mexico. One of his men is the first European to spot the Grand Canyon.

1541 Spaniard Hernando de Soto crosses the Mississippi River.

1579 Sir Francis Drake of England explores California's coastline.

1607 English settlers found Jamestown in Virginia. The colony's leader, John Smith, is captured by Native Americans. According to legend, he is saved by Pocahontas, the daughter of a Native American chief.

1609–1611 Henry Hudson visits the Chesapeake Bay, Delaware Bay, and New York Bay and becomes the first European to sail up the Hudson River.

1620 Pilgrims land at Plymouth, Massachusetts.

1626 Dutchman Peter Minuit buys the island of Manhattan from the Canarsie tribe.

1692 In Massachusetts, accusations of witchcraft lead to the Salem witch trials and the executions of 20 people.

1770 Tensions between British soldiers and colonists erupt in the Boston Massacre, when British troops kill five men.

1773 Colonists protest a tax on tea by dressing up as Native Americans, boarding ships, and dumping tea into Boston Harbor. Known as the Boston Tea Party, the protest angers the British, who pass other harsh taxes.

1775 Paul Revere warns the colonists that the British are coming. The Battle of Lexington and Concord is the first battle of the American Revolution.

The British surrender at Yorktown, Virginia, in 1781.

1776 Drafted by Thomas Jefferson, the Declaration of Independence is signed, and the United States is formed.

1787 The U.S. Constitution is written and submitted to the states for ratification. By the end of the year, Delaware, Pennsylvania, and New Jersey have accepted it.

1789 George Washington becomes the first President of the United States.

1791 The Bill of Rights, written mostly by James Madison, becomes part of the Constitution.

1803 President Thomas Jefferson buys the Louisiana Territory from France, adding 020,000 square miles (2,144,510 sq km) to the United States.

1804–1806 Meriwether Lewis and William Clark explore the Louisiana territory. They reach the Pacific Ocean in 1805.

1812 The War of 1812 breaks out between the United States and Britain because of trade and border disputes, as well as disagreements about freedom of the seas. The Treaty of Ghent ends the war in 1814.

1823 President James Monroe issues the Monroe Doctrine, warning that the Americas are not open for colonization.

1836 Texas declares independence from Mexico. In response, the Mexican army attacks and kills the 189 Texans defending the Alamo.

1838 In what is known as the Trail of Tears, the U.S. government forces 16,000 Cherokees to leave their land in Georgia and relocate to a reservation in Oklahoma. Roughly a quarter of the Cherokees die.

1846 The Mexican-American War begins. At the end of the fighting, in 1848, Mexico gives California and New Mexico (which also includes present-day Arizona, Utah, and Nevada) to the United States. In return, the United States agrees to pay Mexico $15 million.

1848 John Sutter strikes gold in California, kicking off the California gold rush.

1860 Tensions between the North and the South over slavery, taxes, and representation reach a boiling point, and South Carolina secedes from the United States.

1861 Mississippi, Florida, Alabama, Georgia, Louisiana, and Texas secede from the Union, and the Confederate government is formed. The first shots of the American Civil War are fired by Confederate soldiers at Fort Sumter, in South Carolina's Charleston Harbor. Virginia, Arkansas, Tennessee, and North Carolina also secede from the Union.

1862 The Homestead Act encourages settlers to move west by promising 160 acres (647,497 sq m) of land to anyone who remains on the land for five years.

1863 President Abraham Lincoln issues the Emancipation Proclamation, which frees all slaves in the Confederate states. The Battle of Gettysburg is fought. It is the bloodiest battle of the Civil War.

1865 General Robert E. Lee of the Confederacy surrenders to Union General Ulysses S. Grant at Appomattox Court House, in Virginia, ending the Civil War.
   President Lincoln is assassinated at Ford's Theater by John Wilkes Booth, and Andrew Johnson becomes President.
   The 13th Amendment, which puts an end to slavery, is ratified.

1869 The transcontinental railroad is completed.

1890 The Battle of Wounded Knee is the last major defeat for Native American tribes.

1898 The Spanish-American War is fought. At the end of the war, Cuba is independent, and Puerto Rico, Guam, and the Philippines become territories of the United States.

1903 Wilbur and Orville Wright complete their first airplane flight at Kitty Hawk, North Carolina.

1908 Henry Ford, founder of the Ford Motor Company, builds the Model T and sells it for $825, making automobiles much more affordable than ever before.

1917 The United States enters World War I.

1920 With the passage of the 19th Amendment, women get the right to vote.

1929 The U.S. stock market crashes, and the Great Depression begins.

Model T

U.S. History

1941 In a surprise attack, Japan bombs the U.S. fleet at Pearl Harbor, in Hawaii. The United States declares war on Japan. Germany and Italy declare war on the United States.

1945 Germany surrenders on May 7, ending the war in Europe. In August, the U.S. aircraft *Enola Gay* drops an atomic bomb on Hiroshima, Japan. Three days later, a U.S. plane drops an atomic bomb on the city of Nagasaki. The effects are devastating. Six days later, Japan surrenders, ending World War II.

1946 The first bank-issued credit card is developed by John Biggins for the Flatbush National Bank of Brooklyn, in New York City.

1950 North Korean communist forces invade South Korea. U.S. forces enter the Korean War to defend South Korea. Despite three years of bitter fighting, little land changes hands.

1954 In Brown v. Board of Education of Topeka, Kansas, the U.S. Supreme Court declares that segregated schools are unconstitutional.

1955 Rosa Parks is arrested for refusing to give up her bus seat to a white person, leading to a boycott of the entire bus system in Montgomery, Alabama.

1962 The U.S. discovers that the Soviet Union has installed missiles on the island of Cuba that are capable of reaching the U.S. Known as the Cuban Missile Crisis, this event brings the United States and the Soviet Union to the brink of nuclear war. After two weeks of extremely tense negotiations, the crisis comes to a peaceful end.

1963 Martin Luther King Jr. delivers his famous "I Have a Dream" speech to a crowd of more than 250,000 people in Washington, D.C.
President John F. Kennedy is assassinated in Dallas, Texas.

1965 Civil rights advocate and black militant leader Malcolm X is killed.
A race riot in the Watts section of Los Angeles, California, is one of the worst in history.
President Lyndon B. Johnson authorizes air raids over North Vietnam.

Martin Luther King, Jr. Memorial in Washington, D.C.

1968 James Earl Ray shoots and kills Martin Luther King Jr., in Memphis, Tennessee. Riots break out across the country.

1969 Neil Armstrong and Buzz Aldrin, astronauts from NASA's Apollo 11, are the first two people to walk on the moon.

1973 The Vietnam War ends when peace accords are signed. Two years later, North Vietnam takes over Saigon (now Ho Chi Minh City), the capital of South Vietnam.

1974 After his involvement in the Watergate scandal, President Richard Nixon resigns. Gerald Ford becomes president.

1979 Islamic militants storm the U.S. embassy in Tehran, Iran, and 52 Americans are held hostage for 444 days.

1991 After Iraq invades Kuwait, the United States begins bombing raids. The first Persian Gulf War ends quickly as Iraqi forces are driven from Kuwait.

1999 President Bill Clinton is acquitted of impeachment charges.

2000 The election race between Democrat Al Gore and Republican George W. Bush is extremely close, and there are allegations of voter fraud. The U.S. Supreme Court determines the outcome, and Bush is declared the winner.

U.S. History

Firefighters working on September 11, 2001

2001 On September 11, two passenger planes are hijacked and flown into the World Trade Center, in New York City, causing the buildings to collapse. Another plane is flown into the Pentagon, near Washington, D.C. A fourth hijacked plane crashes into a field in Pennsylvania. The United States and Britain respond by attacking the Taliban government in Afghanistan for harboring Osama bin Laden, the alleged mastermind of the attacks. The U.S. government declares the War on Terror.

2003 Along with its allies—Britain and other countries—the United States goes to war in Iraq. Saddam Hussein's government falls quickly, but resistance and fighting continue.

2005 Hurricane Katrina hits the Gulf Coast, destroying parts of Mississippi and Louisiana, and areas along the coast of the southeastern United States. About 80% of New Orleans, Louisiana, is flooded.

2007 Apple introduces the iPhone, revolutionizing the world of mobile and smartphone technology.

2008 A global economic crisis causes a sharp rise in unemployment. Many U.S. homeowners lose their homes.

2009 Barack Obama becomes America's first African-American president. He would go on to win a second term.

2010 A federal law is enacted to overhaul the U.S. health-care system and extend health insurance to the 32 million Americans who did not have it before.

2011 The U.S. secretary of defense announces that the war in Iraq is officially over and that all remaining U.S. troops will leave Iraq by the end of 2011. During the conflict, nearly 4,500 U.S. troops lose their lives in Iraq, and about 30,000 are wounded.

2013 Because of disagreements over the costs of the Affordable Care Act, Congress fails to pass a federal budget. This leads to a 16-day shutdown of the federal government. Some essential services, like mail delivery and military protection, remain up and running.

2014 After decades of tense relations, the U.S. and Cuba restore diplomatic ties.

2015 In a 5–4 decision, the Supreme Court rules that the Constitution guarantees a right to same-sex marriage.

Great Adventures

These three pioneers conquered new heights around the world—and even beyond! Follow their journey and lead them to the famous place where they made history.

Amelia Earhart

Neil Armstrong

Sir Edmund Hillary

Answer:

_____

Along with sherpa Tenzing Norgay, this adventurer was the first person to climb to the top of Mount Everest, the world's tallest mountain, in 1953.

Answer:

_____

After becoming the first person to walk on the moon, In 1969, this astronaut famously said: "That's one small step for man, one giant leap for mankind."

Answer:

_____

This pilot flew solo across the Atlantic Ocean in 1928, a year after Charles Lindbergh completed the first-ever such flight.

Answers on page 277

Inventions and Technology

Interesting Innovations

What makes an invention great? Sometimes, an invention solves a problem you didn't think could be solved. Sometimes, an invention solves a problem you didn't even know you had. And sometimes an invention just makes life more fun. Here are some recent, cool inventions featured in TIME FOR KIDS.

Hoverboards may look fun to zip around on, but they are not always safe.

Buyer Beware

It's known as a hoverboard, but the scooter does not actually hover. Once a rider hops on, the device automatically allows him or her to balance. A rider can speed forward, backward, and around with a shift of body weight. More than 20 companies are making versions of the cool device. But it's dangerous! Britain has outlawed its use on public sidewalks and streets. Amazon is not selling most brands because of safety concerns, including batteries that catch fire. Prices range from $350 to $1,700.

Look Around

Virtual reality is cool. Google Cardboard is even cooler because it can be built using free online instructions. The images come from smartphone apps. Viewers can drive cars or play video games. "We ask people, 'Hey, put your smartphone in this piece of cardboard. It's going to do something amazing,'" says Clay Bavor, a vice president at Google. "And then it does, and they're shocked."

Easy-On Shoes

In 2012, Matthew Walzer, a high school student with a disability, sent a note to Nike. "My dream is to go to college," he wrote, "without having to worry about someone coming to tie my shoes every day." Nike assigned a design team to the challenge. In 2015, they unveiled their solution: the FlyEase. The basketball shoe can be fastened with one hand. The mechanism drew inspiration from "opening and closing a door," says Tobie Hatfield, the shoe's head designer. A pair of Nike FlyEase shoes sells for $130.

Be Creative

Having a hard time choosing an instrument? You might want to try the Artiphon, which can imitate dozens of instruments—not just how they sound but how they're played. It can be strummed like a guitar or tapped like a piano. "We're trying to pave a different path toward musical creativity," says Jacob Gordon, an Artiphon co-founder. The Artiphon costs $399.

The Artiphon can be strummed like a guitar.

An Airport for Drones

As Amazon, Google, and others get ready for drone delivery service, there is one big question: What kinds of home bases will their drones have? Rwanda, in Africa, may have the answer. There workers will soon start work on three drone ports. The goal is to make it easier to transport food, medical supplies, electronics, and other goods through the hilly countryside where road travel is difficult. Construction is set to be completed in 2020.

A Virtual Pencil and Paper

In the 450 years or so since its invention, the pencil has become so common, it's easy to forget how remarkable it is. It can write at any angle. It writes darker when you press harder. Its marks can be erased. It's tough to digitally copy the way it functions. That's what makes Apple's latest effort so impressive. The Apple Pencil allows users to draw, paint, or write on a screen, just as they would on a sheet of paper. The Apple Pencil goes for $99 and the iPad Pro is $799+.

The Apple Pencil functions like a real pencil on a screen.

Have a Ball Coding

Kids need to learn coding. That's why Many created Hackaball. The toy syncs with a mobile app that allows users to program how and when the ball lights up. Users see how the program works. In one test, for example, kids set the ball to change colors at random intervals. Then they used the ball to play a hot-potato-style game. Hackaball is priced at $85.

See-Through Truck

Thousands of people get in car accidents when large vehicles block their view. This is especially true in Argentina, with its narrow roads. That's where Samsung and ad agency Leo Burnett partnered on the Safety Truck. The system relays video footage from in front of a truck to four screens on its back, giving drivers behind a clear view of what's ahead.

An Ocean Vacuum

There's a collection of plastic trash in the middle of the Pacific Ocean that's bigger than Texas—and growing. The present removal method of chasing it with nets is both costly and time-consuming. Instead, the Ocean Cleanup Project proposes a 62-mile-long floating barrier that would use natural currents to trap trash. If next year's trials succeed, a full cleanup operation would aim to start in 2020. Estimates suggest it could reduce the trash by 42% over 10 years.

The Underground Park

"It's not like any park you've ever seen before," says Dan Barasch, of the Lowline. The Lowline is an abandoned trolley terminal in New York City. Barasch and architect James Ramsey are trying to turn it into an acre of lush green space. The key: a "remote skylight" system that captures sunlight from surrounding rooftops and sends it underground. Once there, it's beamed out through a reflective dome, enabling plants to grow. With approvals and funding, the park could open in 2020.

FROM TIME FOR KIDS MAGAZINE

The Foldable Desk

A group creates a handy desk for students in need.

School is not always easy. And without the right supplies, school can be even harder. In some parts of the world, every day is a struggle. Many students in India cannot afford a backpack. They carry their books in their arms or in bags. At school, they sit on the floor because desks and chairs are a luxury. Kids hunch over as they do their assignments on the floor.

Aarambh is a nonprofit organization that help people in the poorest areas of Mumbai, India. Aarambh's founder, Shobha Murthy, wanted to make life easier for schoolchildren. "It was painful for the kids to sit in school," she told TFK. "It was uncomfortable even for us to watch them."

So Aarambh volunteers came up with a unique idea. They would create a schoolbag made of recycled cardboard boxes that with a few folds turned into a desk.

Good Things, Small Packages

To make the Help Desk, volunteers collected used cardboard boxes from stores, offices, and recycling centers. Then they developed a design and cut the boxes. Each Help Desk costs less than 20 cents to make.

Aarambh has given free desks to six schools in western India. More than 2,000 children have received a desk. "They were thrilled," Murthy says. "Some of the kids were crying they were so happy."

Now people all over the world have reached out to Aarambh. They want to volunteer or donate money for the project. "It's a reflection of how much people are thinking of others," Murthy says.

Aarambh hopes to add waterproof material to the Help Desk. With that, it will hold up better in heavy rain. "Aarambh means 'the beginning,'" Murthy says. "And this is just the beginning of bringing happiness to children."

—By Stephanie Kraus

Lean On Me
A student uses a Help Desk to do his work.

INVENTIONS AND TECHNOLOGY

Science

The Scientific Method

The scientific method is a set of steps that all scientists follow to create and conduct experiments. Here is the basic process.

Eureka! Through research and testing, you can draw important conclusions.

1. ASK A QUESTION

Are you concerned about the environment? Do you wish you understood more about the weather? Come up with a question you would like to answer. It could be something fun, such as: How do I make an egg float in water?

2. RESEARCH THE TOPIC

Investigate your topic, and find out whether other scientists have investigated the same question. What you learn will help you design a better experiment.

3. FORM A HYPOTHESIS

A hypothesis is a prediction based on what you have observed and read. Hypotheses are usually put into this format: "If, then, because." For example, "If I add salt to water, then an egg will float, because salt increases the density of water"

4. TEST THE HYPOTHESIS WITH AN EXPERIMENT

Design an experiment to test the hypothesis and write down each step. Come up with a list of the materials you will need (in this case, two containers, two eggs, water, and salt), and gather them. Follow the steps carefully. Record your observations in writing and in pictures.

5. ANALYZE THE RESULTS

What happened in your experiment? When did the egg float and sink? Think about the data you collected. Put your findings into a chart.

6. DRAW A CONCLUSION

Did the results of your experiment support your hypothesis? If not, come up with a new hypothesis, and try the experiment again. Change only one variable in your experiment—for example, the amount of salt you use—and see what results you get.

7. SHARE YOUR FINDINGS

When professional scientists complete an experiment, they often publish a paper or article about what they've found. You can tell your parents, teachers, and friends.

Biology

Biology is the study of life, including single-celled organisms, plants, and animals. Biologists study how they are structured and function, how they grow and reproduce, and how populations change over time.

Key Concepts

1. Living organisms can detect and respond to changes in their environments. Many animals process information through their nervous systems and brains. Plants may not have eyes or ears, but they are still able to sense the environment and respond to light, wind, and touch.

2. Reproduction is the process by which living organisms create new organisms. Some organisms, including many kinds of bacteria, starfish, and mushrooms, can create copies of themselves. For most animals, two individuals combine cells to create a completely new and unique living organism.

3. Living organisms depend on energy to fuel their bodies. Most plants can convert sunlight into energy through a process called photosynthesis. Most animals eat to gain energy.

The double helix of DNA contains important biological information.

4. All life is made up of cells. Organisms can be single-celled or contain quadrillions of them. (The human body is composed of about 40 trillion cells.) Cells combine to carry out a wide array of functions in plants and animals, from building muscles and skin to storing information and energy.

5. DNA includes vital information that determines how an organism looks and acts. Genes, made up of DNA segments, are passed down from generation to generation.

Pioneering Scientist
Charles Darwin

Darwin's research on the similarities and differences between various species led to the groundbreaking theory of evolution. While traveling around the world, Darwin studied plants and animals. He discovered that species were often very similar, but had differences that seemed to fit their environments. He came up with a theory that those species shared a common ancestor, but they had changed—or evolved—their structure and behavior in order to allow them to survive in their unique habitats. In 1859 he published *On the Origin of Species by Means of Natural Selection*, one of the most influential books in the history of science. Darwin's work revolutionized the way humans understand life on Earth.

Some Branches of Biology

Anatomy The study of the parts of living things, their shapes, structures, and relationships to one another.

Botany The study of plant life, including where plants live, how they interact with their environments, and how their internal systems work.

Genetics The study of how DNA is passed from one generation to the next, and how genes (segments of DNA) affect an organism's physical and behavioral traits.

Zoology The study of animals, their evolutionary history, and how they are classified.

Paleontology The study of fossils, which are the remains of prehistoric living things that have been preserved in earth or rock.

Biology in Action

The vaccination shots you get at the doctor's office may sting a little, but they can do a lifetime of good. The body's immune system, a network of cells that defend against harmful infections, can learn to recognize and destroy certain diseases. Vaccines include tiny, harmless amounts of viruses, toxins, or bacterium that give your cells a test run at fighting infections. That means that in the future your body will be able to keep you healthy.

Vaccines train your body to help fight off certain dangerous diseases.

Chemistry

Chemistry is a science concerned with the formation, structure, properties, and interactions of matter, including how forces hold matter together and how atoms form into larger structures.

Key Concepts

1. The basic unit of all matter—whether solid, liquid, gas, or plasma—is the atom. Atoms are made up of a core, called the nucleus, consisting of protons and neutrons. Electrons orbit the nucleus. The number of protons in an atom determines what element it forms. For example, oxygen atoms contain eight protons, silver atoms contain 47, and mercury atoms contain 80.

The core of the atom is called the nucleus.

2. The properties of different materials are a result of the arrangement of their atoms. Certain combinations of elements (basic substances that cannot be broken down into simpler components) are more or less likely to bond. Some elements can bond in different ways.

3. Chemical reactions occur when bonds between atoms are changed. Elements may be combined, detached, or replaced, and new substances are formed. Energy and heat are products of some chemical reactions, such as the reaction that takes place when striking a match.

Water is known as H_2O because it is two hydrogen atoms bonded to one oxygen atom.

80 ml
APPROX
60
40
20

Chemistry in Action

Why do cakes and cookies rise while in the oven? If baking soda is on your ingredient list, a chemical reaction is causing your dessert to expand. Baking soda, known more formally as "sodium bicarbonate," is made up of the elements sodium, hydrogen, carbon, and oxygen. Baking soda reacts chemically with other ingredients, such as milk or sugar, to produce tiny bubbles of gas. Those bubbles expand and widen the ingredient mixture, a key to baking many sweet treats.

SCIENCE

Some Branches of Chemistry

• **Analytical Chemistry** The study of what chemical compounds contain, which can be applied to countless to fields such as crime investigation, environmental study, and chemical safety.

• **Biochemistry** The study of chemical processes that take place in living things, such as the behavior of cells and the effects of medicine.

• **Cosmochemistry** The study of the chemical composition of matter throughout the universe and how those chemical combinations came to be.

• **Inorganic Chemistry** The study of compounds that do not contain carbon-hydrogen bonds, such as metals and minerals.

Pioneering Scientist: Marie Curie

Curie, along with her husband, Pierre, coined the term "radioactivity," which is the giving off of rays of energy when certain elements break apart. Her work led to the establishment of nuclear chemistry. She also helped discover two new radioactive elements, radium and polonium. For her contributions, Curie was the first woman to win two Nobel Prizes.

The Periodic Table

The chemical elements arranged by atomic number

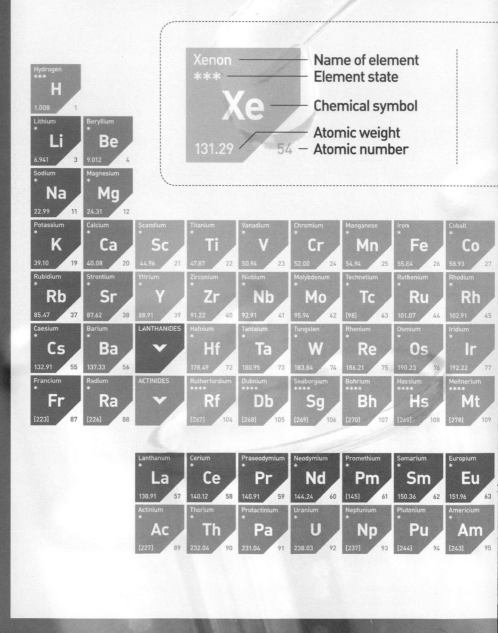

Xenon — Name of element
*** — Element state
Xe — Chemical symbol
131.29 — Atomic weight
54 — Atomic number

Hydrogen *** **H** 1.008 1	

| Lithium * **Li** 6.941 3 | Beryllium * **Be** 9.012 4 |

| Sodium * **Na** 22.99 11 | Magnesium * **Mg** 24.31 12 |

Potassium * **K** 39.10 19	Calcium * **Ca** 40.08 20	Scandium * **Sc** 44.96 21	Titanium * **Ti** 47.87 22	Vanadium * **V** 50.94 23	Chromium * **Cr** 52.00 24	Manganese * **Mn** 54.94 25	Iron * **Fe** 55.84 26	Cobalt * **Co** 58.93 27
Rubidium * **Rb** 85.47 37	Strontium * **Sr** 87.62 38	Yttrium * **Y** 88.91 39	Zirconium * **Zr** 91.22 40	Niobium * **Nb** 92.91 41	Molybdenum * **Mo** 95.94 42	Technetium * **Tc** [98] 43	Ruthenium * **Ru** 101.07 44	Rhodium * **Rh** 102.91 45
Caesium * **Cs** 132.91 55	Barium * **Ba** 137.33 56	LANTHANIDES ▼	Hafnium * **Hf** 178.49 72	Tantalum * **Ta** 180.95 73	Tungsten * **W** 183.84 74	Rhenium * **Re** 186.21 75	Osmium * **Os** 190.23 76	Iridium * **Ir** 192.22 77
Francium * **Fr** [223] 87	Radium * **Ra** [226] 88	ACTINIDES ▼	Rutherfordium **** **Rf** [267] 104	Dubnium **** **Db** [268] 105	Seaborgium **** **Sg** [269] 106	Bohrium **** **Bh** [270] 107	Hassium **** **Hs** [269] 108	Meitnerium **** **Mt** [278] 109

| Lanthanum * **La** 138.91 57 | Cerium * **Ce** 140.12 58 | Praseodymium * **Pr** 140.91 59 | Neodymium * **Nd** 144.24 60 | Promethium * **Pm** [145] 61 | Samarium * **Sm** 150.36 62 | Europium * **Eu** 151.96 63 |
| Actinium * **Ac** [227] 89 | Thorium * **Th** 232.04 90 | Protactinium * **Pa** 231.04 91 | Uranium * **U** 238.03 92 | Neptunium * **Np** [237] 93 | Plutonium * **Pu** [244] 94 | Americium * **Am** [243] 95 |

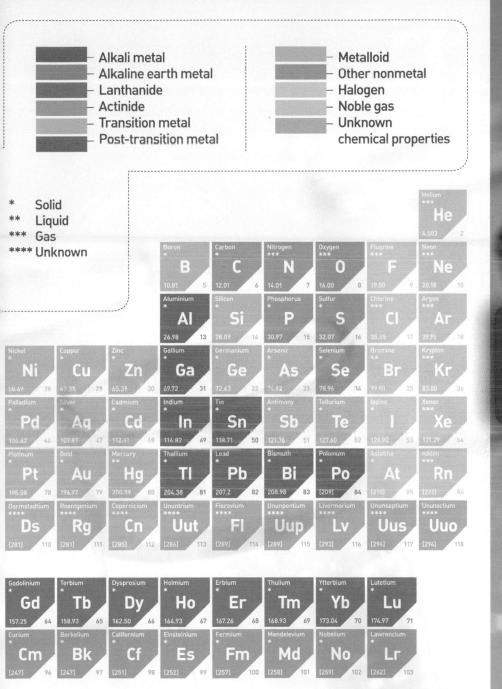

Alkali metal
Alkaline earth metal
Lanthanide
Actinide
Transition metal
Post-transition metal

Metalloid
Other nonmetal
Halogen
Noble gas
Unknown chemical properties

* Solid
** Liquid
*** Gas
**** Unknown

Helium *** He 4.003 2

Boron * B 10.81 5	Carbon * C 12.01 6	Nitrogen *** N 14.01 7	Oxygen *** O 16.00 8	Fluorine *** F 19.00 9	Neon *** Ne 20.18 10
Aluminium * Al 26.98 13	Silicon * Si 28.09 14	Phosphorus * P 30.97 15	Sulfur * S 32.07 16	Chlorine *** Cl 35.45 17	Argon *** Ar 39.95 18

Nickel * Ni 58.69 28	Copper * Cu 63.55 29	Zinc * Zn 65.39 30	Gallium * Ga 69.72 31	Germanium * Ge 72.63 32	Arsenic * As 74.92 33	Selenium * Se 78.96 34	Bromine ** Br 79.90 35	Krypton *** Kr 83.80 36
Palladium * Pd 106.42 46	Silver * Ag 107.87 47	Cadmium * Cd 112.41 48	Indium * In 114.82 49	Tin * Sn 118.71 50	Antimony * Sb 121.76 51	Tellurium * Te 127.60 52	Iodine * I 126.90 53	Xenon *** Xe 131.29 54
Platinum * Pt 196.08 78	Gold * Au 196.97 79	Mercury ** Hg 200.59 80	Thallium * Tl 204.38 81	Lead * Pb 207.2 82	Bismuth * Bi 208.98 83	Polonium * Po [209] 84	Astatine * At [210] 85	Radon *** Rn [222] 86
Darmstadtium **** Ds [281] 110	Roentgenium **** Rg [281] 111	Copernicium **** Cn [285] 112	Ununtrium **** Uut [286] 113	Flerovium **** Fl [289] 114	Ununpentium **** Uup [289] 115	Livermorium **** Lv [293] 116	Ununseptium **** Uus [294] 117	Ununoctium **** Uuo [294] 118

Gadolinium * Gd 157.25 64	Terbium * Tb 158.93 65	Dysprosium * Dy 162.50 66	Holmium * Ho 164.93 67	Erbium * Er 167.26 68	Thulium * Tm 168.93 69	Ytterbium * Yb 173.04 70	Lutetium * Lu 174.97 71
Curium * Cm [247] 96	Berkelium * Bk [247] 97	Californium * Cf [251] 98	Einsteinium * Es [252] 99	Fermium * Fm [257] 100	Mendelevium * Md [258] 101	Nobelium * No [259] 102	Lawrencium * Lr [262] 103

Physics

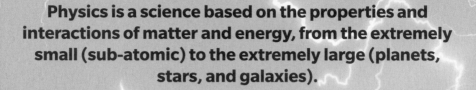

Physics is a science based on the properties and interactions of matter and energy, from the extremely small (sub-atomic) to the extremely large (planets, stars, and galaxies).

Key Concepts

1. Mass, energy, electric charge, and momentum are among the physical properties which cannot be created or destroyed, but can be rearranged or change form. These concepts are known as the conservation laws.

2. All interactions in the universe originate from four forces of nature. **Gravity** is a force that causes matter to be attracted to other matter. The **electromagnetic** force creates magnetic fields and electric currents. The **strong** and **weak** nuclear forces act upon extremely tiny particles within atoms.

3. A wave is a description of the motion that transfers energy. Mechanical waves, such as sound waves or waves in a body of water, require moving matter. Electromagnetic waves, such as radio waves and light, can travel without matter.

4. Albert Einstein's famous $E=mc^2$ equation tells us, among other things, that energy (E) can be converted into mass (m) and vice versa. The c^2 represents the speed of light multiplied by itself. The most destructive weapons in the history of the world were built on this principle, since so little mass is needed to create tremendous energy.

This device, known as Newton's Cradle, demonstrates several laws of physics.

Rainbows occur when sunlight enters raindrops at a certain angle.

Physics in Action

Rainbows are a result of a process known as dispersion. You're able to see a rainbow when sunlight enters individual raindrops and you are positioned at just the right angle (and not facing the sun). The rays of bright light are dispersed, or broken up, into the individual colors formed by different wavelengths of light.

Pioneering Scientist: Ibn al-Haytham

Born around 965 A.D. in modern-day Iraq, al-Haytham made important contributions to the field of optics. For centuries, dating back to the ancient Greeks, the theory of vision was based on the idea that eyes send out rays to objects they are seeing. Al-Haytham is the first known person to correctly take the opposite stance: Light originates in objects and travels in straight lines into the eye.

Some Branches of Physics

• **Acoustics** The study of how sound and vibrations are produced, heard, controlled, and effected.
• **Electromagnetism** The study of the magnetic and electrical charges and how they are related to each other.
• **Mechanics** The study of motion and the forces that produce motion.
• **Optics** The study of the behavior and properties of light, both visible and invisible.
• **Thermodynamics** The study of energy and work as they relate to heat.

Earth Science

Earth science includes the study of the materials and systems that make up our planet and how they interact. It is also the study of the history of our planet and its place within the universe.

Key Concepts

1. The Earth is a complex system of rock (geosphere), water (hydrosphere), air (atmosphere), and life (biosphere). All of Earth's processes are a result of energy and matter flowing between and within these "spheres."

4. The Earth is about 4.5 billion years old. The age is based on measurements from rocks, minerals, and asteroid fragments on Earth, as well as rocks taken from the moon. Evidence for the age of our solar system and galaxy also supports the age estimate.

2. The Earth is constantly changing. Its interior is always in motion, while the surface is made up of dozens of pieces, called tectonic plates, which are always slowly shifting. In fact, all the land on Earth used to be one giant continent, called Pangaea, hundreds of millions of years ago.

3. The Earth orbits the sun because of the gravitational pull of the sun. The Earth is one of four terrestrial planets (along with Mercury, Venus, and Mars), meaning it is relatively small with a rocky surface and metallic interior. Jupiter, Saturn, Uranus, and Neptune are known as Jovian planets. They are larger and farther away from the sun, and are made up mostly of gases.

Mount Aso in Japan is one of Earth's active volcanoes.

Some Branches of Earth Science

Geology The study of the rocks and minerals that form the solid Earth, and the processes which cause them to change.

Hydrology The study of the movement, distribution, occurrence, and properties of water and its relationship with the environment.

Meteorology The study of the atmosphere, the gaseous envelope that surrounds the Earth, and its effects on weather.

Seismology The study of earthquakes, which occur when tectonic plates (pieces of the Earth's surface layers) shift and create vibrations known as seismic waves.

Volcanology The study of the formation, distribution, and classification of volcanoes, as well as the materials emitted during their eruptions.

Pioneering Scientist: Clair Patterson

Patterson spent many years developing a method for determining the age of rocks and minerals by measuring the tiny amounts of lead they contained. Through this process, he came up with the first accurate estimate of the Earth's age—4.5 billion years—in 1953. He also discovered that humans were releasing dangerous amounts of lead into the atmosphere through pollution. Patterson helped convince the U.S. government to monitor and regulate harmful lead pollution, leading to the Clean Air Act of 1970 and the removal of lead from gasoline.

Dams can be an effective way to generate electricity.

Earth Science in Action

The last time you rode in a car, bus, or plane, chances are liquid petroleum fueled your trip. Petroleum is formed when the remains of marine life from millions of years ago mix with other minerals and are exposed to high temperatures and pressures underground.

Petroleum fuels help make cars run.

Food Fight

Companies are using gene science to develop potatoes and other crops. But not everyone wants the new foods.

The J.R. Simplot Company set out to create a better potato. The Idaho-based company developed a super spud called the Innate. The potato is designed to produce less acrylamide. Potatoes make the chemical when they are cooked at high temperatures. Scientists think acrylamide may cause cancer.

The U.S. Department of Agriculture gave Simplot approval to start growing the Innate. But not everyone is ready to buy food made with genetically modified ingredients, or GMOs. Genes are the instructions inside cells that help determine what a living thing looks like: its size, its shape, and other traits. GMOs add or change genes.

Good Enough to Eat?

People who oppose GMOs fear that changing a crop's genes could harm humans and the environment. For that reason, McDonald's will not buy the Innate. McDonald's has served Simplot's potatoes since the 1960s. In a statement, the company said it "does not source genetically modified potatoes."

In November 2014, voters in Maui County, in Hawaii, approved an initiative that put a temporary ban on the cultivation of GMOs. The county wanted scientific studies done to determine the benefits and safety of GMOs.

Two companies challenged the ban in court. Monsanto and Dow Agrosciences grow GMO corn in Maui County. Both say their products are safe and that the ban could cost hundreds of people their jobs. "This ban would have [a negative impact] on the community, the local economy, and on agriculture in Hawaii," Dow said in a statement. In 2015, a judge ruled that the initiative was invalid.

—*By Glenn Greenberg, with AP reporting*

McDonald's decided against using genetically-modified potatoes.

A member of a Monsanto crew works in a cornfield in Kihei, Hawaii. About 90% of all U.S. corn is genetically modified.

What Do I Do?

Scientists can be experts in robots, weather, and even prehistoric plants! See if you can match the scientists to their specialty.

ASTRONOMER

CRIMINOLOGIST

EPIDEMIOLOGIST

GEOLOGIST

LEPIDOPTERIST

MALACOLOGIST

METEOROLOGIST

PALEOBOTANIST

PALEONTOLOGIST

ROBOTICIST

• Designs, builds, and operates robots

Answer:

• Examines diseases and how they spread

Answer:

• Examines stars, planets, comets, asteroids, galaxies, and other things in space

Answer:

• Focuses on the biology and evolution of prehistoric plants

Answer:

• Studies mollusks (such as snails, oysters, and clams)

Answer:

• Studies the remains of organisms that lived long ago

Answer:

• Studies the origins, history, surface, structure, and makeup of Earth

Answer:

• A biologist who focuses on butterflies

Answer:

• Studies weather and climate

Answer:

• Studies criminals and the causes of their behavior

Answer:

SCIENCE

Answers on page 277

Hubble Space Telescope

Space

Space: The Final Frontier

Key moments in the history of space exploration

Yuri Gagarin

1957

October 4
The Soviet Union successfully launches *Sputnik I*, marking the dawn of the space age. The world's first satellite is about the size of a beach ball and weighs about 184 pounds. The event kicks off the great space race between the U.S. and the Soviets.

1958

October 1
The National Aeronautics and Space Administration (NASA) begins operations.
October 11
Pioneer I is the first NASA spacecraft to launch from Cape Canaveral, Florida. It sends back 43 hours of data.

1959

April 9
NASA unveils the U.S.'s first group of astronauts in the Mercury program: John Glenn, Walter Schirra, Alan Shepard, Scott Carpenter, Gordon Cooper, Virgil "Gus" Grissom, and Donald "Deke" Slayton. They are nicknamed the Mercury Seven.

1961

April 12
Russian cosmonaut Yuri Gagarin becomes the first person in space, orbiting the Earth one time during a 108-minute flight.
May 5
Alan Shepard blasts into space on the *Freedom 7* capsule. He is the first American to fly in space.

1962

February 20
John Glenn becomes the first American to circle the Earth. He makes three orbits in the *Friendship 7* spacecraft.

1965

July 14
Mariner 4 arrives at Mars. It passes within 6,118 miles of the planet's surface after an eight-month journey. This mission produces the first close-up images of the red planet.

1969

July 16–24
Apollo 11 completes the first lunar landing mission with astronauts Neil Armstrong, Edwin "Buzz" Aldrin, and Michael Collins. On July 20, Armstrong becomes the first person to walk on the moon. "That's one small step for man, one giant leap for mankind," he famously says.

1970

April 11–17
Apollo 13 lifts off. A problem with the oxygen tank damages the spacecraft, putting the lives of the astronauts in danger. Fortunately, all of the crew members return safely to Earth.

John Glenn

Apollo 13

1975

July 15–24
The Apollo-Soyuz Test Project is the first joint international human space flight effort. The project was designed to test the compatibility of docking systems for American and Soviet spacecraft. It was also meant to open the way for international space rescue.

1981

April 12
Astronauts John Young and Robert Crippen fly the space shuttle *Columbia* on the first flight of the Space Transportation System (STS-1). It becomes the first airplanelike craft to land from orbit and be reused.

1983

June 18–24
American Sally Ride flies on the STS-7 mission aboard the space shuttle *Challenger*. She becomes the first woman astronaut in space.

1986

January 28
The space shuttle *Challenger* is destroyed during its launch. An explosion occurs 73 seconds into the flight. All seven crew members are killed in the blast.

Space Shuttle *Columbia* launches from Kennedy Space Center.

Sally Ride

2003

February 1
The space shuttle *Columbia* breaks up in the atmosphere 15 minutes before its scheduled landing. All crew members of the 16-day mission are killed.

2004

January 3 and 24
NASA successfully lands two Mars exploration rovers, Spirit and Opportunity, on the surface of Mars.
June 30
Following a seven-year, two-billion-mile journey, the Cassini-Huygens spacecraft is the first to go into orbit around Saturn. It was launched from Cape Canaveral on October 15, 1997.

2005

July 26
The space shuttle *Discovery* (STS-114) launches successfully into orbit. It's NASA's first return to human spaceflight after the *Columbia* tragedy.

2006

January 19
The New Horizons spacecraft begins its nine-year trip toward Pluto and the Kuiper Belt.

Mars rovers Spirit and Opportunity land on the planet.

1988

September 29
NASA's 26th shuttle launch, made by *Discovery*, marks the successful return to flight for the space shuttle.

1990

April 24
The Hubble Space Telescope launches from the space shuttle *Columbia* (STS-31). In the years that follow, Hubble makes important discoveries, such as new galaxies.

The Hubble Space Telescope reaches orbit in 1990.

1996

Mir and *Atlantis*

March 22–31
The space shuttle *Atlantis* docks with the Russian space station Mir. U.S. astronaut Shannon Lucid becomes the first woman on the space station. She stays aboard the station for six months.

1998

May 28
The Hubble Space Telescope gives the world its first direct image of what is probably a planet outside our solar system.

November 20
The first module for the International Space Station (ISS), the Russian Zarya module, launches. The ISS is a partnership between several international space agencies.

International Space Station

2011

August 31
The space shuttle program officially ends just over a month after the final shuttle mission, *Atlantis* (STS-135), lands back on Earth at Kennedy Space Center.

Atlantis

2015

March 27
NASA's Twins Study begins as astronaut Scott Kelly blasts into space aboard a Russian Soyuz rocket. Scott's identical twin brother, retired astronaut Mark Kelly, remains on Earth. Scott, along with cosmonaut Mikhail Kornienko, is set to spend a year aboard the ISS. The experiment aims to explore the effects of long-term space flight on the human body

by studying the brothers before, during, and after the mission.

July 14
After a decade-long journey, the New Horizons spacecraft makes its closest-ever approach to Pluto. The craft flew 7,750 miles

above the dwarf planet's surface, about the same distance from New York to Mumbai, India.

September 28
NASA confirms definitive evidence of liquid water on Mars.

Pluto's surface has many colors, including deep red and pale blue.

Rocket Men

The Kelly twins—one in orbit and one on Earth—helped NASA unlock the secrets of long-term space travel.

When Scott Kelly called home from the International Space Station (ISS), whoever answered the phone could have simply hung up on him. The call was welcome, but the line was often bad. That can happen when placing a call from 229 miles above the Earth. "When someone answers, I have to say, 'It's the space station! Don't hang up!'" said Scott.

But his brother, Mark, knew the crackle of an extraterrestrial signal in his ear. Mark is a former astronaut who has been to space four times. Mark is also known for being married to former congresswoman Gabrielle Giffords, who was hurt in an assassination attempt in 2011.

Mark and Scott are identical twins. They have the same genetic makeup. Though they have served a combined seven missions, the brothers have never gone to space together.

A Year in Space

In March 2015, Scott left his family in Houston, Texas, for a one-year stay aboard the ISS. It set a single-mission record for a U.S. astronaut. Scott shared his marathon mission with Russian cosmonaut Mikhail Kornienko. A rotating

Mark Kelly floats inside the International Space Station during a five-day NASA mission in 2008.

cast of 13 other crew members joined them for shorter visits.

The U.S. has long dreamed of sending astronauts to Mars. The biggest problem with reaching this goal is, simply, the human body. We are designed for Earth. In space, bones get brittle, eyeballs lose their shape, hearts beat less efficiently, and balance goes awry. "There's quite a bit of data

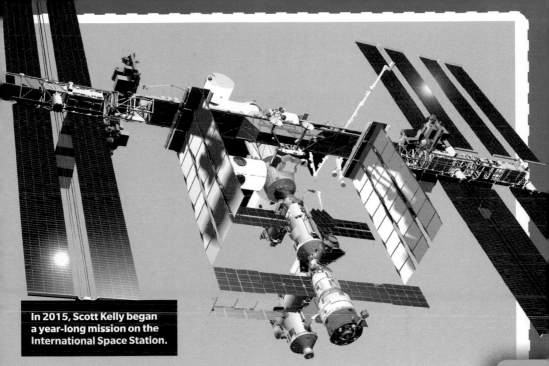

In 2015, Scott Kelly began a year-long mission on the International Space Station.

[on human health] for six months in orbit," says space-station program manager Mike Suffredini. "Do things change at one year?"

NASA needed subjects to test the long-term effects of space. In a perfect experiment, every subject would have a control subject on Earth with the exact same genes. This would help scientists separate the changes that come from being in space from those that are a result of growing the same year older on Earth. In the Kelly brothers—and only the Kelly brothers—NASA had that two-person sample group.

Star Twins

Scott's days on the ISS were packed with science experiments, exercise, and monitoring and fixing the station's systems. The station was stocked with movies and books, and the crew could surf the Internet.

On this flight, Scott and Kornienko were very closely monitored with medical and psychological tests. Mark underwent a similar study on the ground. Scientists hope that comparing the data will shed light on the impact of spending a long time in space.

Scott's mission was equal parts science experiment, endurance test, and human drama. To the Kelly brothers, it was just the latest mile in a journey they've shared for half a century.

—By Jeffrey Kluger
for TIME

Scott Kelly takes a seat in a service module aboard the International Space Station in 2007.

The Solar System

The sun is at the center of our solar system. It consists mostly of ionized gas and supports life on Earth. Planets rotate around the sun. Mercury, Venus, Earth, and Mars are called terrestrial planets because they have solid, rocky bodies. The outer planets, Jupiter, Saturn, Uranus, and Neptune, do not have solid surfaces because they are made up of gases.

Earth
About 70% of Earth is covered with water. Nearly all of it is found in the oceans, which are salt water. Only 3% is drinkable freshwater. Earth has a diameter of 7,962 miles (12,756 km), and its average surface temperature is 59°F (15°C).

Saturn
Known as the ringed planet, Saturn spins very quickly. It takes less than 11 hours for the planet to rotate fully on its axis. Saturn's famous rings are made up of ice and rock.

Mercury
At the closest point in its orbit, Mercury is about 29 million miles (47 million km) from the sun. Because it's so close, Mercury can be seen only within an hour or so of the rising or setting of the sun.

Jupiter
Jupiter is the biggest planet in the solar system. Four of its many moons are planet-sized. Its diameter is 11 times bigger than Earth's.

Venus
Venus is similar in size to Earth but has no oceans. It's covered by a layer of thick clouds, which trap heat in its atmosphere. Its average surface temperature is 864°F (462°C).

Mars
Mars is prone to dust storms that engulf the entire planet. It has two moons and is about 142 million miles (228 million km) from the sun.

Uranus
Uranus was discovered by William Herschel in 1781. With a diameter of 31,763 miles (51,118 km), it is about four times the size of Earth.

Neptune
Neptune was the first planet located by mathematical predictions instead of observation. The planet farthest from the sun, it has an average surface temperature of –353°F (–214°C).

What's in Space?

Stars

The center of our solar system is a star that we call the sun. It is made up of hot balls of gas that are constantly exploding. There would be no life on Earth without the sun, because its heat and energy are what cause the chemical reactions that give us oxygen, water, and food.

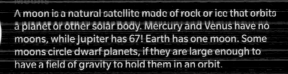

Moons

A moon is a natural satellite made of rock or ice that orbits a planet or other solar body. Mercury and Venus have no moons, while Jupiter has 67! Earth has one moon. Some moons circle dwarf planets, if they are large enough to have a field of gravity to hold them in an orbit.

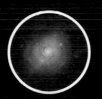

Galaxies

A group of millions of stars (along with dust, gas, and debris) bound together by gravity is known as a galaxy. Galaxies are like the enormous neighborhoods that make up the universe. Our sun and its planets exist in a part of the universe called the Milky Way galaxy.

Comets

A comet is made up of frozen gas, rocks, dust, and ice. It's like a cosmic snowball, orbiting in space. When a comet gets near the sun, it heats up and parts of it begin to melt. Its dust and gases spread out into a formation that sometimes reaches as much as 100 million miles in length.

The Mars Mystery

How did the Red Planet lose its air? The MAVEN spacecraft went on a mission to find out.

Mars was once a warm, wet place, with oceans and rivers. But billions of years ago, the planet lost most of its atmosphere and its water dried up, turning it into the cold, dry desert it is today. What happened?

"We know that something drastic must have happened to change Mars," NASA scientist Jared Espley told TFK. "Our best guess is that the solar wind, a very thin gas that flows from the sun, has been gradually blowing away bits of the air of Mars."

NASA's MAVEN spacecraft was on a mission to search for clues to the mystery of why Mars lost its air and why its climate changed. On September 21, 2014, MAVEN arrived in Mars's orbit after a 10-month journey. The craft orbited the planet for a year and studied its upper atmosphere.

In this artist's view, MAVEN orbits Mars, with Earth in the distance.

Several groups across the country worked together on MAVEN. Espley works for NASA's Goddard Space Flight Center, in Greenbelt, Maryland. This group managed the mission. Espley and other scientists are using measurements that MAVEN collected to learn more about Mars.

MAVEN is 37.5 feet long. That is almost the length of a school bus. The craft is equipped with eight tools. "Most of them are particle detectors—instruments that collect the escaping particles, or bits, from Mars, and count them up," explained Espley. "There are also instruments that will help us understand where the escaping air would go and how it would travel."

MAVEN was not the only craft studying the Red Planet. India's first Mars-bound spacecraft arrived in Mars's orbit just days after MAVEN did. NASA's robot on wheels, the Curiosity rover, is exploring the planet's surface.

Studying Mars is helping NASA prepare for its goal of sending humans there in the 2030s. Mars is the planet in our solar system most like Earth. Espley says it is exciting to study a planet to which people might travel. "This mission has a specific science goal," he says, "but also touches on big-picture questions, such as how the climate or environment of a planet changes over time."

—By Elizabeth Winchester

Out of This World

These photos of astronaut Carlos Noriega on a spacewalk may look similar—but examine them closely and you'll see that not everything is quite the same. Can you spot all 10 differences?

SPACE

Tight end Rob Gronkowski

Serena Williams

Sports

Point guard Stephen Curry

First baseman Miguel Cabrera

BALTIMORE ORIOLES

FOUNDED: 1901
(as the Milwaukee Brewers)

World Series Titles: 3

Last World Series Won: 1983

Big Star: Shortstop Cal Ripken Jr., played in a record 2,632 straight games

BOSTON RED SOX

FOUNDED: 1901

World Series Titles: 8

Last World Series Won: 2013

Big Star: Leftfielder Ted Williams, the last player to hit over .400 in a season (1941)

CHICAGO WHITE SOX

FOUNDED: 1901

World Series Titles: 3

Last World Series Won: 2005

Big Star: DH Frank Thomas, two-time AL MVP (1993 and '94)

CLEVELAND INDIANS

FOUNDED: 1901

World Series Titles: 2

Last World Series Won: 1948

Big Star: Pitcher Bob Feller, seven-time MLB strikeout leader and Hall of Famer

DETROIT TIGERS

FOUNDED: 1901

World Series Titles: 4

Last World Series Won: 1984

Big Star: First baseman **Miguel Cabrera**, 2012 Triple Crown winner (led the league in batting average, home runs, and runs batted in)

Outfielder Babe Ruth

MINNESOTA TWINS

FOUNDED: 1901
(as the Washington Senators)

World Series Titles: 3
Last World Series Won: 1991
Big Star: Catcher Joe Mauer, three-time AL batting champion (2006, '08, '09)

HOUSTON ASTROS

FOUNDED: 1962

World Series Titles: 0
Big Star: Second baseman Craig Biggio, seven-time All-Star and franchise leader in career hits (3,060)

NEW YORK YANKEES

FOUNDED: 1903

World Series Titles: 27
Last World Series Won: 2009
Big Star: Outfielder **Babe Ruth**, holds the highest career slugging percentage in MLB history (.690)

KANSAS CITY ROYALS

FOUNDED: 1969

World Series Titles: 2
Last World Series Won: 2015
Big Star: George Brett, holds the record for most career hits by a third baseman (3,154)

SPORTS

Centerfielder Mike Trout

LOS ANGELES ANGELS OF ANAHEIM

FOUNDED: 1961 (as the Los Angeles Angels)

World Series Titles: 1
Last World Series Won: 2002
Big Star Centerfielder **Mike Trout**, 2012 AL Rookie of the Year and 2014 AL MVP

OAKLAND ATHLETICS

FOUNDED: 1901
(as the Philadelphia Athletics)

World Series Titles: 9
Last World Series Won: 1989
Big Star: Leftfielder Rickey Henderson, holds the MLB record for most career stolen bases (1,406)

SEATTLE MARINERS

FOUNDED: 1977

World Series Titles: 0
Big Star: Pitcher **Felix Hernandez**, two-time American League earned run average leader and 2010 Cy Young Award winner

TAMPA BAY RAYS

FOUNDED: 1998

World Series Titles: 0
Big Star: Evan Longoria, 2008 AL Rookie of the Year and franchise leader in home runs

TEXAS RANGERS

FOUNDED: 1961
(as the Washington Senators)

World Series Titles: 0
Big Star: Pitcher Nolan Ryan, has a record seven career no-hitters

Pitcher Felix Hernandez

TORONTO BLUE JAYS

FOUNDED: 1977

World Series Titles: 2
Last World Series Won: 1993
Big Star: Outfielder Jose Bautista, led the league in home runs in 2010 and '11

National League

ARIZONA DIAMONDBACKS

FOUNDED: 1998

World Series Titles: 1
Last World Series Won: 2001
Big Star: First baseman **Paul Goldschmidt**, three-time All-Star and led the NL in home runs (36) and RBIs (125) in 2013

First baseman Paul Goldschmidt

ATLANTA BRAVES

FOUNDED: 1876
(as the Boston Braves)

World Series Titles: 3
Last World Series Won: 1995
Big Star: Rightfielder Hank Aaron, the career leader in runs batted in (2,297)

CHICAGO CUBS

FOUNDED: 1876

World Series Titles: 2
Last World Series Won: 1908
Big Star: Shortstop **Ernie Banks**, two-time NL MVP and the Cubs' all-time leader in extra-base hits

CINCINNATI REDS

FOUNDED: 1882

World Series Titles: 5
Last World Series Won: 1990
Big Star: Catcher Johnny Bench, 1976 World Series MVP and 10-time Gold Glove winner

COLORADO ROCKIES

FOUNDED: 1993

World Series Titles: 0
Big Star: First baseman Todd Helton, 2000 NL batting champ and the franchise leader in home runs (369)

Shortstop Ernie Banks

Pitcher Matt Harvey

NEW YORK METS

FOUNDED: 1962

World Series Titles: 2
Last World Series Won: 1986
Big Star: Matt Harvey, starting pitcher for the 2013 NL All-Star team at Citi Field, the Mets' home park

LOS ANGELES DODGERS

FOUNDED: 1884
(as the Brooklyn Dodgers)

World Series Titles: 6
Last World Series Won: 1988
Big Star: Second baseman Jackie Robinson, broke MLB's color barrier and won Rookie of the Year in 1947

PHILADELPHIA PHILLIES

FOUNDED: 1883

World Series Titles: 2
Last World Series Won: 2008
Big Star: Third baseman Mike Schmidt, three-time NL MVP and the Phillies' all-time leader in home runs (548) and runs batted in (1,595)

MIAMI MARLINS

FOUNDED: 1993
(as the Florida Marlins)

World Series Titles: 2
Last World Series Won: 2003
Big Star: Rightfielder Giancarlo Stanton, led the NL in home runs in 2014

PITTSBURGH PIRATES

FOUNDED: 1882

World Series Titles: 5
Last World Series Won: 1979
Big Star: Centerfielder Andrew McCutchen, 2013 NL MVP

MILWAUKEE BREWERS

FOUNDED: 1969
(as the Seattle Pilots)

World Series Titles: 0
Big Star: Shortstop Robin Yount, two-time AL MVP

SAN DIEGO PADRES

FOUNDED: 1969

World Series Titles: 0

Big Star: Rightfielder Tony Gwynn, hit .394 in 1994 for the highest single-season batting average since 1941

SAN FRANCISCO GIANTS

FOUNDED: 1883
(as the New York Gothams)

World Series Titles: 8

Last World Series Won: 2014

Big Star: Pitcher **Madison Bumgarner**, set the MLB record for lowest World Series ERA (0.29) among pitchers with at least 25 innings pitched

Pitcher Madison Bumgarner

ST. LOUIS CARDINALS

FOUNDED: 1882

World Series Titles: 11

Last World Series Won: 2011

Big Star: Outfielder **Stan Musial**, has the most career hits by a player who played for only one team (3,630)

WASHINGTON NATIONALS

FOUNDED: 1969
(as the Montreal Expos)

World Series Titles: 0

Big Star: Outfielder Bryce Harper, 2015 NL MVP

Outfielder Stan Musial

Quarterback Joe Flacco

BALTIMORE RAVENS

FOUNDED: 1996

Super Bowl Titles: 2
Last Title Won: Super Bowl XLVII
Big Star: Quarterback **Joe Flacco**, Super Bowl XLVII MVP

BUFFALO BILLS

FOUNDED: 1960

Super Bowl Titles: 0
Big Star: Defensive end Bruce Smith, holds the NFL record for most career sacks (200)

CINCINNATI BENGALS

FOUNDED: 1968

Super Bowl Titles: 0
Big Star: Offensive tackle Anthony Muñoz, named to 11 straight Pro Bowls and nine All-Pro first teams

CLEVELAND BROWNS

FOUNDED: 1946

Super Bowl Titles: 0
Big Star: Fullback Jim Brown, the only player to lead the NFL in rushing for five straight seasons (1957–61)

DENVER BRONCOS

FOUNDED: 1960

Super Bowl Titles: 3
Last Title Won: Super Bowl 50
Big Star: Quarterback John Elway, 1987 NFL MVP

HOUSTON TEXANS

FOUNDED: 2002

Super Bowl Titles: 0
Big Star: Defensive end J.J. Watt, two-time NFL Defensive Player of the Year

INDIANAPOLIS COLTS

FOUNDED: 1953
(as the Baltimore Colts)

Super Bowl Titles: 2
Last Title Won: Super Bowl XLI
Big Star: Quarterback **Johnny Unitas**, three-time NFL MVP

Quarterback Johnny Unitas

Tight end Rob Gronkowski

JACKSONVILLE JAGUARS

FOUNDED: 1995

Super Bowl Titles: 0
Big Star: Wide receiver Jimmy Smith, five-time Pro Bowler who led the NFL in receptions in 1999 (116)

KANSAS CITY CHIEFS

FOUNDED: 1960
(as the Dallas Texans)

Super Bowl Titles: 1
Last Title Won: Super Bowl IV
Big Star: Running back Jamaal Charles, holds NFL records for rushing yards in a quarter (165) and receiving touchdowns by a running back in one game (four)

MIAMI DOLPHINS

FOUNDED: 1966

Super Bowl Titles: 2
Last Title Won: Super Bowl VIII
Big Star: Quarterback Dan Marino, the first QB to throw for 5,000 yards in a season (in 1984)

NEW ENGLAND PATRIOTS

FOUNDED: 1960 (as the Boston Patriots)

Super Bowl Titles: 4
Last Title Won: Super Bowl XLIX
Big Star: Tight end **Rob Gronkowski**, holds the NFL records for single-season yards (1,327) and touchdowns (18) by a tight end

Quarterback Joe Namath

NEW YORK JETS

FOUNDED: 1960

Super Bowl Titles: 1

Last Title Won: Super Bowl III

Big Star: Quarterback **Joe Namath**, led the underdog Jets to the biggest upset in Super Bowl history (over the Colts)

OAKLAND RAIDERS

FOUNDED: 1960

Super Bowl Titles: 3

Last Title Won: Super Bowl XVIII

Big Star: Running back Marcus Allen, the Raiders' all-time leader in rushing yards (8,545) and rushing touchdowns (79) and the Super Bowl XVIII MVP

PITTSBURGH STEELERS

FOUNDED: 1933

Super Bowl Titles: 6

Last Title Won: Super Bowl XLIII

Big Star: Defensive tackle Joe Greene, two-time defensive player of the year and four-time Super Bowl winner

SAN DIEGO CHARGERS

FOUNDED: 1960

(as the Los Angeles Chargers)

Super Bowl Titles: 0

Big Star: Running back LaDainian Tomlinson, holds the mark for most touchdowns in a season (31 in 2006)

TENNESSEE TITANS

FOUNDED: 1960 (as the Houston Oilers)

Super Bowl Titles: 0

Big Star: Running back **Eddie George**, four-time Pro Bowler and 1996 Offensive Rookie of the Year

Running back Eddie George

Wide receiver Larry Fitzgerald

ATLANTA FALCONS

FOUNDED: 1966

Super Bowl Titles: 0

Big Star: Quarterback Matt Ryan, 2008 Offensive Rookie of the Year and the Falcons' all-time leader in passing TDs

CAROLINA PANTHERS

FOUNDED: 1995

Super Bowl Titles: 0

Big Star: Quarterback Cam Newton, holds the mark for single-season rushing TDs by a QB (14 in 2011)

CHICAGO BEARS

FOUNDED: 1920

(as the Decatur Staleys)

Super Bowl Titles: 1

Last Title Won: Super Bowl XX

Big Star: Running back Walter Payton, two-time NFL MVP

DALLAS COWBOYS

FOUNDED: 1960

Super Bowl Titles: 5

Last Title Won: Super Bowl XXX

Big Star: Running back Emmitt Smith, all-time leader in career rushing yards (18,355) and rushing TDs (164)

DETROIT LIONS

FOUNDED: 1930

(as the Portsmouth Spartans)

Super Bowl Titles: 0

Big Star: Wide receiver Calvin Johnson, set the record for receiving yards in a season (1,964 in 2012)

National Football Conference

ARIZONA CARDINALS

FOUNDED: 1920 (as the Chicago Cardinals)

Super Bowl Titles: 0

Big Star: Wide receiver **Larry Fitzgerald**, hold the record for receiving yards in one postseason (546)

Running back Marshall Faulk

Quarterback Aaron Rodgers

GREEN BAY PACKERS

FOUNDED: 1921

Super Bowl Titles: 4
Last Title Won: Super Bowl XLV
Big Star: Quarterback **Aaron Rodgers**, two-time NFL MVP and the all-time leader in career passer rating

LOS ANGELES RAMS

FOUNDED: 1937
(as the Cleveland Rams)

Super Bowl Titles: 1
Last Title Won: Super Bowl XXXIV
Big Star: Running back **Marshall Faulk**, all-time leader in receiving yards by a running back (6,875)

MINNESOTA VIKINGS

FOUNDED: 1961

Super Bowl Titles: 0
Big Star: Quarterback **Fran Tarkenton**, nine-time Pro Bowler and 1975 NFL MVP

NEW ORLEANS SAINTS

FOUNDED: 1967

Super Bowl Titles: 1
Last Title Won: Super Bowl XLIV
Big Star: Quarterback Drew Brees, threw a touchdown pass in 54 straight games, an NFL record

NEW YORK GIANTS

FOUNDED: 1925

Super Bowl Titles: 4

Last Title Won: Super Bowl XLVI

Big Star: Defensive end **Michael Strahan**, holds the NFL single-season record for sacks (22½)

Defensive end Michael Strahan

SAN FRANCISCO 49ERS

FOUNDED: 1946

Super Bowl Titles: 5

Last Title Won: Super Bowl XXIX

Big Star: Wide receiver Jerry Rice, NFL's all-time leader in TDs (208), receptions (1,549), and receiving yards (22,895)

PHILADELPHIA EAGLES

FOUNDED: 1933

Super Bowl Titles: 0

Big Star: Quarterback Donovan McNabb, six-time Pro Bowler

SEATTLE SEAHAWKS

FOUNDED: 1976

Super Bowl Titles: 1

Last Title Won: Super Bowl XLVIII

Big Star: Including the playoffs, quarterback Russell Wilson has won more games in his first three seasons (42) than any QB in NFL history

TAMPA BAY BUCCANEERS

FOUNDED: 1976

Super Bowl Titles: 1

Last Title Won: Super Bowl XXXVII

Big Star: Linebacker Derrick Brooks, scored four defensive touchdowns and won Defensive Player of the Year and a Super Bowl in the 2002 season

WASHINGTON REDSKINS

FOUNDED: 1932
(as the Boston Braves)

Super Bowl Titles: 3

Last Title Won: Super Bowl XXVI

Big Star: Cornerback Darrell Green, seven-time Pro Bowler and the Redskins' leader in career interceptions (54)

ATLANTA HAWKS

FOUNDED: 1946
(as the Tri-Cities Blackhawks)

NBA Titles: 1

Last Title Won: 1958

Big Star: Forward Dominique Wilkins, nine-time All-Star and two-time slam dunk champion

BOSTON CELTICS

FOUNDED: 1946

NBA Titles: 17

Last Title Won: 2008

Big Star: Center Bill Russell, 11-time NBA champion and five-time MVP

BROOKLYN NETS

FOUNDED: 1967
(as the New Jersey Americans of the ABA)

NBA Titles: 0

Big Star: Center Brook Lopez, 2013 All-Star and member of the 2009 NBA All-Rookie first team

CHARLOTTE HORNETS

FOUNDED: 1988

NBA Titles: 0

Big Star: Point guard Muggsy Bogues, shortest player in NBA history (5'3")

CHICAGO BULLS

FOUNDED: 1966

NBA Titles: 6

Last Title Won: 1998

Big Star: Michael Jordan, NBA's all-time scoring leader (30.1 points per game) and holds the record for Finals MVP awards (six)

CLEVELAND CAVALIERS

FOUNDED: 1970

NBA Titles: 0

Big Star: Forward **LeBron James**, four-time NBA MVP, two-time Finals MVP, and the all-time scoring leader among active players (27.3 points per game through 2014–15 season)

Guard Michael Jordan

Point guard Isiah Thomas

DETROIT PISTONS

FOUNDED: 1948 (as the Fort Wayne Pistons of the BAA)

NBA Titles: 3

Last Title Won: 2004

Big Star: Point guard **Isiah Thomas**, 1990 Finals MVP

INDIANA PACERS

FOUNDED: 1967

NBA Titles: 0

Big Star: Guard Reggie Miller, Pacers' all-time leader in points (25,279), assists (4,141), and steals (1,505)

MIAMI HEAT

FOUNDED: 1988

NBA Titles: 3

Last Title Won: 2013

Big Star: Guard Dwyane Wade, three-time NBA champion and 2006 Finals MVP

Forward LeBron James

MILWAUKEE BUCKS

FOUNDED: 1968

NBA Titles: 1

Last Title Won: 1971

Big Star: Guard Sidney Moncrief, two-time NBA defensive player of the year

NEW YORK KNICKS

FOUNDED: 1946

NBA Titles: 2

Last Title Won: 1973

Big Star: Center Patrick Ewing, 11-time All-Star and two-time Olympic gold medalist

ORLANDO MAGIC

FOUNDED: 1989

NBA Titles: 0

Big Star: Center Shaquille O'Neal, 1992–93 Rookie of the Year and 15-time All-Star

PHILADELPHIA 76ERS

FOUNDED: 1949
(as the Syracuse Nationals)

NBA Titles: 3

Last Title Won: 1983

Big Star: Guard Allen Iverson, 2000–01 NBA MVP, led the league in steals per game three years in a row (2000–01 to 2002–03)

TORONTO RAPTORS

FOUNDED: 1995

NBA Titles: 0

Big Star: Guard-forward Vince Carter, eight-time All-Star

Point guard John Wall

WASHINGTON WIZARDS

FOUNDED: 1961 (as the Chicago Packers)

NBA Titles: 1

Last Title Won: 1978

Big Star: Point guard **John Wall**, the last rookie to average more than 15 points and eight assists per game

Western Conference

DALLAS MAVERICKS

FOUNDED: 1980

NBA Titles: 1

Last Title: 2011

Big Star: Forward **Dirk Nowitzki**, 2006–07 MVP and the 2010–11 Finals MVP

GOLDEN STATE WARRIORS

FOUNDED: 1946 (as the Philadelphia Warriors)

NBA Titles: 4

Last Title Won: 2015

Big Star: Point guard **Stephen Curry**, broke his own NBA record for three-pointers made in a season in 2015–16.

Point guard Stephen Curry

Forward Dirk Nowitzki

DENVER NUGGETS

FOUNDED: 1967

NBA Titles: 0

Big Star: Forward Alex English, eight-time All-Star and the Nuggets' all-time leader in points (21,645)

HOUSTON ROCKETS

FOUNDED: 1967
(as the San Diego Rockets)

NBA Titles: 2

Last Title: 1995

Big Star: Center Hakeem Olajuwon, won MVP, Defensive Player of the Year and Finals MVP in 1993–94

LOS ANGELES CLIPPERS

FOUNDED: 1970

NBA Titles: 0

Big Star: Forward Blake Griffin, five-time All-Star and 2010–11 Rookie of the Year

LOS ANGELES LAKERS

FOUNDED: 1947
(as the Minneapolis Lakers)

NBA Titles: 16

Last Title Won: 2010

Big Star: Point guard Magic Johnson, five-time NBA champion and three-time Finals MVP

MEMPHIS GRIZZLIES

FOUNDED: 1995
(as the Vancouver Grizzlies)

NBA Titles: 0

Big Star: Forward Marc Gasol, 2012–13 NBA Defensive Player of the Year and 2014–15 All-NBA first team

MINNESOTA TIMBERWOLVES

FOUNDED: 1989

NBA Titles: 0

Big Star: Forward Kevin Garnett, nine-time All-Defensive first team

Center Anthony Davis

NEW ORLEANS PELICANS

FOUNDED: 2002

NBA Titles: 0

Big Star: Center **Anthony Davis**, two-time NBA leader in blocks per game (2.8 in 2013–14 and 2.9 in 2014–15).

OKLAHOMA CITY THUNDER

FOUNDED: 1967
(as the Seattle Super Sonics)

NBA Titles: 1

Last Title Won: 1979

Big Star: Forward Kevin Durant, 2013–14 NBA scoring leader (32.0 points per game) and 2013–14 MVP

PHOENIX SUNS

FOUNDED: 1968

NBA Titles: 0

Big Star: Point guard **Steve Nash**, back-to-back MVP (2004–05 and 2005–06)

Point guard Steve Nash

PORTLAND TRAIL BLAZERS

FOUNDED: 1970

NBA Titles: 1

Last Title Won: 1977

Big Star: Guard Clyde Drexler, 10-time All-Star and Trail Blazers' all-time leader in points (18,040)

SACRAMENTO KINGS

FOUNDED: 1945
(as the Rochester Royals)

NBA Titles: 1

Last Title Won: 1951

Big Star: Point guard Oscar Robertson, only player in NBA history to average a triple-double in a season

Center-forward Tim Duncan

SAN ANTONIO SPURS

FOUNDED: 1967

NBA Titles: 5

Last Title Won: 2014

Big Star: Center-forward **Tim Duncan**, three-time Finals MVP

UTAH JAZZ

FOUNDED: 1974

NBA Titles: 0

Big Star: Point guard John Stockton, all-time leader in assists (15,806)

ATLANTA DREAM

FOUNDED: 2008

WNBA Titles: 0

Big Star: Guard-forward Angel McCoughtry, four-time All-Star and two-time WNBA Peak Performer in scoring (2012 and '13)

CHICAGO SKY

FOUNDED: 2006

WNBA Titles: 0

Big Star: Guard-forward Elena Delle Donne, 2015 MVP and three-time All-Star

CONNECTICUT SUN

FOUNDED: 1999

WNBA Titles: 0

Big Star: Forward Chiney Ogwumike, 2014 first overall pick of the WNBA draft and Rookie of the Year

NEW YORK LIBERTY

FOUNDED: 1997

WNBA Titles: 0

Big Star: Guard Teresa Weatherspoon, two-time WNBA Defensive Player of the Year and four-time All-Star

WASHINGTON MYSTICS

FOUNDED: 1998

WNBA Titles: 0

Big Star: Forward Chamique Holdsclaw, six-time All-Star and set the WNBA record for rebounds in a game (24 in 2003).

INDIANA FEVER

FOUNDED: 2000

WNBA Titles: 1

Last Title Won: 2012

Big Star: Forward **Tamika Catchings**, five-time WNBA Defensive Player of the Year, 2011 MVP, and 2012 Finals MVP

Forward Tamika Catchings

PHOENIX MERCURY

FOUNDED: 1997

WNBA Titles: 3

Last Title Won: 2014

Big Star: Guard **Diana Taurasi**, active leader in career scoring average (20.1 points per game), 2009 MVP, and two-time Finals MVP

Guard Diana Taurasi

Western Conference

SAN ANTONIO STARS

FOUNDED: 1997

WNBA Titles: 0

Big Star: Guard Becky Hammon, six-time All-Star

LOS ANGELES SPARKS

FOUNDED: 1997

WNBA Titles: 2

Last Title Won: 2002

Big Star: Center Lisa Leslie, three-time MVP and the first WNBA player to dunk in a game (in 2002)

SEATTLE STORM

FOUNDED: 2000

WNBA Titles: 2

Last Title Won: 2010

Big Star: Forward-center Lauren Jackson, three-time MVP and 2010 Finals MVP

MINNESOTA LYNX

FOUNDED: 1999

WNBA Titles: 3

Last Title Won: 2015

Big Star: Forward Maya Moore, 2013 Finals MVP, 2014 MVP, and 2014 WNBA Peak Performer in scoring (23.9 points per game).

TULSA SHOCK

FOUNDED: 1998

WNBA Titles: 3

Last Title Won: 2008

Big Star: Guard Riquna Williams, first player in WNBA history to score 50 points in a game

Defenseman Seth Jones

BOSTON BRUINS

FOUNDED: 1924

Stanley Cup Titles: 6

Last Cup Won: 2011

Big Star: Defenseman Bobby Orr, the only blueliner to lead the NHL in scoring (120 points in 1969–70 and 135 in 1974–75)

COLUMBUS BLUE JACKETS

FOUNDED: 2000

Stanley Cup Titles: 0

Big Star: Defenseman **Seth Jones**, fourth overall pick of the 2013 NHL draft.

BUFFALO SABRES

FOUNDED: 1970

Stanley Cup Titles: 0

Big Star: Center Gilbert Perreault, franchise leader in points (1,326)

DETROIT RED WINGS

FOUNDED: 1926

Stanley Cup Titles: 11

Last Cup Won: 2008

Big Star: Right wing **Gordie Howe**, most games played in NHL history (1,767)

CAROLINA HURRICANES

FOUNDED: 1979
(as the Hartford Whalers)

Stanley Cup Titles: 1

Last Cup Won: 2006

Big Star: Center Ron Francis, second in career assists (1,249)

Right wing Gordie Howe

MONTREAL CANADIENS

FOUNDED: 1917

Stanley Cup Titles: 24
Last Cup Won: 1993
Big Star: Right wing Maurice Richard, winner of eight Stanley Cups and first player to score 50 goals in a season

NEW JERSEY DEVILS

FOUNDED: 1974 (as the Kansas City Scouts)

Stanley Cup Titles: 3
Last Cup Won: 2003
Big Star: Goalie **Martin Brodeur**, four-time Vezina Trophy winner (2003, '04, '07, '08)

Goalie Martin Brodeur

NEW YORK ISLANDERS

FOUNDED: 1972

Stanley Cup Titles: 4
Last Cup Won: 1983
Big Star: Right wing Mike Bossy, holds mark for most consecutive 50-goal seasons (nine)

FLORIDA PANTHERS

FOUNDED: 1993

Stanley Cup Titles: 0
Big Star: Center Olli Jokinen, Panthers captain (2003–04 to '07–08) and franchise leader in goals (188) and points (419)

NEW YORK RANGERS

FOUNDED: 1926

Stanley Cup Titles: 4
Last Cup Won: 1994
Big Star: Center Mark Messier, captain of the 1994 Stanley Cup team and second in the NHL in career points (1,887)

OTTAWA SENATORS

FOUNDED: 1992

Stanley Cup Titles: 0

Big Star: Right wing Daniel Alfredsson, franchise leader in goals (426), assists (682), and points (1,108)

PHILADELPHIA FLYERS

FOUNDED: 1967

Stanley Cup Titles: 2

Last Cup Won: 1975

Big Star: Center Bobby Clarke, three-time Hart Trophy winner and franchise leader in assists (852) and points (1,210)

PITTSBURGH PENGUINS

FOUNDED: 1967

Stanley Cup Titles: 3

Last Cup Won: 2009

Big Star: Center Mario Lemieux, second all-time in points per game (1.88)

TAMPA BAY LIGHTNING

FOUNDED: 1992

Stanley Cup Titles: 1

Last Cup Won: 2004

Big Star: Right wing Martin St. Louis, franchise leader in assists (588) and points (953) and Hart Trophy winner in 2003–04

TORONTO MAPLE LEAFS

FOUNDED: 1917

Stanley Cup Titles: 13

Last Cup Won: 1967

Big Star: Defenseman Tim Horton, winner of four Stanley Cups

WASHINGTON CAPITALS

FOUNDED: 1974

Stanley Cup Titles: 0

Famous Player: Left wing **Alexander Ovechkin**, Capitals' leader in goals and points, and three-time Hart Trophy winner (2008, '09, '13)

Center Jonathan Toews

Western Conference

ANAHEIM DUCKS

FOUNDED: 1993

Stanley Cup Titles: 1
Last Cup Won: 2007
Big Star: Right wing Teemu Selanne, 10-time All-Star and ranked 11th on all time goals list (684)

ARIZONA COYOTES

FOUNDED: 1979
(as the Winnipeg Jets)

Stanley Cup Titles: 0
Big Star: Right wing Shane Doan, franchise leader in games played

CALGARY FLAMES

FOUNDED: 1972

Stanley Cup Titles: 1
Last Cup Won: 1989
Big Star: Right wing Jarome Iginla, had 11-straight 30-goal seasons

CHICAGO BLACKHAWKS
FOUNDED: 1926
Stanley Cup Titles: 6
Last Cup Won: 2015
Big Star: Center **Jonathan Toews**, has won a Stanley Cup and gold medals in the Olympics and World Championships

COLORADO AVALANCHE

FOUNDED: 1979
(as the Quebec Nordiques)

Stanley Cup Titles: 2
Last Cup Won: 2001
Big Star: Goalie **Patrick Roy**, three-time Conn Smythe (1986, '93, 2001) and Vezina (1989, '90, '92) winner

Goalie Patrick Roy

DALLAS STARS

FOUNDED: 1967
(as the Minnesota North Stars)

Stanley Cup Titles: 1
Last Cup Won: 1999
Big Star: Center Mike Modano, has the most career goals (561) and points (1,374) for an American-born player

Center Wayne Gretzky

EDMONTON OILERS

FOUNDED: 1979

Stanley Cup Titles: 5
Last Cup Won: 1990
Big Star: Center **Wayne Gretzky**, career leader in goals (894) and assists (1,963)

MINNESOTA WILD

FOUNDED: 2000

Stanley Cup Titles: 0
Big Star: Center Mikko Koivu, franchise leader in assists and points

NASHVILLE PREDATORS

FOUNDED: 1998

Stanley Cup Titles: 0
Big Star: Defenseman Shea Weber, Olympic gold medalist; has the most points for a blueliner in franchise history

Goalie Jonathan Quick

LOS ANGELES KINGS

FOUNDED: 1967

Stanley Cup Titles: 2
Last Cup Won: 2014
Big Star: Goalie **Jonathan Quick**, Conn Smythe Trophy winner in 2011–12

Left wing Patrick Marleau

ST. LOUIS BLUES

FOUNDED: 1967

Stanley Cup Titles: 0

Big Star: Right wing Brett Hull, Hart Trophy winner (1990–91) and one of five players to score 50 goals in 50 games

VANCOUVER CANUCKS

FOUNDED: 1970

Stanley Cup Titles: 0

Big Star: Center Henrik Sedin, winner of the Hart and Art Ross (for most points in a season) trophies in 2009–10

SAN JOSE SHARKS

FOUNDED: 1991

Stanley Cup Titles: 0

Big Star: Left wing **Patrick Marleau**, franchise leader in goals and points

WINNIPEG JETS

FOUNDED: 1999
(as the Atlanta Thrashers)

Stanley Cup Titles: 0

Big Star: Left wing Ilya Kovalchuk, franchise leader in goals (328), assists (287) and points (615)

Jordan Spieth

Major Tournaments

MASTERS TOURNAMENT

FIRST PLAYED: 1934

Played In: April
Location: Augusta National Golf Club in Georgia (U.S.)
2017 Tournament: April 6–9
Most championships: Jack Nicklaus (6)
Best score (to par): -18 by Tiger Woods (1997) and **Jordan Spieth** (2015)

U.S. OPEN

FIRST PLAYED: 1895

Played In: June
Location: Various U.S. locations
2017 Tournament: June 15–18 (Erin Hills in Erin, Wisc.)
Most championships: Jack Nicklaus, Ben Hogan, Bobby Jones, Willie Anderson (4 each)
Best score (to par): -16 by Rory McIlroy (2011)

THE BRITISH OPEN

FIRST PLAYED: 1860

Played In: July
Location: United Kingdom (England, Scotland, Northern Ireland)
2017 Tournament: July 20–23 (Royal Birkdale Golf Club in Southport, England)
Most championships: Harry Vardon (6)
Best score (to par): -19 by Tiger Woods (2000)

PGA CHAMPIONSHIP

FIRST PLAYED: 1916

Played In: August
Location: Various U.S. locations
2017 Tournament: August 17–20 (Quail Hollow Club in Charlotte, NC)
Most championships: Jack Nicklaus, Walter Hagen (5 each)
Best score (to par): -20 by Jason Day (2015)

Grand Slam Tournaments

Serena Williams

FRENCH OPEN
FIRST PLAYED: 1891

Surface: Clay
Played in: May/June
Location: Roland Garros Stadium (Paris, France)
Most Open Era women's singles championships: Chris Evert (7)
Most Open Era men's singles championships: Rafael Nadal (9)

WIMBLEDON
FIRST PLAYED: 1877

Surface: Grass
Played In: June/July
Location: All England Lawn Tennis and Croquet Club (London, England)
Most Open Era ladies' singles championships:
Martina Navratilova (9)
Most Open Era gentlemen's singles championships: Pete Sampras and Roger Federer (7 each)

U.S. OPEN
FIRST PLAYED: 1881

Surface: Hardcourt
Played In: August/September
Location: USTA Billie Jean King National Tennis Center (Flushing, NY, United States)
Most Open Era women's singles championships: Chris Evert and Serena Williams (6 each)
Most Open Era men's singles championships: Jimmy Connors, Pete Sampras, and Roger Federer (5 each)

AUSTRALIAN OPEN
FIRST PLAYED: 1905

Surface: Hardcourt
Played In: January
Location: Melbourne Park (Melbourne, Australia)
Most Open Era women's singles championships: Serena Williams (6)
Most Open Era men's singles championships: Novak Djokovic (5)

FIFA Men's World Cup

Pelé of Brazil

1930
Host: Uruguay
Final: Uruguay beats Argentina, 4–2

1934
Host: Italy
Final: Italy beats Czechoslovakia, 2–1 (Extra Time)

1938
Host: France
Final: Italy beats Hungary, 4–2

1950
Host: Brazil
Final: Uruguay beats Brazil, 2–1

1954
Host: Switzerland
Final: West Germany beats Hungary, 3–2

1958
Host: Sweden
Final: Brazil beats Sweden, 5–2

1962
Host: Chile
Final: Brazil beats Czechoslovakia, 3–1
Golden Ball Winner: Garrincha, Brazil

1966
Host: England
Final: England beats West Germany, 4–2 (Extra Time)
Golden Ball Winner: Bobby Charlton, England

1970
Host: Mexico
Final: Brazil beats Italy, 4–1
Golden Ball Winner: Pelé, Brazil

1974
Host: West Germany
Final: West Germany beats Netherlands, 2–1
Golden Ball Winner: Johan Cruyff, Netherlands

1978
Host: Argentina
Final: Argentina beats Netherlands, 3–1 (Extra Time)
Golden Ball Winner: Mario Kempes, Argentina

1982
Host: Spain
Final: Italy beats West Germany, 3–1
Golden Ball Winner: Paolo Rossi, Italy

Bobby Charlton of England

Diego Maradona of Argentina

1986

Host: Mexico
Final: Argentina beats West Germany, 3–2
Golden Ball Winner: Diego Maradona, Argentina

1990

Host: Italy
Final: West Germany beats Argentina, 1–0
Golden Ball Winner: Salvatore Schillaci, Italy

1994

Host: United States
Final: Brazil beats Italy, 0–0 (Penalty Kicks)
Golden Ball Winner: Romário, Brazil Brazil

1998

Host: France
Final: France beats Brazil, 3–0
Golden Ball Winner: Ronaldo, Brazil

2002

Host: South Korea & Japan
Final: Brazil beats Germany, 2–0
Golden Ball Winner: Oliver Kahn, Germany

2006

Host: Germany
Final: Italy beats France, 1–1 (Penalty Kicks)
Golden Ball Winner: Zinedine Zidane, France

2010

Host: South Africa
Final: Spain beats Netherlands, 1–0 (Extra Time)
Golden Ball Winner: Diego Forlán, Uruguay

2014

Host: Brazil
Final: Germany beats Argentina, 1–0 (Extra Time)
Golden Ball Winner: Lionel Messi, Argentina

Lionel Messi of Argentina

FIFA Women's World Cup

Carli Lloyd of the U.S.

1991
Host: China
Final: United States beats Norway, 2–1
Golden Ball Winner: Carin Jennings, United States

1995
Host: Sweden
Final: Norway beats Germany, 2–0
Golden Ball Winner: Hege Riise, Norway

1999
Host: United States
Final: United States beats China, 0–0 (Penalty Kicks)
Golden Ball Winner: Sun Wen, China

2003
Host: United States
Final: Germany beats Sweden, 2–1 (Extra Time)
Golden Ball Winner: Birgit Prinz, Germany

2007
Host: China
Final: Germany beats Brazil, 2–0
Golden Ball Winner: Marta, Brazil

2011
Host: Germany
Final: Japan beats United States, 2–2 (Penalty Kicks)
Golden Ball Winner: Homare Sawa, Japan

2015
Host: Canada
Final: United States beats Japan, 5–2
Golden Ball Winner: Carli Lloyd, United States

Marta of Brazil

Olympic Makeover

New rules could cut costs and add to the thrill of the games.

In 2012, London, England, hosted the Olympics.

Game on! The International Olympic Committee (IOC) says major changes are in store for the international sporting extravaganza. There will be added sports and events. In addition, the IOC hopes new rules will make the Summer and Winter Olympic Games less expensive to produce and more exciting for fans.

The changes were approved as part of a plan called Olympic Agenda 2020. Athletes, countries, and even the United Nations helped develop the rules, the biggest changes to the games in decades.

The IOC also says it will launch a digital channel to promote Olympic sporting events in the years between the games. "The channel will engage audiences, especially young audiences, in the power of what sport can do," says IOC president Thomas Bach.

Go for the Gold

The plan got past one big hurdle. The IOC has dropped the cap of 28 sports, which will allow new sporting events to be played in the Summer Games. This clears the way for Japan to ask that baseball and softball be

On Deck Softball may make a comeback in the 2020 Summer Games.

part of the 2020 Summer Olympics, in Tokyo. Both sports were dropped after the 2008 games, but are hugely popular in Japan.

Other sports, such as squash and karate, may be added, and existing sports could get new events. "We have to find a way to introduce new sports that are relevant to young people," John Coates, IOC's vice president, said in a statement.

The plan also allows for future games to be hosted by two cities or countries at once, as a way to reduce costs. Being a host nation comes at a high price. Bach pushed for the shake-up. "Now is the time for change," he said at a recent event. "We have to adapt to the modern world."

—*By Melanie Kletter*

Capitol Hill in Washington, D.C.

The United States

American Goldfinch

Alabama

- **Capital:** Montgomery
- **Largest City:** Birmingham
- **Postal Code:** AL
- **Land area:** 50,750 square miles (131,443 sq km)
- **Population (2014):** 4,849,377
- **Entered union (rank):** December 14, 1819 (22)
- **Motto:** Audemus jura nostra defendere. (We dare maintain our rights.)
- **Tree:** Southern longleaf pine
- **Flower:** Camellia
- **Bird: Yellowhammer**
- **Nicknames:** Yellowhammer State, Cotton State, Heart of Dixie
- **Famous Natives:** Rosa Parks, civil rights leader, Hank Williams, country singer and songwriter; Mia Hamm, soccer player; Bo Jackson, multi-sport athlete

Fun Fact: One of the most important moments in the American civil rights movement came when Rosa Parks, an African-American woman, refused to give up her seat in the front of the bus in Montgomery, Alabama. Her actions ushered in the Montgomery Bus Boycott and later helped end public segregation in the south.

Alaska

- **Capital:** Juneau
- **Largest City:** Anchorage
- **Postal Code:** AK
- **Land area:** 570,374 square miles (1,477,267 sq km)
- **Population (2013):** 736,732
- **Entered union (rank):** January 3, 1959 (49)
- **Motto:** North to the future.
- **Tree:** Sitka spruce
- **Flower: Forget-me-not**
- **Bird:** Willow ptarmigan
- **Nicknames:** The Last Frontier, Land of the Midnight Sun
- **Famous Natives:** Howard Rock, newspaper editor and activist; Jewel, singer and songwriter; Curt Schilling, baseball player

Fun Fact: Alaska is the only state in the country where the Northern Lights (also known as aurora borealis) are visible throughout the year. The natural phenomenon, which is caused by ions interacting with the magnetic force of the atmosphere, makes bright lights and patterns appear in the night sky.

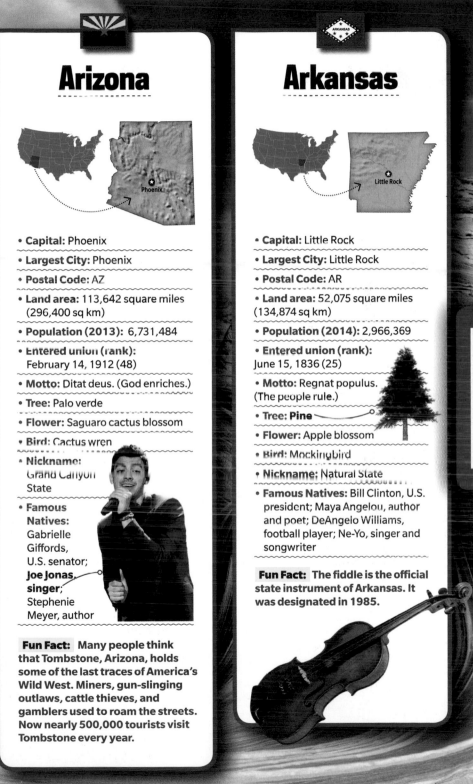

Arizona

- **Capital:** Phoenix
- **Largest City:** Phoenix
- **Postal Code:** AZ
- **Land area:** 113,642 square miles (296,400 sq km)
- **Population (2013):** 6,731,484
- **Entered union (rank):** February 14, 1912 (48)
- **Motto:** Ditat deus. (God enriches.)
- **Tree:** Palo verde
- **Flower:** Saguaro cactus blossom
- **Bird:** Cactus wren
- **Nickname:** Grand Canyon State
- **Famous Natives:** Gabrielle Giffords, U.S. senator; **Joe Jonas,** singer; Stephenie Meyer, author

Fun Fact: Many people think that Tombstone, Arizona, holds some of the last traces of America's Wild West. Miners, gun-slinging outlaws, cattle thieves, and gamblers used to roam the streets. Now nearly 500,000 tourists visit Tombstone every year.

Arkansas

- **Capital:** Little Rock
- **Largest City:** Little Rock
- **Postal Code:** AR
- **Land area:** 52,075 square miles (134,874 sq km)
- **Population (2014):** 2,966,369
- **Entered union (rank):** June 15, 1836 (25)
- **Motto:** Regnat populus. (The people rule.)
- **Tree:** Pine
- **Flower:** Apple blossom
- **Bird:** Mockingbird
- **Nickname:** Natural State
- **Famous Natives:** Bill Clinton, U.S. president; Maya Angelou, author and poet; DeAngelo Williams, football player; Ne-Yo, singer and songwriter

Fun Fact: The fiddle is the official state instrument of Arkansas. It was designated in 1985.

California

- **Capital:** Sacramento
- **Largest City:** Los Angeles
- **Postal Code:** CA
- **Land area:** 155,973 square miles (403,970 sq km)
- **Population (2014):** 38,802,500
- **Entered union (rank):** September 9, 1850 (31)
- **Motto:** Eureka! (I have found it!)
- **Tree:** California redwood
- **Flower:** Golden poppy
- **Bird:** California valley quail
- **Nicknames:** Golden State
- **Famous Natives:** Ronald Reagan, U.S. president; Sally Ride, astronaut; Steve Jobs, co-founder of Apple; Katy Perry, pop singer; Alex Morgan, U.S. women's national soccer team player; Adam Levine, musician

Fun Fact: California is home to both the highest point in the continental United States (Mt. Whitney, 14,495 feet) and the lowest (Death Valley, 282 feet below sea level). The two points are just 85 miles apart!

Colorado

- **Capital:** Denver
- **Largest City:** Denver
- **Postal Code:** CO
- **Land area:** 103,730 square miles (268,660 sq km)
- **Population (2014):** 5,355,866
- **Entered union (rank):** August 1, 1876 (38)
- **Motto:** Nil sine numine. (Nothing without the deity.)
- **Tree:** Colorado blue spruce
- **Flower:** Rocky Mountain columbine
- **Bird: Lark bunting**
- **Nicknames:** Centennial State
- **Famous Natives:** Dwight Eisenhower, U.S. president; Roy Halladay, baseball player; Amy Adams, actress

Fun Fact: A mesa is a flat-topped mountain. Grand Mesa, in Colorado, is the largest mesa in the world.

Connecticut

Hartford

Bridgeport

- **Capital:** Hartford
- **Largest City:** Bridgeport
- **Postal Code:** CT
- **Land area:** 5,018 square miles (12,997 sq km)
- **Population (2014):** 3,596,677
- **Entered union (rank):** January 9, 1788 (5)
- **Motto:** Qui transtulit sustinet. (He who transplanted still sustains.)
- **Tree:** White oak
- **Flower:** Mountain laurel
- **Bird:** American robin
- **Nicknames:** Constitution State, Nutmeg State
- **Famous Natives:** George W. Bush, U.S. president; P.T. Barnum, circus founder; **Joey Logano, race car driver**

Fun Fact: The oldest newspaper in the U.S. is Connecticut's *Hartford Courant*, which has been in print since 1764.

Delaware

Wilmington

Dover

- **Capital:** Dover
- **Largest City:** Wilmington
- **Postal Code:** DE
- **Land area:** 1,955 square miles (5,063 sq km)
- **Population (2014):** 935,614
- **Entered union (rank):** December 7, 1787 (1)
- **Motto:** Liberty and independence.
- **Tree:** American holly
- **Flower:** Peach blossom
- **Bird:** Blue hen chicken
- **Nicknames:** Diamond State, First State, Small Wonder
- **Famous Natives:** Henry Heimlich, doctor and inventor of the Heimlich maneuver; Joe Biden, U.S. vice president; Elena Delle Donne, basketball player

Fun Fact: Thanks to the efforts of a second grade classroom in Milford, Delaware, the ladybug was adopted as the official state bug of Delaware in 1974.

Florida

Jacksonville
★ Tallahassee

- **Capital:** Tallahassee
- **Largest City:** Jacksonville
- **Postal Code:** FL
- **Land area:** 53,927 square miles (139,670 sq km)
- **Population (2014):** 19,893,297
- **Entered union (rank):** March 3, 1845 (27)
- **Motto:** In God we trust.
- **Tree: Sabal palm (cabbage palmetto)**
- **Flower:** Orange blossom
- **Bird:** Mockingbird
- **Nickname:** Sunshine State
- **Famous Natives:** Zora Neale Hurston, author; Ariana Grande, singer and actress; Victoria Justice, actress

Fun Fact: Cape Canaveral, Florida, is home to NASA's Kennedy Space Center. Many famous missions have launched from Cape Canaveral, including the Apollo missions and the Space Shuttle program.

Georgia

★ Atlanta

- **Capital:** Atlanta
- **Largest City:** Atlanta
- **Postal Code:** GA
- **Land area:** 57,919 square miles (150,010 sq km)
- **Population (2014):** 10,097,343
- **Entered union (rank):** January 2, 1788 (4)
- **Motto:** Wisdom, justice, and moderation.
- **Tree:** Live oak
- **Flower:** Cherokee rose
- **Bird: Brown thrasher**
- **Nicknames:** Peach State, Empire State of the South
- **Famous Natives:** Martin Luther King Jr., civil rights activist; Jimmy Carter, U.S. president; Ray Charles, singer

Fun Fact: On the final Saturday of the annual Georgia Peach Festival, Peach County employees bake the "World's Largest Peach Cobbler." It takes about 90 pounds (40 kg) of butter to make the 11 by 5 foot (3.4 by 1.5 m) dessert.

Hawaii

Honolulu

PACIFIC OCEAN

- **Capital:** Honolulu (on the island of Oahu)
- **Largest City:** Honolulu
- **Postal Code:** HI
- **Land area:** 6,423 square miles (16,636 sq km)
- **Population (2014):** 1,419,561
- **Entered union (rank):** August 21, 1959 (50)
- **Motto:** Ua mau ke ea o ka aina i ka pono. (The life of the land is perpetuated in righteousness.)
- **Tree:** Kuku'i (candlenut)
- **Flower:** Yellow hibiscus
- **Bird:** Nene (Hawaiian goose)
- **Nickname:** Aloha State
- **Famous Natives:** Bethany Hamilton, professional surfer; Bruno Mars, musician; **Barack Obama, U.S. president**

Fun Fact: There are no skyscrapers or towers on the Hawaiian island of Kauai. In fact, no building can be constructed that is taller than a palm tree.

Idaho

Boise

- **Capital:** Boise
- **Largest City:** Boise
- **Postal Code:** ID
- **Land area:** 82,751 square miles (214,325 sq km)
- **Population (2014):** 1,634,464
- **Entered union (rank):** July 3, 1890 (43)
- **Motto:** Esto perpetua. (Let it be perpetual.)
- **Tree:** Western white pine
- **Flower:** Syringa
- **Bird:** Mountain bluebird
- **Nickname:** Gem State
- **Famous Natives:** Gutzon Borglum, Mount Rushmore sculptor; Picabo Street, skier

Fun Fact: Idaho's mountains are full of minerals. Alongside these minerals are some rare and beautiful gemstones, including star garnet (the official state gem), opal, zircon, and jade.

Illinois

- **Capital:** Springfield
- **Largest City:** Chicago
- **Postal Code:** IL
- **Land area:** 55,593 square miles (143,986 sq km)
- **Population (2014):** 12,880,580
- **Entered union (rank):** December 3, 1818 (21)
- **Motto:** State sovereignty, national union
- **Tree:** White oak
- **Flower:** Purple violet
- **Bird:** Cardinal
- **Nicknames:** Prairie State, Land of Lincoln
- **Famous Natives:** Michelle Obama, First Lady; Carol Moseley Braun, first African-American female U.S. senator; **Anthony Davis, basketball player**

Fun Fact: Each year, a local plumber's union in Chicago, Illinois, temporarily dyes the Chicago River bright green to celebrate the city's St. Patrick's Day parade.

Indiana

- **Capital:** Indianapolis
- **Largest City:** Indianapolis
- **Postal Code:** IN
- **Land area:** 35,870 square miles (92,903 sq km)
- **Population (2014):** 6,596,855
- **Entered union (rank):** December 11, 1816 (19)
- **Motto:** The crossroads of America
- **Tree:** Tulip tree (yellow poplar)
- **Flower:** Peony
- **Bird:** Cardinal
- **Nicknames:** Hoosier State, Crossroads of America
- **Famous Natives:** Madam C.J. Walker, entrepreneur; Michael Jackson, pop singer; Larry Bird, basketball player; DaMarcus Beasley, soccer player; John Green, author

Fun Fact: One of Indiana's most historic sites is the Levi Coffin Home, which was an important stop on the Underground Railroad. More than 2,000 escaped slaves stayed in the home on their way to Canada.

Iowa

- **Capital:** Des Moines
- **Largest City:** Des Moines
- **Postal Code:** IA
- **Land area:** 55,875 square miles (144,716 sq km)
- **Population (2014):** 3,107,126
- **Entered union (rank):** December 28, 1846 (29)
- **Motto:** Our liberties we prize, and our rights we will maintain.
- **Tree:** Oak
- **Flower:** Wild prairie rose
- **Bird:** Eastern goldfinch (American goldfinch)
- **Nickname:** Hawkeye State
- **Famous Natives:** Amelia Earhart, aviator; Shawn Johnson, gymnast; Lolo Jones, track and field and bobsled athlete; Ashton Kutcher, actor

Fun Fact: Iowa is the only state bordered to the east and west by parallel rivers. The Mississippi River is on Iowa's eastern border, and the Missouri River is to the west.

Kansas

- **Capital:** Topeka
- **Largest City:** Wichita
- **Postal Code:** KS
- **Land area:** 81,823 square miles (211,922 sq km)
- **Population (2014):** 2,904,021
- **Entered union (rank):** January 29, 1861 (34)
- **Motto:** Ad astra per aspera (To the stars through difficulties)
- **Tree:** Cottonwood
- **Flower:** Sunflower
- **Bird:** Western meadowlark
- **Nicknames:** Sunflower State, Jayhawk State, Wheat State
- **Famous Natives:** Langston Hughes, author and poet; Janelle Monae, R&B and soul musician; Barry Sanders, football player

Fun Fact: With an average wind speed of 13.9 miles per hour, Dodge City, Kansas, is the windiest city in the United States.

UNITED STATES

Kentucky

Louisville

★ Frankfort

- **Capital:** Frankfort
- **Largest City:** Louisville
- **Postal Code:** KY
- **Land area:** 39,732 square miles (102,906 sq km)
- **Population (2014):** 4,413,457
- **Entered union (rank):** June 1, 1792 (15)
- **Motto:** United we stand, divided we fall.
- **Tree:** Tulip poplar
- **Flower:** Goldenrod
- **Bird: Cardinal**
- **Nickname:** Bluegrass State
- **Famous Natives:** Jennifer Lawrence, actress; George Clooney, actor; Garrett A. Morgan, inventor of the traffic light and the gas mask; Muhammad Ali, boxer

Fun Fact: Fort Knox, Kentucky, is home to the United States Bullion Depository, where the treasury keeps its supply of gold, as well as other precious items belonging to or entrusted to the federal government.

Louisiana

Baton Rouge ★

New Orleans

- **Capital:** Baton Rouge
- **Largest City:** New Orleans
- **Postal Code:** LA
- **Land area:** 43,566 square miles (112,836 sq km)
- **Population (2014):** 4,649,676
- **Entered union (rank):** April 30, 1812 (18)
- **Motto:** Union, justice, and confidence
- **Tree:** Bald cypress
- **Flower:** Magnolia
- **Bird:** Eastern brown pelican
- **Nickname:** Pelican State
- **Famous Natives:** **Peyton Manning, football player;** Louis Armstrong, musician; Ellen DeGeneres, talk show host; Hunter Hayes, country singer

Fun Fact: The country's largest Mardi Gras celebration is held each February in New Orleans, Louisiana, and features a parade of music and pageantry. The holiday comes from an ancient custom of food and fun before Lent, a Catholic time of prayer and sacrifice.

Maine

- **Capital:** Augusta
- **Largest City:** Portland
- **Postal Code:** ME
- **Land area:** 30,865 square miles (79,940 sq km)
- **Population (2014):** 1,330,089
- **Entered union (rank):** March 15, 1820 (23)
- **Motto:** Dirigo. (I lead.)
- **Tree:** **White pine**
- **Flower:** White pine cone and tassel
- **Bird:** Black-capped chickadee
- **Nickname:** Pine Tree State
- **Famous Natives:** Henry Wadsworth Longfellow, author and poet; Anna Kendrick, actress; Stephen King, author

Fun Fact: Maine is the largest state in New England. It is about the same size as the other five states (Connecticut, Massachusetts, New Hampshire, Rhode Island, and Vermont) combined.

Maryland

- **Capital:** Annapolis
- **Largest City:** Baltimore
- **Postal Code:** MD
- **Land area:** 9,775 square miles (25,317 sq km)
- **Population (2014):** 5,976,407
- **Entered union (rank):** April 28, 1788 (7)
- **Motto:** Fatti maschii, parole femine (Manly deeds, womanly words)
- **Tree:** White oak
- **Flower:** Black-eyed Susan
- **Bird:** Baltimore oriole
- **Nicknames:** Free State, Old Line State
- **Famous Natives:** Michael Phelps, swimmer and Olympic gold medalist; Francis Scott Key, composer of the national anthem; Kevin Durant, basketball player

Fun Fact: The state sport of Maryland is jousting. Once enjoyed by medieval knights, jousting involves two contestants, mounted on horses, charging each other and attempting to dismount each other with a lance.

Massachusetts

- **Capital:** Boston
- **Largest City:** Boston
- **Postal Code:** MA
- **Land area:** 7,838 square miles (20,300 sq km)
- **Population (2014):** 6,745,408
- **Entered union (rank):** February 6, 1788 (6)
- **Motto:** Ense petit placidam sub libertate quietem. (By the sword we seek peace, but peace only under liberty.)
- **Tree:** American elm
- **Flower:** Mayflower
- **Bird:** Black-capped chickadee
- **Nicknames:** Bay State, Old Colony State, Baked Bean State
- **Famous Natives:** Benjamin Franklin, inventor and statesman; Theodor Geisel (Dr. Seuss), author; **Chris Evans, actor**

Fun Fact: The Boston terrier was designated the official state dog of Massachusetts in 1979. A combination of an English bulldog and an English terrier, the Boston terrier was the first purebred dog developed in America.

Michigan

- **Capital:** Lansing
- **Largest City:** Detroit
- **Postal Code:** MI
- **Land area:** 56,809 square miles (147,135 sq km)
- **Population (2014):** 9,909,877
- **Entered union (rank):** January 26, 1837 (26)
- **Motto:** Si quaeris peninsulam amoenam circumspice. (If you seek a pleasant peninsula, look about you.)
- **Tree:** White pine
- **Flower:** Apple blossom
- **Bird:** American robin
- **Nicknames:** Wolverine State, Great Lakes State
- **Famous Natives:** Henry Ford, automaker, Taylor Lautner, actor; Magic Johnson, basketball player; Kristen Bell, actress

Fun Fact: Michigan Stadium, the home of the University of Michigan Wolverines football team, is the largest football stadium in the United States. Often called "The Big House," the stadium can fit 109,901 people inside.

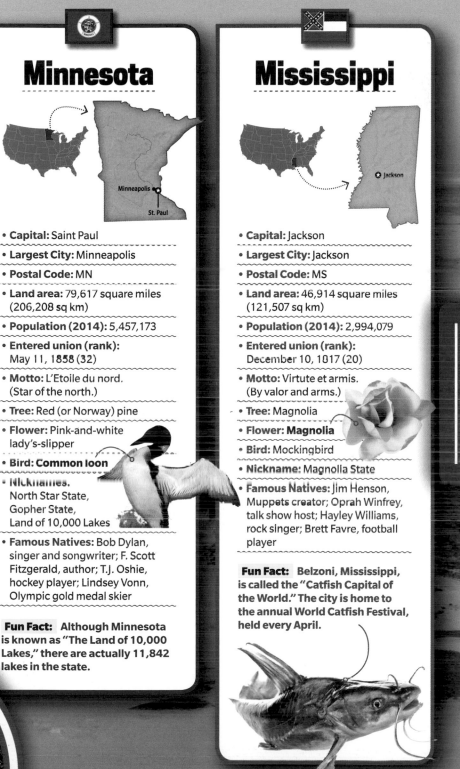

Minnesota

- **Capital:** Saint Paul
- **Largest City:** Minneapolis
- **Postal Code:** MN
- **Land area:** 79,617 square miles (206,208 sq km)
- **Population (2014):** 5,457,173
- **Entered union (rank):** May 11, 1858 (32)
- **Motto:** L'Etoile du nord. (Star of the north.)
- **Tree:** Red (or Norway) pine
- **Flower:** Pink-and-white lady's-slipper
- **Bird: Common loon**
- **Nicknames:** North Star State, Gopher State, Land of 10,000 Lakes
- **Famous Natives:** Bob Dylan, singer and songwriter; F. Scott Fitzgerald, author; T.J. Oshie, hockey player; Lindsey Vonn, Olympic gold medal skier

Fun Fact: Although Minnesota is known as "The Land of 10,000 Lakes," there are actually 11,842 lakes in the state.

Mississippi

- **Capital:** Jackson
- **Largest City:** Jackson
- **Postal Code:** MS
- **Land area:** 46,914 square miles (121,507 sq km)
- **Population (2014):** 2,994,079
- **Entered union (rank):** December 10, 1817 (20)
- **Motto:** Virtute et armis. (By valor and arms.)
- **Tree:** Magnolia
- **Flower: Magnolia**
- **Bird:** Mockingbird
- **Nickname:** Magnolia State
- **Famous Natives:** Jim Henson, Muppets creator; Oprah Winfrey, talk show host; Hayley Williams, rock singer; Brett Favre, football player

Fun Fact: Belzoni, Mississippi, is called the "Catfish Capital of the World." The city is home to the annual World Catfish Festival, held every April.

Missouri

- **Capital:** Jefferson City
- **Largest City:** Kansas City
- **Postal Code:** MO
- **Land area:** 68,898 square miles (178,446 sq km)
- **Population (2014):** 6,063,589
- **Entered union (rank):** August 10, 1821 (24)
- **Motto:** Salus populi suprema lex esto. (The welfare of the people shall be the supreme law.)
- **Tree:** Flowering dogwood
- **Flower:** Hawthorn
- **Bird:** Bluebird
- **Nickname:** Show Me State
- **Famous Natives:** **Mark Twain**, author; Tennessee Williams, playwright; Walter Cronkite, journalist

Fun Fact: Missouri's state rock is mozarkite. It comes in many colors, including red, pink, purple, green, gray, and brown.

Montana

- **Capital:** Helena
- **Largest City:** Billings
- **Postal Code:** MT
- **Land area:** 145,556 square miles (376,990 sq km)
- **Population (2014):** 1,023,579
- **Entered union (rank):** November 8, 1889 (41)
- **Motto:** Oro y plata. (Gold and silver.)
- **Tree:** Ponderosa pine
- **Flower:** **Bitterroot**
- **Bird:** Western meadowlark
- **Nickname:** Treasure State
- **Famous Natives:** Phil Jackson, basketball coach; Gary Cooper, actor

Fun Fact: The state butterfly of Montana is the mourning cloak. Its name refers to the dark clothing people traditionally wear while in mourning, the period of sadness after the death of a loved one. These butterflies can often blend in with tree bark to hide from predators.

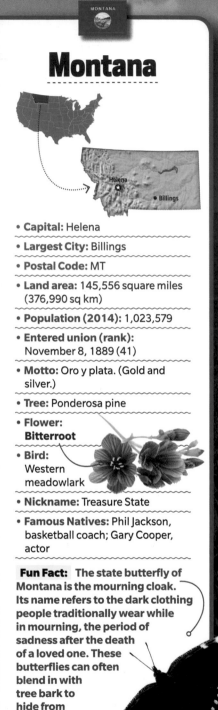

Nebraska

- **Capital:** Lincoln
- **Largest City:** Omaha
- **Postal Code:** NE
- **Land area:** 76,878 square miles (199,114 sq km)
- **Population (2014):** 1,881,503
- **Entered union (rank):** March 1, 1867 (37)
- **Motto:** Equality before the law.
- **Tree:** Eastern cottonwood
- **Flower:** Goldenrod
- **Bird:** **Western meadowlark**
- **Nicknames:** Cornhusker State, Beef State
- **Famous Natives:** Standing Bear, Native American civil rights advocate; Fred Astaire, dancer, singer and actor; Andy Roddick, tennis player; Nicholas Sparks, author

Fun Fact: In 1927, Kool-Aid was invented by Edwin Perkins in Hastings, Nebraska. The brand's mascot, Kool-Aid Man, has his footprints preserved in cement near Hasting's Visitors Center.

Nevada

- **Capital:** Carson City
- **Largest City:** Las Vegas
- **Postal Code:** NV
- **Land area:** 109,806 square miles (284,397 sq km)
- **Population (2014):** 2,839,099
- **Entered union (rank):** October 31, 1864 (36)
- **Motto:** All for our country.
- **Tree:** Single-leaf piñon pine
- **Flower:** Sagebrush
- **Bird:** Mountain bluebird
- **Nicknames:** Sagebrush State, Silver State, Battle Born State
- **Famous Natives:** Adam Hicks, author and singer; **Bryce Harper, baseball player;** DeMarco Murray, football player

Fun Fact: At the end of every summer, thousands of people gather at Nevada's Black Rock Desert for the Burning Man festival. They set up a temporary city and spend a week making music, art, and celebrating community. Then they pack up and go home, trying not to leave anything behind.

New Hampshire

- **Capital:** Concord
- **Largest City:** Manchester
- **Postal Code:** NH
- **Land area:** 8,969 square miles (23,230 sq km)
- **Population (2014):** 1,326,813
- **Entered union (Rank):** June 21, 1788 (9)
- **Motto:** Live free or die.
- **Tree: White birch (canoe birch or paper birch)**
- **Flower:** Purple lilac
- **Bird:** Purple finch
- **Nickname:** Granite State
- **Famous Natives:** Alan Shepard, astronaut; Bode Miller, skier and Olympic medalist; Seth Meyers, comedian

Fun Fact: New Hampshire has only 18 miles of coastline, the shortest amount for any ocean-touching U.S. state.

New Jersey

- **Capital:** Trenton
- **Largest City:** Newark
- **Postal Code:** NJ
- **Land area:** 7,419 square miles (19,215 sq km)
- **Population (2014):** 8,938,175
- **Entered union (rank):** December 18, 1787 (3)
- **Motto:** Liberty and prosperity.
- **Tree:** Red oak
- **Flower:** Common meadow violet
- **Bird:** Eastern goldfinch (American goldfinch)
- **Nickname:** Garden State
- **Famous Natives:** Buzz Aldrin, astronaut; **Mike Trout, baseball player**; Frank Sinatra, singer

Fun Fact: In 1870, the first boardwalk in the world was built along the beach in Atlantic City, New Jersey.

New Mexico

- **Capital:** Santa Fe
- **Largest City:** Albuquerque
- **Postal Code:** NM
- **Land area:** 121,365 square miles (314,335 sq km)
- **Population (2014):** 2,085,572
- **Entered union (rank):** January 6, 1912 (47)
- **Motto:** Crescit eundo. (It grows as it goes.)
- **Tree:** Piñon pine
- **Flower: Yucca**
- **Bird:** Roadrunner
- **Nicknames:** Land of Enchantment, Cactus State
- **Famous Natives:** Geronimo, Apache leader; Willow Shields, actress; Arian Foster, football player

Fun Fact: New Mexico's White Sands National Monument is actually not made from sand at all. The 275-square-mile (710 km) park is composed entirely of gypsum crystals.

New York

- **Capital:** Albany
- **Largest City:** New York City
- **Postal Code:** NY
- **Land area:** 47,224 square miles (122,310 sq km)
- **Population (2014):** 19,746,227
- **Entered union (rank):** July 26, 1788 (11)
- **Motto:** Excelsior. (Ever upward.)
- **Tree:** Sugar maple
- **Flower:** Rose
- **Bird: Bluebird**
- **Nickname:** Empire State
- **Famous Natives:** Franklin D. Roosevelt, U.S. president; Jonas Salk, researcher who discovered the polio vaccine; Jimmy Fallon, comedian; Lea Michelle, actress

Fun Fact: The first pizzeria in the United States is said to have opened in New York City in 1897.

North Carolina

- **Capital:** Raleigh
- **Largest City:** Charlotte
- **Postal Code:** NC
- **Land area:** 48,708 square miles (126,154 sq km)
- **Population (2014):** 9,943,964
- **Entered union (rank):** November 21, 1789 (12)
- **Motto:** Esse quam videri (To be rather than to seem)
- **Tree:** Pine
- **Flower:** Flowering dogwood
- **Bird:** Cardinal
- **Nickname:** Tar Heel State
- **Famous Natives:** Andrew Johnson, U.S. president; Dale Earnhardt, Jr., race car driver; Michael Jordan, basketball player

Fun Fact: The first miniature golf course in the United States was built in Fayetteville, North Carolina.

North Dakota

- **Capital:** Bismarck
- **Largest City:** Fargo
- **Postal Code:** ND
- **Land area:** 68,994 square miles (178,694 sq km)
- **Population (2014):** 739,482
- **Entered union (rank):** November 2, 1889 (39)
- **Motto:** Liberty and union, now and forever, one and inseparable
- **Tree:** American elm
- **Flower: Wild prairie rose**
- **Bird:** Western meadowlark
- **Nicknames:** Sioux State, Flickertail State, Peace Garden State, Rough Rider State
- **Famous Natives:** Roger Maris, baseball player; Kellan Lutz, actor; Ronda Rousey, MMA fighter and Olympic medalist

Fun Fact: North Dakota leads the United States in both honey production and sunflower growth.

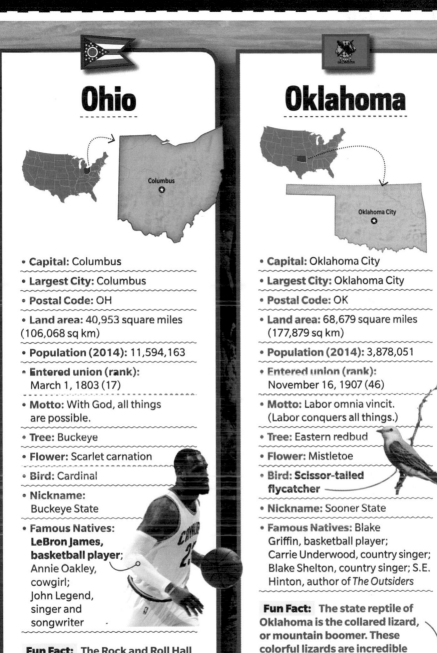

Ohio

Columbus

- **Capital:** Columbus
- **Largest City:** Columbus
- **Postal Code:** OH
- **Land area:** 40,953 square miles (106,068 sq km)
- **Population (2014):** 11,594,163
- **Entered union (rank):** March 1, 1803 (17)
- **Motto:** With God, all things are possible.
- **Tree:** Buckeye
- **Flower:** Scarlet carnation
- **Bird:** Cardinal
- **Nickname:** Buckeye State
- **Famous Natives:** **LeBron James, basketball player;** Annie Oakley, cowgirl; John Legend, singer and songwriter

Fun Fact: The Rock and Roll Hall of Fame is located in Cleveland, Ohio. The 2015 inductees include Ringo Starr, Joan Jett & the Blackhearts, Bill Withers, and Green Day.

Oklahoma

Oklahoma City

- **Capital:** Oklahoma City
- **Largest City:** Oklahoma City
- **Postal Code:** OK
- **Land area:** 68,679 square miles (177,879 sq km)
- **Population (2014):** 3,878,051
- **Entered union (rank):** November 16, 1907 (46)
- **Motto:** Labor omnia vincit. (Labor conquers all things.)
- **Tree:** Eastern redbud
- **Flower:** Mistletoe
- **Bird:** **Scissor-tailed flycatcher**
- **Nickname:** Sooner State
- **Famous Natives:** Blake Griffin, basketball player; Carrie Underwood, country singer; Blake Shelton, country singer; S.E. Hinton, author of *The Outsiders*

Fun Fact: The state reptile of Oklahoma is the collared lizard, or mountain boomer. These colorful lizards are incredible sprinters. They can move as fast as 16 miles (26 km) per hour for short distances.

UNITED STATES

Oregon

- **Capital:** Salem
- **Largest City:** Portland
- **Postal Code:** OR
- **Land area:** 96,003 square miles (248,648 sq km)
- **Population (2014):** 3,970,239
- **Entered union (rank):** February 14, 1859 (33)
- **Motto:** Alis volat propriis. (She flies with her own wings.)
- **Tree:** Douglas fir
- **Flower:** Oregon grape
- **Bird:** Western meadowlark
- **Nickname:** Beaver State
- **Famous Natives:** Linus Pauling, chemist and Nobel Prize winner; Kevin Love, basketball player; Dick Fosbury, track and field athlete who invented the Fosbury Flop, a revolutionary high jump technique

Fun Fact: It is illegal for drivers to pump their own gas in the state of Oregon. (The same law applies in New Jersey.)

Pennsylvania

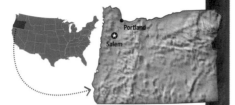

- **Capital:** Harrisburg
- **Largest City:** Philadelphia
- **Postal Code:** PA
- **Land area:** 44,820 square miles (116,084 sq km)
- **Population (2014):** 12,787,209
- **Entered union (rank):** December 12, 1787 (2)
- **Motto:** Virtue, liberty, and independence.
- **Tree:** Hemlock
- **Flower:** Mountain laurel
- **Bird:** Ruffed grouse
- **Nickname:** Keystone State
- **Famous Natives:** Betsy Ross, seamstress who sewed the first American flag; Louisa May Alcott, author; Will Smith, actor; **Taylor Swift, singer and songwriter**

Fun Fact: Pennsylvania is the only original colony that does not border the Atlantic Ocean.

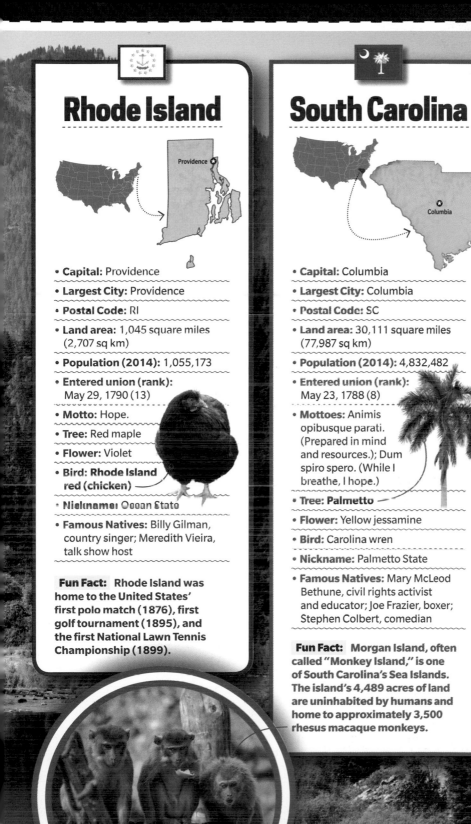

Rhode Island

Providence

- **Capital:** Providence
- **Largest City:** Providence
- **Postal Code:** RI
- **Land area:** 1,045 square miles (2,707 sq km)
- **Population (2014):** 1,055,173
- **Entered union (rank):** May 29, 1790 (13)
- **Motto:** Hope.
- **Tree:** Red maple
- **Flower:** Violet
- **Bird: Rhode Island red (chicken)**
- **Nickname:** Ocean State
- **Famous Natives:** Billy Gilman, country singer; Meredith Vieira, talk show host

Fun Fact: Rhode Island was home to the United States' first polo match (1876), first golf tournament (1895), and the first National Lawn Tennis Championship (1899).

South Carolina

Columbia

- **Capital:** Columbia
- **Largest City:** Columbia
- **Postal Code:** SC
- **Land area:** 30,111 square miles (77,987 sq km)
- **Population (2014):** 4,832,482
- **Entered union (rank):** May 23, 1788 (8)
- **Mottoes:** Animis opibusque parati. (Prepared in mind and resources.); Dum spiro spero. (While I breathe, I hope.)
- **Tree: Palmetto**
- **Flower:** Yellow jessamine
- **Bird:** Carolina wren
- **Nickname:** Palmetto State
- **Famous Natives:** Mary McLeod Bethune, civil rights activist and educator; Joe Frazier, boxer; Stephen Colbert, comedian

Fun Fact: Morgan Island, often called "Monkey Island," is one of South Carolina's Sea Islands. The island's 4,489 acres of land are uninhabited by humans and home to approximately 3,500 rhesus macaque monkeys.

South Dakota

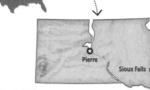

- **Capital:** Pierre
- **Largest City:** Sioux Falls
- **Postal Code:** SD
- **Land area:** 75,898 square miles (196,575 sq km)
- **Population (2014):** 853,175
- **Entered union (rank):** November 2, 1889 (40)
- **Motto:** Under God the people rule.
- **Tree: Black Hills spruce**
- **Flower:** Pasqueflower
- **Bird:** Ring-necked pheasant
- **Nicknames:** Mount Rushmore State, Coyote State
- **Famous Natives:** Sitting Bull, Sioux chief; Becky Hammon, basketball player and coach; Tom Brokaw, journalist; Brock Lesnar, professional wrestler

Fun Fact: Jewel Cave, located in the Black Hills, is the third longest cave in the world. About 175 miles of passageways have been surveyed and mapped, making up only an estimated 5% of the cave.

Tennessee

- **Capital:** Nashville
- **Largest City:** Memphis
- **Postal Code:** TN
- **Land area:** 41,220 square miles (106,760 sq km)
- **Population (2014):** 6,549,352
- **Entered union (rank):** June 1, 1796 (16)
- **Motto:** Agriculture and commerce.
- **Tree:** Tulip poplar
- **Flower:** Iris
- **Bird: Mockingbird**
- **Nickname:** Volunteer State
- **Famous Natives:** Davy Crockett, folk hero and politician; Al Gore, U.S. vice president; Dolly Parton, musician and actress; Pat Summitt, basketball coach; Reese Witherspoon, actress

Fun Fact: Nashville's Centennial Park is home to a full-size replica of the Parthenon, a famous temple in Athens, Greece. Originally constructed in 1897 for Tennessee's state fair, the building now functions as an art museum.

Texas

Austin ★ • Houston

- **Capital:** Austin
- **Largest City:** Houston
- **Postal Code:** TX
- **Land area:** 261,914 square miles (678,357 sq km)
- **Population (2014):** 6,956,958
- **Entered union (rank):** December 29, 1845 (28)
- **Motto:** Friendship.
- **Tree:** Pecan
- **Flower:** Texas bluebonnet
- **Bird:** Mockingbird
- **Nickname:** Lone Star State
- **Famous Natives:** Lyndon B. Johnson, U.S. president; Sandra Day O'Connor, Supreme Court Justice; George Foreman, boxer; **Demi Lovato, pop singer;** Jordan Spieth, golfer

Fun Fact: Rodeo is the official state sport of Texas. The state's largest rodeo takes place in Houston and brings in more than 2.5 million visitors each year.

Utah

Salt Lake City ★

- **Capital:** Salt Lake City
- **Largest City:** Salt Lake City
- **Postal Code:** UT
- **Land area:** 82,168 square miles (212,815 sq km)
- **Population (2014):** 2,942,902
- **Entered union (rank):** January 4, 1896 (45)
- **Motto:** Industry.
- **Tree:** Blue spruce
- **Flower:** Sego lily
- **Bird:** California gull
- **Nickname:** Beehive State
- **Famous Natives:** Philo Farnsworth, inventor of the television; Julianne Hough, dancer, actress, and singer

Fun Fact: More dinosaur fossil records have been found in Utah than any other state. It is also home to the world's most complete record of prehistoric life and geologic history.

Vermont

- **Capital:** Montpelier
- **Largest City:** Burlington
- **Postal Code:** VT
- **Land area:** 9,249 square miles (23,956 sq km)
- **Population (2014):** 626,562
- **Entered union (rank):** March 4, 1791 (14)
- **Motto:** Freedom and unity.
- **Tree:** Sugar maple
- **Flower:** Red clover
- **Bird: Hermit thrush**
- **Nickname:** Green Mountain State
- **Famous Natives:** John Deere, founder of the tractor company John Deere and Company; Hannah Teter, Olympic snowboarder; Robert Frost, poet

Fun Fact: Vermont produces 500,000 gallons of maple syrup each year, more than any other state in the country.

Virginia

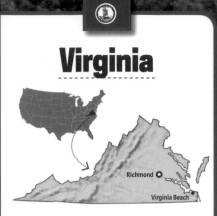

- **Capital:** Richmond
- **Largest City:** Virginia Beach
- **Postal Code:** VA
- **Land area:** 39,598 square miles (102,559 sq km)
- **Population (2014):** 8,326,289
- **Entered union (rank):** June 25, 1788 (10)
- **Motto:** Sic semper tyrannis. (Thus always to tyrants.)
- **Tree: Flowering dogwood**
- **Flower:** American dogwood
- **Bird:** Cardinal
- **Nicknames:** The Old Dominion, Mother of Presidents
- **Famous Natives:** Gabby Douglas, gymnast and Olympic gold medalist; Ella Fitzgerald, jazz singer; Pharrell Williams, singer; Russell Wilson, football player

Fun Fact: The Pentagon, located in Arlington, is the largest office building in the world. It has 5.1 million square feet of working space—more than twice that of the Empire State Building.

Washington

- **Capital:** Olympia
- **Largest City:** Seattle
- **Postal Code:** WA
- **Land area:** 66,582 square miles (172,447 sq km)
- **Population (2014):** 7,061,530
- **Entered union (rank):** November 11, 1889 (42)
- **Motto:** Al-ki (an Indian word meaning "by and by" or "hope for the future").
- **Tree:** Western hemlock
- **Flower:** Coast rhododendron
- **Bird:** Willow goldfinch
- **Nickname:** Evergreen State
- **Famous Natives:** Bill Gates, co-founder of Microsoft; Macklemore, rapper; Apolo Anton Ohno, speed skater, most decorated Winter Olympian of all time; Chris Pratt; actor

Fun Fact: Washington is home to five major volcanoes: Mount Baker, Glacier Peak, Mount Ranier, Mount Adams, and Mount St. Helens, whose eruption in 1980 was the first to occur on the continental United States since 1915.

West Virginia

- **Capital:** Charleston
- **Largest City:** Charleston
- **Postal Code:** WV
- **Land area:** 24,087 square miles (62,385 sq km)
- **Population (2014):** 1,850,326
- **Entered union (rank):** June 20, 1863 (35)
- **Motto:** Montani semper liberi. (Mountaineers are always free.)
- **Tree:** Sugar maple
- **Flower:** Rhododendron
- **Bird:** Cardinal
- **Nickname:** Mountain State
- **Famous Natives:** Brad Paisley, country musician; Randy Moss, football player

Fun Fact: The dome on West Virginia's capitol building is 292 feet tall, higher than the Nation's capitol building in Washington, D.C., which measures 288 feet tall.

Wisconsin

Wyoming

- **Capital:** Madison
- **Largest City:** Milwaukee
- **Postal code:** WI
- **Land area:** 54,314 square miles (140,673 sq km)
- **Population (2014):** 5,757,564
- **Entered union (rank):** May 29, 1848 (30)
- **Motto:** Forward.
- **Tree:** Sugar maple
- **Flower:** Wood violet
- **Bird:** American robin
- **Nicknames:** Badger State, Dairy State

- **Famous Natives:** Georgia O'Keeffe, artist; **Mark Ruffalo, actor**; Frank Lloyd Wright, architect

Fun Fact: Wisconsin is the dairy capital of the United States. It is home to 1.27 million cows, who produce 13% of the country's entire milk supply and 25% of its cheese.

- **Capital:** Cheyenne
- **Largest City:** Cheyenne
- **Postal Code:** WY
- **Land area:** 97,105 square miles (251,502 sq km)
- **Population (2014):** 584,153
- **Entered union (rank):** July 10, 1890 (44)
- **Motto:** Equal rights.
- **Tree:** Plains cottonwood
- **Flower: Indian paintbrush**
- **Bird:** Meadowlark
- **Nicknames:** Big Wyoming, Equality State, Cowboy State
- **Famous Natives:** Travis Rice, snowboarder; Resi Stiegler, alpine ski racer

Fun Fact: Yellowstone became the United States' first National Park in 1872—20 years before Montana, Idaho, and Wyoming became states!

Washington, D.C.
THE NATION'S CAPITAL

The District of Columbia, which covers the same area as the city of Washington, is the capital of the United States. The seat of the U.S. government was transferred from Philadelphia, Pennsylvania, to Washington, D.C., on December 1, 1800.

- **Land area:** 68.25 square miles (177 sq km)
- **Population (2013):** 646,449
- **Motto:** Justitia omnibus. (Justice for all.)
- **Tree:** Scarlet oak
- **Flower:** American beauty rose
- **Bird: Wood thrush**
- **Famous Native:** John Philip Sousa, composer

U.S. Territories

- **Puerto Rico** is in the Caribbean Sea, about 1,000 miles (1,609 km) southeast of Miami, Florida. The U.S. took possession of Puerto Rico in 1898. It consists of the island of Puerto Rico plus the islets of Vieques, Culebra, and Mona. Its capital is San Juan, located on the main island's northern coast. Puerto Rico has an estimated population of 3.5 million.

- **American Samoa**, a group of islands in the South Pacific Ocean, is situated about halfway between Hawaii and New Zealand. It has a land area of 76 square miles (197 sq km) and a population of approximately 54,000.

- **Guam**, in the North Pacific Ocean, was given to the U.S. by Spain in 1898. It has a land area of 210 square miles (544 sq km) and a population of approximately 162,000.

- **U.S. Virgin Islands**, which include Saint Croix, Saint Thomas, Saint John, and many other islands, are located in the Caribbean Sea, east of Puerto Rico. Together, they have a land area of 134 square miles (346 sq km) and a population of about 104,000.

- **The Northern Mariana Islands**, located in the North Pacific Ocean, have been administered by the U.S. since the end of World War II. They have a land area of 179 square miles (464 sq km) and a population of around 52,000.

El Morro Fortress overlooks San Juan Bay in Puerto Rico.

The Three Branches of the U.S. Government

Under this structure, the nation's government operates on a system of checks and balances

1. Executive Branch

- Made up of the president, the vice president, and the cabinet

- The president signs bills into laws or vetoes (rejects) them.

- He or she also nominates Supreme Court justices

2. Legislative Branch

- Made up of the members of the House of Representatives and the Senate (which together form the Congress)

- Writes bills and votes on whether or not to make the bills into laws

- Collects taxes

- Declares war

- Confirms, or approves, Supreme Court justices

3. Judicial Branch

- Interprets laws and decides how they should be applied

- Decides whether laws agree with the Constitution

- Evaluates whether Executive Orders are constitutional

The purpose of this structure is to create a separation of powers among three equally important branches. The three branches of government have different responsibilities, but they work together to keep any one branch from becoming too powerful. For example, the legislative branch creates laws, but the judicial branch can strike down a law if it conflicts with the spirit of the Constitution.

1. THE EXECUTIVE TRIO

Together, the president, the vice president, and the cabinet make up the executive branch of the government.

• **The president** is the leader of the nation and the commander in chief of the U.S. Armed Forces.

• **The vice president** presides over the Senate but casts a vote only in the event of a tie. If the president dies, resigns, or is removed from office, the vice president assumes the office of president. Like the president, the vice president must be a native-born U.S. citizen, must be at least 35 years old, and must have lived in the United States for at least 14 years.

• **The cabinet** is made up of 15 department heads who advise the president. Cabinet secretaries are nominated by the president, then each nominee is questioned by the Senate. These interviews are known as confirmation hearings. Each nominee must be confirmed, or approved, by a majority of 51 or more senators. Here are the cabinet departments, along with their Web addresses:

Agriculture
usda.gov

Commerce
commerce.gov

Defense
defense.gov

Education
ed.gov

Energy
energy.gov

Health and Human Services
hhs.gov

Homeland Security
dhs.gov

Housing and Urban Development
hud.gov

Interior
doi.gov

Justice (Attorney General)
justice.gov

Labor
dol.gov

State
state.gov

Transportation
dot.gov

Treasury
treasury.gov

Veterans Affair
va.gov

The White House

2. THE HOUSE OF REPRESENTATIVES

This chamber includes 435 representatives.

The larger a state's population, the more representatives it has. Representatives are elected to two-year terms. The Speaker of the House presides over the sessions.

THE HOUSE OF REPRESENTATIVES HAS THE FOLLOWING SPECIAL POWERS AND RESPONSIBILITIES:

- **Create** bills that allow the government to collect taxes.

- **Elect** the president in the event that no candidate receives a majority of electoral votes.

- **Create** bills that empower the government to spend money.

- **Vote** to impeach the president, vice president, or other elected official. This means to formally charge a public official with wrongdoing.

GUESS WHAT?
To run for the House of Representatives, a candidate must be at least 25 years old.

Coming Together The House and Senate listen to a speech during a joint session.

THE SENATE

This chamber includes 100 senators, two for each state.

Senators are elected to six-year terms, with one-third of the Senate being elected every even-numbered year. The vice president (or president pro tempore, in the vice president's absence) presides over the sessions.

THE SENATE HAS THE FOLLOWING SPECIAL POWERS AND RESPONSIBILITIES:

- **Ratify,** or approve, treaties made by the president. This requires a two-thirds vote of all the senators.

- **Accept** or reject (by majority vote of all senators) the president's appointments of Supreme Court justices and federal judges, ambassadors, and other high-level executive-branch officials.

- **Hold** trials of officials impeached by the House of Representatives and convict or acquit them. A two-thirds vote of all senators is needed for conviction.

GUESS WHAT?

To run for the Senate, a person must be at least 30 years old.

UNITED STATES

Meeting Hall
A replica of the U.S. Senate chamber at the Edward Kennedy Institute.

The U.S. Capitol

3. THE COURT SYSTEM

The U.S. Supreme Court and federal courts decide how an established law should be carried out.

• There are many federal courts around the country. Known as the lower courts, these include U.S. district courts, courts of appeals, bankruptcy courts, and others. There are also special courts, some of which handle appeals for veterans and members of the armed services.

The Supreme Court is the highest court in the country. Most of the cases that the Supreme Court hears come from the lower courts. A person with a legal claim can petition, or ask, the Supreme Court to review a decision from a lower court. The Supreme Court also hears cases in which one state sues another or a state sues the national government.

• **The Supreme Court** has the power to declare a law unconstitutional. The court consists of eight associate justices and a chief justice. All decisions are made by a majority vote of the justices.

Supreme Court justices and federal judges are appointed by the president and confirmed by the Senate. They serve for life or until they decide to resign or retire.

THE JUSTICES IN 2015

Top Row (from left to right): Sonia Sotomayor, Stephen G. Breyer, Samuel A. Alito Jr., Elena Kagan

Bottom Row (from left to right): Clarence Thomas, Antonin Scalia*, Chief Justice John G. Roberts, Anthony M. Kennedy, Ruth Bader Ginsberg

*Died in 2016

The U.S. Supreme Court

Famous Supreme Court Cases

Since its first session in 1790, the U.S. Supreme Court has made many significant legal rulings that changed U.S. history. One of its most famous was the case of Brown v. Board of Education, in 1954. The Supreme Court declared that racial segregation in public schools is unconstitutional, a victory for civil rights in the U.S. Here are some other noteworthy Supreme Court cases.

• **Marbury v. Madison (1803)**
Established the Constitution's precedence over any other law and the Supreme Court's power to decide what a law is.

• **Dred Scott v. Sandford (1857)**
Said that a slave was not a U.S. citizen and that Congress could not outlaw slavery. In 1868, the 14th Amendment overturned the decision by granting citizenship to those born in the U.S., regardless of color.

• **Plessy v. Ferguson. (1896)**
Upheld a Louisiana court decision that racial segregation was legal. This decision was overturned by the Supreme Court's ruling on Brown v. Board of Education in 1954.

• **Miranda v. Arizona (1966)**
Determined that suspected criminals must be read their constitutional rights before being questioned by law enforcement officers.

• **Bush v. Gore (2000)**
Overturned a Florida Supreme Court decision to manually recount the state's votes in the presidential election, which originally gave a slight lead to George W. Bush over Al Gore. The decision was based on the fact that the process of counting votes varies from state to state and the Supreme Court didn't have jurisdiction in the way the process was regulated. As a result, Bush won the election.

• **National Federation of Independent Business v. Sebelius (2012)**
Upheld the mandate that most Americans were required to have health insurance. President Barack Obama had overhauled the healthcare system to try to ensure that all Americans have access to medical coverage. The decision upheld the Affordable Care Act.

• **Obergefell v. Hodges (2015)**
Declared that the Constitution guaranteed a nationwide right to same-sex marriage. Previously, only a handful of states had legalized same-sex marriage.

DAILY NEWS
HISTORIC RULING
BUSH WINS
U.S. SUPREME COURT REJECTS...OUNT

The Bush v. Gore decision prevented a recount in the 2000 presidential election.

FROM TIME FOR KIDS MAGAZINE

10 Questions

→ For Kerry Sautner

TFK's Brenda Iasevoli spoke to Kerry Sautner, of the Constitution Center, in Philadelphia, Pennsylvania, to learn more about the U.S. Constitution.

1. What is the Constitution?
The Constitution established the framework of our government. It contains the rights and freedoms that "we the people" enjoy today.

2. How was it created?
Our Founding Fathers spent months, in Philadelphia, deciding how our government should work. They had lots of arguments and made lots of compromises. After signing the Constitution, in 1787, they sent it to the people for approval.

3. Why is it important?
It is the supreme law of the land. It is the law that all citizens live by.

4. Why was the Bill of Rights added?
The Bill of Rights is the first 10 amendments to the Constitution. These amendments protect our most cherished civil liberties, including freedom of speech, religion, and assembly.

5. How has the Constitution lasted for so many years?
We have the ability to make changes to the Constitution when it is necessary for our country and its future.

6. Why do we celebrate the anniversary of the document's signing?
In 2004, Senator Robert Byrd passed a bill naming September 17 the day citizens celebrate the signing and learn more about our founding document.

7. How does the Constitution Center celebrate the day?
We have the biggest "we the people" birthday cake you've ever seen! Each year, civic heroes visit the center to talk to students about our country's history.

8. Why should kids care about such an old document?
It affects our daily life and spells out how we all have a voice in our government and need to

get involved in our communities.

9. What's the best way to celebrate Constitution Day?
Celebrate your right to be an active participant in our democracy. Organize a fundraiser for your community, or pass out a petition about something important to you. Read the Constitution! It is only four pages long, and it's a great way to honor the Founding Fathers.

10. How can kids learn more about the document?
Visit *constitutioncenter.org/ constitutionday*

Kerry Sautner is vice president of education at the Constitution Center.

1. GEORGE WASHINGTON

SERVED 1789–1797
Political Party: Independent
Lived: February 22, 1732–
December 14, 1799
Vice President: John Adams
First Lady: Martha Dandridge Custis

GUESS WHAT?
In 1978, 179 years after his death, the U.S. Army promoted Washington to the rank of General of the Armies of the United States, declaring no officer could ever receive a higher rank.

2. JOHN ADAMS
SERVED 1797–1801
Political Party: Federalist
Lived: October 30, 1735–July 4, 1826
Vice President: Thomas Jefferson
First Lady: Abigail Smith

GUESS WHAT? Adams was the first president to live in the White House. The nation's capital was moved from Philadelphia to Washington, D.C., in 1800.

3. THOMAS JEFFERSON
SERVED 1801–1809
Political Party: Democratic-Republican
Lived: April 13, 1743–July 4, 1826
Vice Presidents: Aaron Burr, George Clinton
First Lady: Martha Wayles Skelton

GUESS WHAT? After his presidency, Jefferson founded the University of Virginia, the first non-religiously-affiliated university in the U.S.

4. JAMES MADISON
SERVED 1809–1817
Political Party: Democratic-Republican
Lived: March 16, 1751–June 28, 1836
Vice Presidents: George Clinton, Elbridge Gerry
First Lady: Dolley Payne Todd

GUESS WHAT? Madison often wrote letters in codes and ciphers, fearing unauthorized people would read his correspondences to colleagues, including Thomas Jefferson.

5. JAMES MONROE

SERVED 1817–1825
Political Party: Democratic-Republican
Lived: April 28, 1758–July 4, 1831
Vice President: Daniel D. Tompkins
First Lady: Elizabeth "Eliza" Kortright

GUESS WHAT?

Monroe supported the establishment of Liberia, an African nation for free slaves. The capital city, Monrovia, is named after him.

6. JOHN QUINCY ADAMS
SERVED 1825–1829
Political Party: Democratic-Republican
Lived: July 11, 1767–February 23, 1848
Vice President: John C. Calhoun
First Lady: Louisa Catherine Johnson

GUESS WHAT? John Quincy Adams was the son of the second President, making him the first son of a President to also serve in the White House.

★

7. ANDREW JACKSON
SERVED 1829–1837
Political Party: Democratic
Lived: March 15, 1767–June 8, 1845
Vice Presidents: John C. Calhoun, Martin Van Buren
First Lady: Emily Donelson

GUESS WHAT? Jackson was the first President to face an assassination attempt. Both of the would-be-killer's guns misfired, and Jackson was able to club the attacker with his cane and escape unharmed.

★

8. MARTIN VAN BUREN
SERVED 1837–1841
Political Party: Democratic
Lived: December 5, 1782–July 24, 1862
Vice President: Richard M. Johnson
First Lady: Hannah Hoes

GUESS WHAT? Van Buren was the first American-born president. He was born in Kinderhook, New York, after the U.S. gained freedom; all previous Presidents were born when the states were still a British colony.

9. WILLIAM HENRY HARRISON
SERVED 1841
Political Party: Whig
Lived: February 9, 1773–April 4, 1841
Vice President: John Tyler
First Lady: Anna Tuthill Symmes

GUESS WHAT? Harrison's campaign was run based on his military valor. He fought in the Northwest Indian War in the 1790s and led U.S. forces to victory over Native American warriors at the Battle of Tippecanoe in 1811. Harrison died 32 days into his presidency of complications from pneumonia.

★

10. JOHN TYLER
SERVED 1841–1845
Political Party: Whig
Lived: March 29, 1790–January 18, 1862
Vice President: None
First Ladies: Letitia Christian (died 1842), Julia Gardiner

GUESS WHAT? After Harrison died, Tyler became the first vice president to take over after a presidential death.

★

11. JAMES K. POLK
SERVED 1845–1849
Political Party: Democratic
Lived: November 2, 1795–June 15, 1849
Vice President: George M. Dallas
First Lady: Sarah Childress

GUESS WHAT? Between the Mexican-American War (1846-1848) and the Oregon Treaty with Great Britain (1846), the U.S. expanded westward by more than one million square miles during Polk's single term in office.

12. ZACHARY TAYLOR

SERVED 1849–1850
Political Party: Whig
Lived: November 24, 1784–July 9, 1850
Vice President: Millard Fillmore
First Lady: Margaret Mackall Smith

GUESS WHAT? Taylor is one of nine U.S. presidents who are descendants of Mayflower passengers. He got sick while in office and died a year into his presidency.

★

13. MILLARD FILLMORE

SERVED 1850–1853
Political Party: Whig
Lived: January 7, 1800–March 8, 1874
Vice President: None
First Lady: Abigail Powers

GUESS WHAT? Fillmore took office after Zachary Taylor died. Even though he was Taylor's vice president, the two had never met before Fillmore was added to the ticket.

14. FRANKLIN PIERCE

SERVED 1853–1857
Political Party: Democratic
Lived: November 23, 1804–October 8, 1869
Vice President: William R. King
First Lady: Jane Means Appleton

GUESS WHAT? Pierce recited a 3,319-word inaugural address entirely from memory.

★

15. JAMES BUCHANAN

SERVED 1857–1861
Political Party: Democratic
Lived: April 23, 1791–June 1, 1868
Vice President: John C. Breckinridge
First Lady: Harriet Lane

GUESS WHAT? Buchanan never married. His niece, Harriet Lane, whom he cared for after she was orphaned at age 11, handled hostess duties in the White House and used her position and popularity to advocate for Native American rights.

16. ABRAHAM LINCOLN

SERVED 1861–1865
Political Party: Republican
Lived: February 12, 1809–April 15, 1865
Vice Presidents: Hannibal Hamlin, Andrew Johnson
First Lady: Mary Todd

Lincoln is a National Wrestling Hall of Fame honoree. He had only one recorded defeat in a dozen years as a grappler.

17. ANDREW JOHNSON
SERVED 1865–1869
Political Parties: Union, Democratic
Lived: December 29, 1808–July 31, 1875
Vice President: None
First Lady: Eliza McCardle

GUESS WHAT? When Southern states were breaking away from the U.S. in the early 1860s, a precursor to the Civil War, Johnson, representing Tennessee, was the only southern senator to remain loyal to the Union government.

★

18. ULYSSES S. GRANT
SERVED 1869–1877
Political Party: Republican
Lived: April 27, 1822–July 23, 1885
Vice Presidents: Schuyler Colfax, Henry Wilson
First Lady: Julia Boggs Dent

GUESS WHAT? Grant was Commanding General of the Union Army during the Civil War. He accepted the Confederacy's surrender in April of 1865, ending the war.

★

19. RUTHERFORD B. HAYES
SERVED 1877–1881
Political Party: Republican
Lived: October 4, 1822–January 17, 1893
Vice President: William A. Wheeler
First Lady: Lucy Ware Webb

GUESS WHAT? Hayes was the first president to have a telephone in the White House.

20. JAMES A. GARFIELD
SERVED 1881
Political Party: Republican
Lived: November 19, 1831–September 19, 1881
Vice President: Chester A. Arthur
First Lady: Lucretia Rudolph

GUESS WHAT? Garfield was ambidextrous (he could write with either hand) and reportedly could write two different languages at the same time.

★

21. CHESTER A. ARTHUR
SERVED 1881–1885
Political Party: Republican
Lived: October 5, 1829–November 18, 1886
Vice President: None
First Lady: Ellen Lewis Herndon

GUESS WHAT? In 1884, Arthur organized the International Meridian Conference, which helped standardize time and dates among different countries.

★

22. GROVER CLEVELAND
SERVED 1885–1889
Political Party: Democratic
Lived: March 18, 1837–June 24, 1908
Vice President: Thomas A. Hendricks
First Lady: Frances Folsom

GUESS WHAT? In 1886, Cleveland became the first president to get married in the White House.

23. BENJAMIN HARRISON

SERVED 1889–1893
Political Party: Republican
Lived: August 20, 1833–March 13, 1901
Vice President: Levi P. Morton
First Lady: Caroline Lavinia Scott (died 1892)

GUESS WHAT?

Harrison is the only grandchild of a president to also rise to the rank of president. His grandfather William was the ninth president of the U.S.

24. GROVER CLEVELAND
SERVED 1893–1897
Political Party: Democratic
Lived: March 18, 1837–June 24, 1908
Vice President: Adlai E. Stevenson
First Lady: Frances Folsom

GUESS WHAT? Cleveland is the only president to serve non-consecutive terms, meaning he was elected twice, but not twice in a row.

★

25. WILLIAM MCKINLEY
SERVED 1897–1901
Political Party: Republican
Lived: January 29, 1843–
September 14, 1901
Vice Presidents: Garret A. Hobart, Theodore Roosevelt
First Lady: Ida Saxton

GUESS WHAT? As an 18-year-old, McKinley served under Rutherford B. Hayes in the Civil War.

26. THEODORE ROOSEVELT

SERVED 1901–1909
Political Party: Republican
Lived: October 27, 1858–January 6, 1919
Vice President: Charles W. Fairbanks
First Lady: Edith Kermit Carow

GUESS WHAT?

For his work establishing a peace treaty between Russia and Japan, Roosevelt became the first U.S. president to win a Nobel Peace Prize, in 1906. Wilson, Carter, and Obama have also won the award.

27. WILLIAM H. TAFT
SERVED 1909–1913
Political Party: Republican
Lived: September 15, 1857–March 8, 1930
Vice President: James S. Sherman
First Lady: Helen Herron

GUESS WHAT? After his presidency, Taft served as chief justice of the Supreme Court from 1921 until shortly before his death in 1930. He is the only American to serve as both president and chief justice.

28. WOODROW WILSON
SERVED 1913–1921
Political Party: Democratic
Lived: December 28, 1856–February 3, 1924
Vice President: Thomas R. Marshall
First Ladies: Ellen Axson (died 1914), Edith Bolling Galt

GUESS WHAT? Wilson appears on the $100,000 bill, the largest denomination ever printed. It was only used for transactions between Federal Reserve banks.

★

UNITED STATES

29. WARREN G. HARDING
SERVED 1921–1923
Political Party: Republican
Lived: November 2, 1865–August 2, 1923
Vice President: Calvin Coolidge
First Lady: Florence Kling

GUESS WHAT? In 1922, Harding became the first president to be broadcast via radio.

★

31. HERBERT C. HOOVER
SERVED 1929–1933
Political Party: Republican
Lived: August 10, 1874–October 20, 1964
Vice President: Charles Curtis
First Lady: Lou Henry

GUESS WHAT? Hoover had 11 pets: nine dogs and two alligators.

30. CALVIN COOLIDGE
SERVED 1923–1929
Political Party: Republican
Lived: July 4, 1872–January 5, 1933
Vice President: Charles G. Dawes
First Lady: Grace Anna Goodhue

GUESS WHAT? Coolidge's father, a notary public, swore in his son at his presidential inauguration.

32. FRANKLIN D. ROOSEVELT

SERVED 1933–1945
Political Party: Democratic
Lived: January 30, 1882–
April 12, 1945
Vice Presidents: John Garner, Henry Wallace, Harry S Truman
First Lady: Anna Eleanor Roosevelt

GUESS WHAT?

FDR was the only president elected four times. In 1951, the 22nd Amendment to the Constitution limited future presidents to serving no more than 10 years.

33. HARRY S TRUMAN

SERVED 1945–1953
Political Party: Democratic
Lived: May 8, 1884–December 26, 1972
Vice President: Alben W. Barkley
First Lady: Elizabeth "Bess" Virginia Wallace

GUESS WHAT? Truman's middle name is "S"; it doesn't stand for anything and thus doesn't have a period after it. His parents chose the letter in honor of his two grandfathers, both of whom had S as one of their initials.

★

34. DWIGHT D. EISENHOWER

SERVED 1953–1961
Political Party: Republican
Lived: October 14, 1890–March 28, 1969
Vice President: Richard M. Nixon
First Lady: Mamie Geneva Doud

GUESS WHAT? When Alaska and Hawaii became a states in 1959, Eisenhower became the first president of 50 states.

★

35. JOHN F. KENNEDY

SERVED 1961–1963
Political Party: Democratic
Lived: May 29, 1917–November 22, 1963
Vice President: Lyndon B. Johnson
First Lady: Jacqueline Lee Bouvier

GUESS WHAT? JFK was awarded the Purple Heart military honor for surviving and heroically rescuing a crewmate from a World War II naval attack.

37. RICHARD NIXON

SERVED 1969–1974
Political Party: Republican
Lived: January 9, 1913–April 22, 1994
Vice Presidents: Spiro T. Agnew, Gerald R. Ford
First Lady: Thelma Catherine "Pat" Ryan

GUESS WHAT? Nixon played the piano, accordion, clarinet, saxophone, and violin. He played a piano piece he composed on a popular TV show in 1963.

★

38. GERALD R. FORD

SERVED 1974–1977
Political Party: Republican
Lived: July 14, 1913–December 26, 2006
Vice President: Nelson A. Rockefeller
First Lady: Elizabeth "Betty" Bloomer

GUESS WHAT? Ford won two national championships playing center and linebacker for the University of Michigan football team. Despite interest from NFL teams, he decided to enter law school.

★

39. JIMMY CARTER

SERVED 1977–1981
Political Party: Democratic
Born: October 1, 1924
Vice President: Walter F. Mondale
First Lady: Rosalynn Smith

GUESS WHAT? Carter was the first president who was born in a hospital.

36. LYNDON B. JOHNSON

SERVED 1963–1969
Political Party: Democratic
Lived: August 27, 1908–January 22, 1973
Vice President: Hubert H. Humphrey
First Lady: Claudia "Lady Bird" Taylor

GUESS WHAT?

Johnson was sworn in while aboard Air Force One after Kennedy's death. District judge Sarah Hughes, a friend of LBJ's, administered the oath of office, making her the first female to do so.

40. RONALD REAGAN

SERVED 1981–1989

Political Party: Republican
Lived: February 6, 1911–June 5, 2004
Vice President: George H.W. Bush
First Lady: Nancy Davis

GUESS WHAT? Reagan loved jelly beans. The Jelly Belly company created a blueberry flavor so that red, white, and blue jelly beans could be served at his 1981 inauguration.

★

41. GEORGE H.W. BUSH

SERVED 1989–1993

Political Party: Republican
Born: June 12, 1924
Vice President: J. Danforth Quayle
First Lady: Barbara Pierce

GUESS WHAT? Bush was captain of the Yale University baseball team. He appeared in the first two College World Series as Yale's first baseman.

42. WILLIAM JEFFERSON CLINTON

SERVED 1993–2001

Political Party: Democratic
Born: August 19, 1946
Vice President: Albert Gore Jr.
First Lady: Hillary Rodham

GUESS WHAT? Clinton is the only President who received a Rhodes Scholarship, a highly prestigious award he used to study at the University of Oxford in England after he graduated from Georgetown University.

★

43. GEORGE W. BUSH

SERVED 2001–2009

Political Party: Republican
Born: July 6, 1946
Vice President: Richard B. Cheney
First Lady: Laura Welch

GUESS WHAT? From 1989 to 1994, Bush was part owner of the Texas Rangers baseball team.

44. BARACK OBAMA

SERVED 2009–2016
Political Party: Democratic
Born: August 4, 1961
Vice President: Joseph R. Biden
First Lady: Michelle Robinson

GUESS WHAT?

Shortly after taking office, Obama had the White House tennis courts adapted so that he could use them for basketball games, as well.

Presidential Shake-Ups

If a U.S. president dies while in office, becomes too ill to continue serving, or is removed from office for any other reason, the vice president is next in line to lead the country. In the history of the United States, this has happened nine times.

Lyndon Johnson is sworn in following President John F. Kennedy's death.

DEATH OF A PRESIDENT

Four U.S. presidents have died of natural causes while in office.
• In 1841, William Henry Harrison died after only 32 days in office. John Tyler took over.
• Zachary Taylor died from an illness in 1850. Millard Fillmore became president.
• After Warren Harding had a heart attack in 1923, Calvin Coolidge took the top job.
• While serving his fourth term in office, Franklin Roosevelt suffered a stroke and died. Harry Truman became president in 1945.

IMPEACHMENT

If the members of the House of Representatives vote to impeach a president, or formally charge him with wrongdoing, then the president must stand trial before the Senate. Two-thirds of all senators must agree in order to convict. One president has left office after being impeached.
• In 1974, Richard Nixon was impeached for his role in covering up a break-in known as the Watergate burglary. He resigned and left office. Gerald Ford became president.

Richard Nixon leaves office after being impeached.

ASSASSINATION

Four U.S. presidents have been assassinated, or killed, while in office.
• In 1865, John Wilkes Booth shot and killed Abraham Lincoln. Andrew Johnson was later sworn in.
• Charles Guiteau shot James Garfield in 1881. Vice President Chester Arthur became president.
• Theodore Roosevelt became president after William McKinley was shot by Leon Czolgosz during the Buffalo Pan-American Exposition in 1901.
• Lyndon Johnson was sworn in as president aboard Air Force One after John F. Kennedy's death in 1963.

The Presidents' Mountain

The faces of four presidents inspire visitors to Mount Rushmore.

George Washington and Abraham Lincoln are celebrated on Presidents' Day. But both men are honored every day at Mount Rushmore National Memorial. Their faces, and those of Thomas Jefferson and Theodore Roosevelt, are carved into a granite cliff in South Dakota's Black Hills.

"The monument is overpowering and moving," park ranger Blaine Kortemeyer told TFK. Because the sculpture features leaders from the first 150 years of the nation, it is an ideal place to learn about history, says Kortemeyer.

MONUMENT MEN

In 1923, South Dakota historian Doane Robinson suggested sculpting statues into the Black Hills. Artist Gutzon Borglum came up with the idea to carve U.S. presidents. He chose the four leaders he felt best represented the country.

Washington stands for the birth of the nation. Jefferson, the third president, nearly doubled the size of the U.S. with the Louisiana Purchase. Lincoln, the 16th president, led the nation through the Civil War. Roosevelt, the 26th, pushed for the creation of the Panama Canal, a waterway that connects the Atlantic and Pacific Oceans.

Borglum studied masks, paintings, and photos of the men. He created models of the faces. Workers used the models to figure out how much rock to remove. From 1927 to 1941, they used dynamite and drills to blast out 90% of the rock.

Gutzon Borglum designs Mount Rushmore.

Mount Rushmore gets nearly 3 million visitors each year. Park rangers travel to local schools to teach kids about the memorial.

Each autumn, workers fix cracks in the monument and seal it to protect it from ice and snow. That way, Borglum's historic work will continue to inspire Americans for generations.
—*By Elizabeth Winchester*

It took 400 drillers and carvers 14 years to create Mount Rushmore. Each face is 60 feet tall.

Road Trip

The United States is full of breathtaking landmarks and places. Take a cross-country trip and see if you can match each American treasure to its location.

Mount Rushmore
Location: _____

Grand Canyon
Location: _____

Washington Monument
Location: _____

Gateway Arch
Location: _____

Golden Gate Bridge
Location: _____

Empire State Building
Location: _____

1) St. Louis, Missouri

2) New York, New York

3) San Francisco, California

4) Arizona

5) Keystone, South Dakota

6) Washington, D.C.

Answers

Page 26 Mystery Person: Jane Goodall

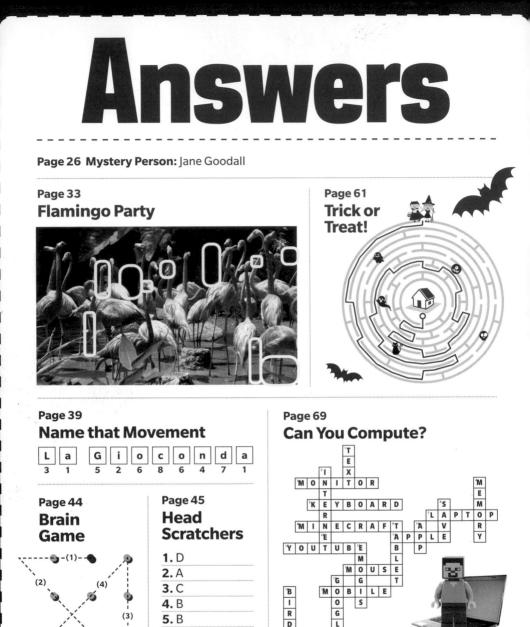

Page 33

Flamingo Party

Page 61

Trick or Treat!

Page 39

Name that Movement

L	a	G	i	o	c	o	n	d	a
3	1	5	2	6	8	6	4	7	1

Page 44

Brain Game

Page 45

Head Scratchers

1. D
2. A
3. C
4. B
5. B
6. C
7. B
8. A

Page 48 Mystery Person: J.K. Rowling

Page 51

The Wisdom of Words

KINDNESS IS
THE LANGUAGE
WHICH THE
DEAF CAN HEAR
AND THE BLIND
CAN SEE

Page 69

Can You Compute?

Page 109

Where in the World?

Taj Mahal
Location:
3) Agra, India

Victoria Falls
Location:
6) Kazungula, Zambia

Big Ben
Location:
4) London, England

Al Khazneh Temple
Location:
5) Petra, Jordan

Notre Dame Cathedral
Location:
2) Paris, France

Christ the Redeemer
Location:
1) Rio de Janeiro, Brazil

Page 119
Save the Planet

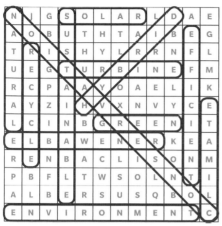

Page 123
Mystery Person: Emma Watson

Page 133
Double Take

Page 159
Mystery Person: Mahatma Gandhi

Page 165
Great Adventures

Amelia Earhart Neil Armstrong Sir Edmund Hillary

Page 185
What Do I Do?

Designs, builds, and operates robots
Answer: Roboticist

Examines diseases and how they spread
Answer: Epidemiologist

Examines stars, planets, comets, asteroids, galaxies, and other things in space
Answer: Astronomer

Focuses on the biology and evolution of prehistoric plants
Answer: Paleobotanist

Studies mollusks (such as snails, oysters, and clams)
Answer: Malacologist

Studies the remains of organisms that lived long ago
Answer: Paleontologist

Studies the origins, history, surface, structure, and makeup of Earth
Answer: Geologist

A biologist who focuses on butterflies
Answer: Lepidopterist

Studies weather and climate
Answer: Meteorologist

Studies criminals and the causes of their behavior
Answer: Criminologist

Page 195
Out of This World

Page 275
Road Trip

Mount Rushmore
Location: 5) Keystone, South Dakota

Grand Canyon
Location: 4) Arizona

Washington Monument
Location: 6) Washington D.C.

Gateway Arch
Location: 1) St. Louis, Missouri

Golden Gate Bridge
Location: 3) San Francisco, California

Empire State Building
Location: 2) New York, New York

Photo Credits

Front Cover
Washington Post/Getty Images (Bei Bei); bluebay/Shutterstock (space module); William Thomas Cain/Getty Images (Yousafzai); Ezra Shaw/Getty Images (Curry); Jason LaVeris/FilmMagic/Getty Images (Swift); Theo Wargo/WireImage/Getty Images (Miranda)

Contents
Page 3: Anthony Behar-Pool/Getty Images (Obama and Castro); Thomas Samson/AFP/Getty Images (Paris attacks); Andrey Armyagov/Shutterstock (gold fish); Universal History Archive/UIG/Getty images (Starry Night); cristovao/Shutterstock (boy); pbombaert/Shutterstock (paint); Eric Isselee/Shutterstock (snake)
Page 4: urfin/Shutterstock (book); Dmytro Balkhovitin/Shutterstock (fireworks); arturasker/Shutterstock (Big Ben); ArtisticPhoto/Shutterstock (flags); Neveshkin Nikolay (game controller)
Page 5: Stockr/Shutterstock (wind turbine); Larry Bussaca/Getty Images (Swift); morganlane/Shutterstock (globe); Anan Kaewkhammul (kangaroo); RTimages/Shutterstock (recycling bin)
Page 6: Library of Congress/Prints and Photographs Division (Albertosaurus); Courtesy Hackaball (Hackaball); Africa Studio/Shutterstock (test tubes); Monkey Business Images/Shutterstock (chemistry experiment); NASA (rover); NASA/JPL-Caltech/T. Pyle (SSC); Nerthuz/Shutterstock (space shuttle); Naeblys/Shutterstock (cell); Laurie O'Keefe/Photo Researchers/Getty Images (nautiloids)
Page 7: Fernando Medina/NBAE/Getty Images (James); Jeff Zelevansky/Getty Images (Gronkowski); The Asahi Shimbun/Getty Images (Williams); Alison Hancock/Shutterstock (U.S. Capitol); ronnybas/Shutterstock (Monument Valley); Andrey Eremin/Shutterstock (gavel)

A Look Back
Pages 8–9: Washington Post/Getty Images (Bei Bei); Anthony Behar-Pool/Getty Images (Obama and Castro); Thomas Samson/Getty Images (Paris)
Page 10: ksl/Shutterstock (flag); Thomas Imo/Getty Images (Kerry and Zarif); Jeff J Mitchell/Getty Images (migrants)
Page 11: Anthony Behar-Pool/Getty Images (Obama and Castro); Thomas Samson/Getty Images (Paris); Omar Havana/Getty Images (Nepal)
Page 12: Jessica McGowan/Getty Images (Army); Gail Johnson/Shutterstock (Denali); Sergiy Palamarchuk/Shutterstock ($10 bill)
Page 13: Jiri Flogel/Shutterstock (Confederate flag); Alex Wong/Getty Images (Ryan); Matt Rourke-Pool/Getty Images (Pope Francis)
Page 14: Washington Post/Getty Images (Bei Bei); NASA Ames Research Center/Brian Day (super blood moon eclipse)
Page 15: NASA/JPL-Caltech/Univ. of Arizona (Mars); starmaro/Shutterstock (mammoth)
Page 16: Nathaniel S. Butler/NBAE/Getty Images (Curry); Horsephotos/Getty Images (American Pharoah); Patrick Smith/Getty Images (Super Bowl)
Page 17: RSPCA (Chris the Sheep); PlusONE/Shutterstock (coins); Yayayoyo/Shutterstock (emoji)

Animals
Pages 18–19: anekoho/Shutterstock (butterflies); Gerald A. DeBoer/Shutterstock (raccoons); Andrey Armyagov/Shutterstock (goldfish)
Page 20: worldswildlifewonders/Shutterstock (frog); Petr Jilek/Shutterstock (eagle)
Page 21: Eric Isselee/Shutterstock (snake); Willyam Bradberry/Shutterstock (shark); Philip Ellard/Shutterstock (elephants)
Page 22: Anna Lurye/Shutterstock (jellyfish); Vilainecrevette/Shutterstock (sea urchins); Stepan Bormotov/Shutterstock (snail)
Page 23: anekoho/Shutterstock (butterflies); Vilainecrevette/Shutterstock (sponges); Maryna Pleshkun/Shutterstock (worm)
Page 24: Science Source/Getty Images
Page 25: Science Source/Getty Images (3)
Page 26: Gerald A. DeBoer (raccoons); Michel Porro/Getty Images (Goodall)
Page 27: Sam DCruz/Shutterstock (antelope); Ethan Daniels (sea stars); Ethan Daniels/The Image Bank/Getty Images (anglerfish)
Pages 28–29: rebeccaashworth/Shutterstock (Labrador); Valerio Pardi/Shutterstock (Persian Cat); Photok.dk/Shutterstock (guinea pig); Andrey Armyagov/Shutterstock (gold fish); Rita Kochmarjova/Shutterstock (German Shepherd)
Page 30–31: Don Heiny for TIME For Kids (3)
Page 32: abc7/Shutterstock (cheetah); Vilainecrevette/Shutterstock (sloth)
Page 33: Alexander Chaikin/Shutterstock (flamingos)

Art
Page 34: Universal History Archive/UIG/Getty images (Cafe Terrace at Night); Zadorozhnyi Viktor/Shutterstock (paint brushes)
Page 35: Kinez Riza/Nature/AFP/Getty Images; Maps by Joe Lemonnier for TIME For Kids
Page 36: DEA Picture Library/Getty Images (The Last Supper); Universal Images Group/Getty Images (The Milkmaid)
Page 37: Fine Art Images/Heritage Images/Getty Images (Madame Georges Charpentier and Her Children); Hans Namuth/Getty Images (Lichtenstein)
Page 38: pbombaert/Shutterstock (paint tube); Kennet Havgaard/Getty Images (Sistine Chapel); Claude Monet/Getty Images (Water Lilies); Photo 12/Getty Images (Three Musicians); Alberto Pizzoli/Getty Images (Kahlo self-portrait); Universal History Archive/Getty Images (Reflection of the Big Dipper)
Page 39: Oscity/Shutterstock (Les Demoiselles d'Avignon); Print Collector/Getty Images (Liberty Leading the People); Universal History Archive/Getty Images (The Scream, Starry Night); Emmanuel Dunand/Getty Images (Campbell Soup Can); DEA / G. Nimatallah/Getty Images (The Birth of Venus); DEA Picture Library/Getty Images (The Calling of St. Matthew); Francois Lochon/Gamma-Rapho/Getty Images (Venus de Milo);

Body and Health
Page 40: Alena Ozerova/Shutterstock (girl brushing teeth); Pressmaster/Shutterstock (family on bike); Denys Prykhodov/Shutterstock (girl sleeping)
Page 42: d8nn/Shutterstock
Page 43: Syda Productions/Shutterstock (boy at chalkboard); Denys Prykhodov/Shutterstock (girl sleeping)
Page 44: cristovao/Shutterstock (boy)
Page 45: Crystal Home/Shutterstock (background)

Books
Page 46: Ermolaev Alexander/Shutterstock
Page 50: David Levine (Levine); Don Heiny for TIME For Kids (Suiter)

Calendar and Holidays
Page 52: Elena Zajchikova/Shutterstock
Page 53: I love photo/Shutterstock (girl at chalkboard); Lorelyn Medina/Shutterstock (calendar)
Pages 54–55: pavelgr/Shutterstock (background)
Pages 56–57: Dmytro Balkhovitin/Shutterstock (fireworks); tomazul/Shutterstock (Martin Luther King Jr. Memorial); Tyler Olson/Shutterstock (kids reading); Neirfy/Shutterstock (flowers); gkuna/Shutterstock (oceans); M. Unal Ozmen/Shutterstock (ice cream); Andriy Solovyov/Shutterstock (park); Jeroen van den Broek/Shutterstock (guide dog); Veronika Matejkova/Shutterstock (breast cancer awareness); wavebreakmedia/Shutterstock (military family)
Pages 58–59: mariacristinaravaglio/iStockphoto.com (Basler Fasnacht); Charles Lewis/The Buffalo News/AP (Dyngus Day); Prakash Mathema/AFP/Getty Images (Gai Jatra); Ulet Ifansasti/Getty Images (Eid al-Fitr)
Page 60: Pedro Armestre/AFP/Getty Images (eating grapes); Sandra van der Steen/Shutterstock (oliebol); Richard Griffin/Shutterstock (potato); bonchan/Shutterstock (Japanese new year); Kozak/Shutterstock (cake)
Page 61: Shutterstock

Computers and Games
Page 62: Ollyy/Shutterstock (boy); Neveshkin Nikolay/Shutterstock (game controller)
Page 63: Andrew Burton/Getty Images (microchip); Science & Society Picture Library/Getty Images (Apple II)
Page 64: Science & Society Picture Library/Getty Images (IBM PC); Canadapanda/Shutterstock (Apple Watch); David Paul Morris/Getty Images (Jobs)
Page 65: Code.org
Page 68: Neveshkin Nikolay/Shutterstock (game controller); Stefano Tinti/Shutterstock (video game)
Page 69: bontom/Shutterstock (emoji); Lilu330/Shutterstock (bird); CTR Photos/Shutterstock (Lego figure); Vtls/Shutterstock (laptop)

Countries
Pages 70–71: zhu difeng/Shutterstock (Great Wall); ArtisticPhoto/Shutterstock (flags)
Page 72: turtix/Shutterstock (Niagara Falls); Matej Hudovernik/Shutterstock (Statue of Liberty); Guido Amrein, Switzerland/Shutterstock (Perito Moreno Glacier); rangizzz/Shutterstock (photograph frames); Shahid Khan/Shutterstock (Trafalgar Square); Mihai Simonia (Empire State Building); vitmark/Shutterstock (Machu Picchu); Zdravinjo/Shutterstock (boy with camera)
Page 73: Marina99/Shutterstock (St. Basil's Cathedral); Veronika Galkina/Shutterstock (Colloseum); zhu difeng/Shutterstock (Great Wall); platongkoh/Shutterstock (Angkor Wat Temple); Aleksandar Todorovic/Shutterstock (Sydney Opera House); oneinchpunch/Shutterstock (Hollywood Walk of Fame); INTERPIXELS/Shutterstock (Eiffel Tower); f8grapher/Shutterstock (Union Square); Nort/Shutterstock (Sphinx)
Page 74: Giraffe Manor (2)
Page 75: Travelpix Ltd/Getty Images (UN building); Yuriy Boyko/Shutterstock (logo)
Pages 76–77: Anna Jedynak/Shutterstock
Pages 78–79: Kiev.Victor/Shutterstock
Pages 80–81: zhu difeng/Shutterstock
Pages 82–83: Monika Hrdinova/Shutterstock
Pages 84–85: PRUSSIA ART/Shutterstock
Pages 86–87: Kiev.Victor/Shutterstock
Pages 88–89: West Coast Scapes/Shutterstock
Pages 90–91: Sean Pavone/Shutterstock

Pages 92–93: Dudarev Mikhail/Shutterstock
Pages 94–95: eAlisa/Shutterstock
Pages 96–97: Alfonso de Tomas/
Shutterstock
Pages 98–99: Sallorr/Shutterstock
Pages 100–101: haveseen/Shutterstock
Pages 102–103: laraslk/Shutterstock
Pages 104–105: Fedor Selivanov/
Shutterstock
Pages 106–107: arturasker/Shutterstock
Page 108: Galyna Andrushko/Shutterstock
Page 109: RuthChoi/Shutterstock (Taj
Mahal); Vadim Petrakov/Shutterstock
(Victoria Falls); S.Borisov/Shutterstock (Big
Ben); dmitry_islentev/Shutterstock (Christ
the Redeemer); WDG Photo/Shutterstock
(Notre Dame Cathedral); kyoshida0710/
Shutterstock (Al Khazneh Temple)

Energy and the Environment
Page 110: Stockr/Shutterstock
Page 111: jonson/Shutterstock (solar panels); RTimages/Shutterstock (recycling bins)
Pages 112–113: Kletr/Shutterstock (nuclear
plant); Denys Prykhodov/Shutterstock
(pipe); LIUSHENGFILM/Shutterstock
(petroleum plant); pixelman/Shutterstock
(coal); tchara/Shutterstock (wood); Stockr/
Shutterstock (wind turbine)
Pages 114–115: foxbat/Shutterstock (solar
collectors); Andrew Zarivny/Shutterstock
(Hoover Dam); Stockr/Shutterstock;
N.Minton/Shutterstock (Geothermal power
station)
Page 116: Bobby Bascomb/Pulitzer Center
on Crisis Reporting; Map by Joe Lemonnier
for TIME for Kids
Page 117: Chones/Shutterstock (bulb);
Madlen/Shutterstock (plant); Shell114/
Shutterstock (washer); RTimages/Shutter-
stock (recycling bins)
Page 118: Justin Sullivan/Getty Images
(Don Pedro Lake); Dan Holm/ Shutterstock
(Brown)
Page 119: Mykola Mazuryk/Shutterstock
(background)

Entertainment
Page 120: Kevork Djansezian/Getty Images
(Sheeran); Larry Busacca/Getty Images
(Swift)
Page 121: Tommaso Boddi/WireImage/
Getty Images (Stone); Karwai Tang/
WireImage/Getty Images (BB8)
Page 122: C Flanigan/FilmMagic/Getty
Images (2)
Page 123: Tommaso Boddi/WireImage/
Getty Images (Stone); Lloyd Bishop/NBC/
NBCU Photo Bank/Getty Images (Stiller);
Jason Merritt/Getty Images (Watson)
Page 124: David Roark/Disney Parks/Getty
Images (Austin and Ally); Victor Chavez/
WireImage/Getty Images (SpongeBob)
Page 125: Trae Patton/NBC/NBCU Photo
Bank/Getty Images (The Voice); Dan Mac-
Medan/WireImage/Getty Images (VEEP)
Page 126: Kevork Djansezian/Getty Images
(Sheeran)
Page 127: Christopher Polk/KCA2015/Getty
Images (Jonas); Kevin Mazur/WireImage/
Getty Images (One Direction); Alexander
Tamargo/Getty Images (Gomez)
Page 128: Larry Busacca/Getty Images
(Swift)
Page 129: Larry Busacca/Getty Images
(Swift); Big Machine (album covers)
Page 130: David Redfern/Redferns/Getty
Images (The Beatles); Kevin Mazur/Getty
Images (Mars)
Page 131: Phil Dent/Redferns/Getty Images
(Jackson); Lucasfilm Ltd. (Star Wars)
Page 132: Alexander Tamargo/Getty Images
(The Big Bang Theory); FOX/Getty Images
(The Simpsons)
Page 133: Tommaso Boddi/WireImage/
Getty Images

Geography
Page 134: cobalt88/Shutterstock
(compass); LIUSHENGFILM/Shutterstock
(background); Anan Kaewkhammul/
Shutterstock (kangaroo)
Page 135: morganlane/Shutterstock (globe)
Page 136: tobkatrina/Shutterstock (Death
Valley); Vadim Petrakov/Shutterstock
(Mount Aconcagua)
Page 137: Daniel Prudek/Shutterstock
(Mount Everest); Incredible Arctic (Arctic);
Quality Master/Shutterstock (Atlantic);
Andrey Armyagov/Shutterstock (Indian);
BlueOrange Studio/Shutterstock (Pacific);
Tsuguliev/Shutterstock (Southern); Alberto
Loyo/Shutterstock (Lake Eyre)
Page 138: Fotos593/Shutterstock (volcano);
plena/Shutterstock (Pangaea)
Page 139: Page 139: Peter West for TIME for
Kids (Bjerklie); Maps by Joe Lemonnier for
Time for Kids; Peter Rejcek/NSF (penguins)
Pages 140–151: Maps by Joe Lemonnier and
Joe Lertola

History
Page 152: Lisa S./Shutterstock
Page 153: robert_s/Shutterstock (globe);
Fernando Garcia Esteban/Shutterstock
(background); Lauren O'Keefe/Photo
Researchers/Getty Images (Nautiloid); Ken
Schulze/Shutterstock (fossil)
Page 154: Library of Congress, Prints and
Photographs Division (Albertosaurus);
Studio Barcelona/Shutterstock
(background); life_in_a_pixel/Shutterstock
(prehistoric man)
Page 155: DEA/G. DAGLI ORTI/De Agos-
tini/Getty Images (The Trojan War); Fedor
Selivanov/Shutterstock (background)
Page 156: Jeff Baumgart/Shutterstock
(background); Dario Lo Presti/Shutterstock
(Mayan statue)
Page 157: David Smart/Shutterstock
(background); walter_g/Shutterstock
(Fabergé egg)
Page 158: pxl.store/Shutterstock (back-
ground); Library of Congress, Prints and
Photographs Division (The Boxer Rebellion)
Page 159: BMCL/Shutterstock
(background); Dinodia Photos/Getty
Images (Gandhi)
Page 160: Shutterstock (background);
Nigel Waldron/WireImage/Getty Images
(Yousafzai)
Page 161: kamomeen/Shutterstock (back-
ground); Library of Congress, Prints and
Photographs Division (Washington)
Page 162: MarkauMark/Shutterstock
(background); Stanislaw Tokarski/Shutter-
stock (Model T)
Page 163: Rudy Balasko (background);
kropic1/Shutterstock (Martin Luther King
Jr. memorial)
Page 164: IndustryAndTravel/Shutterstock
(background); Anthony Correia/Shutter-
stock (firefighters)
Page 165: Akos Nagy/Shutterstock (back-
ground); Everett Historical/Shutterstock
(Earhart); NASA (Armstrong); neftali/Shut-
terstock (Hillary); Serban Bogdan/Shutter-
stock (map); godrick/Shutterstock (moon);
Daniel Prudek/Shutterstock (Everest)

Inventions and Technology
Page 166: 4Max/Shutterstock (back-
ground); Andrey Burmakin/Shutterstock
(drawing); Nike (sneakers)
Page 167: Lenscap Photography/
Shutterstock (hoverboard); Alexandru Nika/
Shutterstock (Google Cardboard)
Page 168: Nike (sneakers); Artiphon (girl
with Artiphon)
Page 169: 4Max/Shutterstock (back-
ground); dny3d/Shutterstock (drone);
Apple (Apple Pencil); Hackaball (Hackaball)
Page 170: Samsung (truck); Fotos593/

Shutterstock (ocean)
Page 171: Courtesy AARAMBH (2)

Science
Page 172: Monkey Business Images/
Shutterstock
Page 173: VectorFrenzy/Shutterstock
(background); ilikestudio/Shutterstock
(researcher); Digital Media Pro/Shutter-
stock (boy)
Pages 174–175: Sashkin/Shutterstock
(background); Diana Taliun/Shutterstock
(plant); Nicku/Shutterstock (Darwin); Image
Point Fr/Shutterstock (vaccine); Leigh
Prather/Shutterstock (DNA)
Pages 176–177: zhu difeng/Shutterstock
(background); Africa Studio/Shutterstock
(test tubes); valdis torms/Shutterstock
(atom; Poznyakov/Shutterstock (girl baking
cookies); Everett Historical/Shutterstock
(Curie); totojang1977/Shutterstock (water)
Pages 178–179: Africa Studio/Shutterstock
(background); Alhovik (Periodic Table)
Pages 180–181: Ase/Shutterstock (back-
ground); Boris15/Shutterstock (atom);
TTstudio/Shutterstock (rainbow); Fred
Stein Archive/Archive Photos/Getty Images
(Einstein); etorres/Shutterstock (Newton's
Cradle)
Pages 182–183: PETRUK VIKTOR/Shutter-
stock (background); robert_s/Shutterstock
(Earth); Sergey Novikov/Shutterstock (boy
in car); Constantine Androsoff/Shutterstock
(dam); gnoparus/Shutterstock (Mount Aso)
Page 184: Luke Sharrett/Bloomberg/Getty
Images (fries); Matthew Thayer/The Maui
News/AP (Monsanto)
Page 185: zhu difeng/Shutterstock

Space
Page 186: sripfoto/Shutterstock (back-
ground); NASA (Hubble Space Telescope);
Nerthuz/Shutterstock (space shuttle)
Page 187: NASA (3)
Page 188: sripfoto/Shutterstock (back-
ground); NASA (3)
Page 189: NASA (Hubble Space Telescope,
Mir and Atlantis, International Space
Station); NASA photo/Tom Tschida
(Discovery); NASA/JHUAPL/SwRI (Pluto)
Page 190: Barry Wilmore/NASA
Page 191: NASA/AP (Kelly); Naeblys/Shut-
terstock (ISS)
Page 192: NASA/JPL-Caltech/T. Pyle (SSC)
Page 193: NASA/JPL-Caltech/GSFC/JAXA
(sun); NASA/JPL-Caltech/Space Science
Institute (moons); NASA & ESA, Acknowl-
edgements: Judy Schmidt (galaxy); NASA/
MSFC/MEO/Aaron Kingery (comet)
Page 194: NASA/AP (MAVEN); NASA/
Hubble Heritage Team/AP (Mars)
Page 195: NASA

Sports
Page 196: Jeff Zelevansky/Getty Images
(Gronkowski); The Asahi Shimbun/Getty
Images (Williams)
Page 197: Nathaniel S. Butler/NBAE/Getty
Images (Curry)
Page 198: David Lee/Shutterstock (back-
ground); Chris Covatta/Getty Images
Page 199: Louis Van Oeyen/Western
Reserve Historical Society/Getty Images
(Ruth); Rob Carr/Getty Images (Trout)
Page 200: David Lee/Shutterstock
(background); Otto Greule Jr/Getty Images
(Hernandez); Ralph Freso/Getty Images
(Goldschimidt); Photo File/MLB Photos/
Getty Images (Banks)
Page 202: David Lee/Shutterstock (back-
ground); Rob Carr/Getty Images (Harvey)
Page 203: Ezra Shaw/Getty Images
(Bumgarner); Hulton Archive/Getty Images
(Musial)
Page 204: Benoit Daoust/Shutterstock
(background); Timothy A. Clary/AFP/Getty

Images (Flacco); Tony Tomsic/Getty Images (Unitas)
Page 205: Jeff Zelevansky/Getty Images (Gronkowski)
Page 206: Benoit Daoust/Shutterstock (background); Diamond Images/Getty Images (Namath); Doug Pensinger/Getty Images (George)
Page 207: Christian Petersen/Getty Images (Fitzgerald)
Page 208: Benoit Daoust/Shutterstock (background); Christian Petersen/Getty Images (Rodgers); Albert Dickson/Sporting News/Getty Images (Faulk)
Page 209: Dilip Vishwanat/Getty Images (Strahan)
Page 210: Torsak Thammachote/Shutterstock (background); Fernando Medina/NBAE/Getty Images (James); Nathaniel S. Butler/NBAE/Getty Images (Jordan)
Page 211: Andrew D. Bernstein/NBAE/Getty Images (Thomas)
Page 212: Torsak Thammachote/Shutterstock (background); Ned Dishman/NBAE/Getty Images (Wall)
Page 213: Noah Graham/NBAE via Getty Images) Ronald Martinez/Getty Images (Nowitzki)
Page 214: Torsak Thammachote/Shutterstock (background); Rocky Widner/NBAE Getty Images (Davis)
Page 215: Melissa Majchrzak/NBAE/Getty Images (Nash); Robert Sullivan/AFP/Getty Images (Duncan)
Page 216: Torsak Thammachote/Shutterstock (background); Ron Hoskins/NBAE/Getty Images (Catchings)
Page 217: Barry Gossage/NBAE/Getty Images (Taurasi)
Page 218: vkilikov/Shutterstock (background); Jamie Sabau/NHLI/Getty Images (Jones); Denis Brodeur/NHLI/Getty Images (Howe)
Page 219: Andy Marlin/NHLI/Getty Images (Brodeur)
Page 220: vkilikov/Shutterstock (background); Patrick McDermott/NHLI/Getty Images (Ovechkin)
Page 221: Bruce Bennett/Getty Images (Toews); Denis Brodeur/NHLI via Getty Images (Roy)
Page 222: vkilikov/Shutterstock (background); B Bennett/Bruce Bennett Studios/Getty Images (Gretzky); Bill Smith/NHLI/Getty Images (Quick)
Page 223: Don Smith/NHLI/Getty Images (Marleau)
Page 224: Wuttichok Panichiwarapun/ Shutterstock (background); Andrew Redington/Getty Images (Spieth)
Page 225: Sutichak/Shutterstock (background); The Asahi Shimbun/Getty Images (Williams)
Page 226: hxdbzxy/Shutterstock (background); Popperfoto/Getty Images (Pele); Hulton Archive/Getty Images (Charlton)
Page 227: Allsport UK /Allsport/Getty Images (Maradona); VI Images/Getty Images (Messi)
Page 228: hxdbzxy/Shutterstock (background); Stuart Franklin - FIFA/FIFA/Getty Images (Lloyd); Joel Auerbach/Getty Images (Marta)
Page 229: Miguel Medina/AFP/Getty Images (London); David Eulitt/Kansas City Star/MCT/Getty Images (softball)

United States
Pages 230–231: Alison Hancock/Shutterstock (Capitol Hill); ronnybas/Shutterstock (Monument Valley); StevenRussellSmithPhotos/Shutterstock (American Goldfinch)
Pages 232–233: STILLFX/Shutterstock (flag); ronnybas/Shutterstock (background); xpixel/Shutterstock (Yellowhammer); Le Do/Shutterstock

(forget-me-not); Universal History Archive/UIG/Getty Images (Northern Lights); Peter Kramer/NBC/NBCU Photo Bank/Getty Images (Jonas); colour/Shutterstock (violin); ukmooney/Shutterstock (pine tree)
Pages 234–235: STILLFX/Shutterstock (flag); tobkatrina/Shutterstock (background); Mariusz S. Jurgielewicz/Shutterstock (Mount Whitney); creighton359/iStockphoto.com (lark bunting); Jeff Curry/Getty Images (Logano); grass-lifeisgood/Shutterstock (peach blossom); Valentina Proskurina/Shutterstock (ladybug)
Pages 236–237: STILLFX/Shutterstock (flag); Pavel Tvrdy/Shutterstock (background); DK Arts/Shutterstock (sabal palm); Joe Raedle/Getty Images (Cape Canaveral); Dennis W. Donohue/Shutterstock (thrasher); Ron Sachs - Pool/Getty Images (Obama); Valentina Razumova/Shutterstock (Syringa); Rob McKay/Shutterstock (bluebird)
Pages 238–239: STILLFX/Shutterstock (flag); Carol M. Highsmith/Buyenlarge/Getty Images (background); Layne Murdoch Jr./NBAE/Getty Images (Davis); Felix Koch/Cincinnati Museum Center/Getty Images (Levi Coffin Home); StevenRussellSmithPhotos/Shutterstock (American Goldfinch); Ian 2010/Shutterstock (sunflower)
Pages 240–241: STILLFX/Shutterstock (flag); Zack Frank/Shutterstock (background); Birds and Dragons/Shutterstock (cardinal); Oleksiy Mark/Shutterstock (gold); Dustin Bradford/Getty Images (Manning); DK Arts/Shutterstock (pine); Matt McClain for The Washington Post/Getty Images (jousting)
Pages 242–243: STILLFX/Shutterstock (flag); John McLaird/Shutterstock (background); Jeffrey Mayer/WireImage/Getty Images (Evans); Leon Halip/Getty Images (Michigan); Mike Truchon/Shutterstock (loon); AN NGUYEN/Shutterstock (magnolia); QiuJu Song/Shutterstock (catfish)
Pages 244–245: STILLFX/Shutterstock (flag); Zvone/Shutterstock (background); Everett Historical/Shutterstock (Twain); de2marco/Shutterstock (bitterroot); MarkMirror/Shutterstock (butterfly); Tom Reichner/Shutterstock (meadowlark); John Horsley/Photoshot/Getty Images (Burning Man); G Fiume/Getty Images (Harper)
Pages 246–247: STILLFX/Shutterstock (flag); Weldon Schloneger/Shutterstock (background); Vaclav Volrab/Shutterstock (tree); Harry How/Getty Images (Trout); Stacey Welu/Shutterstock (Yucca); Alexey Stiop/Shutterstock (sand); Steve Byland (bluebird)
Pages 248–249: STILLFX/Shutterstock (flag); Wollertz/Shutterstock (background) Zerbor/Shutterstock (pine); Kartouchken/Shutterstock (mini golf); Christopher D. Allsop/Shutterstock (rose); David Liam Kyle/NBAE/Getty Images (James); Joe Farah (lizard); Cindi Bateman/Shutterstock (flycatcher)
Pages 250–251: STILLFX/Shutterstock (flag); Zack Frank/Shutterstock (background); Marynka/Shutterstock (Oregon Grape); Jon Kopaloff/FilmMagic/Getty Images (Swift); Rinelle/Shutterstock (chicken); Oleg Senkov/Shutterstock (monkeys); Parinya Feungchan/Shutterstock (palm)
Pages 252–252: STILLFX/Shutterstock (flag); ronnybas/Shutterstock (background); Planner/Shutterstock (fir); Steve Byland/Shutterstock (mockingbird); Jenny Anderson/WireImage/Getty Images (Lovato); Diane Garcia/Shutterstock (rodeo); fredlyfish4/123RF.com (sego lily); Giorgio Rossi/Shutterstock (dinosaur)
Pages 254–255: STILLFX/Shutterstock

(flag); DonLand/Shutterstock (background); Double Brow Imagery/Shutterstock (Hermit thrush); Jiri Hera/Shutterstock (maple syrup); aimintang/Getty Images (Flowering dogwood); LouLouPhotos/Shutterstock (rhododendron); Science Source/USGS/Getty Images (Mount St. Helens); Randy Miramontez/Shutterstock (Paisley)
Page 256: STILLFX/Shutterstock (flag); Zack Frank/Shutterstock (background); JStone /Shutterstock (Ruffalo); Checubus/Shutterstock (geyser); Frank Hearron/Shutterstock (Indian paintbrush)
Page 257: Songquan Deng/Shutterstock (background); Golubev Dmitrii/Shutterstock (thrush); Adam Parent/Shutterstock (Lincoln Memorial); Gary Ives/Shutterstock (Puerto Rico)
Page 258: STILLFX/Shutterstock (flag); eric1513/Shutterstock (Capitol)
Page 259: Miljan Mladenovic/Shutterstock (White House)
Pages 260–261: STILLFX/Shutterstock (flag); Drop of Light/Shutterstock (House); Paul Hakimata Photography (Capitol); David L. Ryan/The Boston Globe/Getty Images (Senate)
Page 262: STILLFX/Shutterstock (flag); Tim Sloan/AFP/Getty Images (Justices); Joe Ravi/Shutterstock (Supreme Court)
Page 263: Andrey Eremin/Shutterstock (gavel); Chris Hondros/Newsmakers/Getty Images (newspaper)
Page 264: Getty Images (Constitution); Courtesy National Constitution Center (Sautner)
Page 265: STILLFX/Shutterstock (flag); Everett Historical/Shutterstock (4)
Pages 266–267: STILLFX/Shutterstock (flag); Everett Historical/Shutterstock (12)
Pages 268–269: STILLFX/Shutterstock (flag); Everett Historical/Shutterstock (12)
Page 270: STILLFX/Shutterstock (flag); Everett Historical/Shutterstock (2); Library of Congress Prints and Photographs Division (Hoover); Stock Montage/Getty Images (Roosevelt)
Page 271: Library of Congress Prints and Photographs Division (6); Joseph Sohm/Shutterstock (Carter)
Page 272: STILLFX/Shutterstock (flag); Joseph Sohm/Shutterstock (Reagan, Clinton, Obama); 360b/Shutterstock (George H.W. Bush); Christopher Halloran/Shutterstock (George W. Bush)
Page 273: Universal History Archive/Getty Images (Johnson); Dirck Halstead/Liaison/Getty Images (Nixon)
Page 274: ullstein bild/Getty Images) (Borglum); Joe Sohn/Visions Of America/Getty Images (Mount Rushmore)
Page 275: photo.ua/Shutterstock (Mount Rushmore); kojihirano/Shutterstock (Grand Canyon); Amalia Ferreira-Espinoza/Shutterstock (Washington Monument); Ffooter/Shutterstock (Gateway Arch); somchaij/Shutterstock (Golden Gate Bridge); Matej Kastelic/Shutterstock (Empire State Building)

Answers
Pages 276–277: Alexander Chaikin/Shutterstock (flamingos); Shutterstock (maze); CTR Photos/Shutterstock (Lego figure); Tommaso Boddi/WireImage/Getty Images (Modern Family); Everett Historical/Shutterstock (Earhart); NASA (Armstrong); neftali/Shutterstock (Hillary); Serban Bogdan/Shutterstock (map); godrick/Shutterstock (moon); Daniel Prudek/Shutterstock (Everest); NASA (astronaut)

Back Cover
lazyllama/Shutterstock (flame); Lucasfilm Ltd. (Star Wars); Taina Sohlman/Shutterstock (Tesla)

Index